Iconoclasm in European Cinema

Iconoclasm in European Cinema

The Ethics and Aesthetics of Image Destruction

Chiara Quaranta

EDINBURGH
University Press

Edinburgh University Press is one of the leading university presses in the UK. We publish academic books and journals in our selected subject areas across the humanities and social sciences, combining cutting-edge scholarship with high editorial and production values to produce academic works of lasting importance. For more information visit our website: edinburghuniversitypress.com

We are committed to making research available to a wide audience and are pleased to be publishing an Open Access ebook edition of this title.

© Quaranta, 2023 under a Creative Commons Attribution-NonCommercial-NoDerivatives (CC-BY-NC-ND) licence.

Edinburgh University Press Ltd
13 Infirmary Street, Edinburgh, EH1 1LT

Typeset in 10/14 Warnock Pro by
Cheshire Typesetting Ltd, Cuddington, Cheshire

A CIP record for this book is available from the British Library

SBN 978 1 4744 9445 8 (hardback) ISBN 978 1 4744 9446 5 (paperback)
ISBN 978 1 4744 9447 2 (webready PDF)
ISBN 978 1 4744 9448 9 (epub)

The right of Chiara Quaranta to be identified as author of this work has been asserted in accordance with the Copyright, Designs and Patents Act 1988 and the Copyright and Related Rights Regulations 2003 (SI No. 2498).

Contents

List of Figures	vii
Acknowledgements	viii
Introduction	1
Prologue: The *Eikōn-Eidōlon* Dichotomy from Plato to Film	23

Part I: Cinematic Iconoclasm as Critique: The Image as *Eidōlon*

1.	Aural Cinema: Isidore Isou's *Traité de bave et d'éternité*	37
2.	An Aesthetics of Displeasure: Guy Debord's Destructive Oeuvre	55
3.	Towards a Radical Voice: Carmelo Bene's *Our Lady of the Turks*	73
4.	In Search of a True Image: Jean-Luc Godard's *Histoire(s) du cinéma*	94

Part II: Cinematic Iconoclasm as an Ethics of (In)visibility: The *Eikōn* as Iconoclastic

5.	Impossible Encounters: Marguerite Duras's *Le Navire Night*	115
6.	Blind Vision, Aural Resonances: Derek Jarman's *Blue*	136
7.	Crumbling Faces: Ingmar Bergman's *Cries and Whispers*	154
8.	Blocks of Suffering: Krzysztof Kieślowski's *Three Colours: Blue*	172

Conclusion: A Communal Vision through Broken Images	189

Notes 195
Glossary 201
Bibliography 205
Filmography 223
Index 226

Figures

1.1	Chiseled image of Isidore Isou	48
1.2	Chiseled image of military personnel	49
1.3	Chiseled filmstrip	50
2.1	Static shot of a photograph of a cinema audience	64
2.2	Static shot of a photograph of Alice Becker-Ho and text 'and the living re-encounters the living'	70
3.1	Burnt medium close-up of Carmelo Bene	87
3.2	Extreme close-up of Lydia Mancinelli and red filters	88
3.3	Partially out-of-focus close-up of Carmelo Bene	90
3.4	A breast disguised amidst the vegetation	92
4.1	Text superimposed on a detail from Fra Angelico's *The Mocking of Christ* superimposed on Godard in his study room	106
4.2	Detail from Fra Angelico's *The Mocking of Christ*	107
4.3	Still frame of Brunella Bovo superimposing on the shot of Fra Angelico's *The Mocking of Christ*	108
4.4	Ingrid Bergman in absorbed prayer superimposed on a blue-tinted still frame of Birger Malmsten and Doris Svedlund	110
4.5	Layered superimposition of green-tinted still frame of Birger Malmsten and Doris Svedlund, Godard in his study room, and text	111
5.1	Actors in *Le Navire Night* (Marguerite Duras, 1979)	131
7.1	Close-up of Agnes in pain	165
7.2	Extreme close-up of Maria and David in front of the mirror	166
7.3–7.5	From Karin's facial close-up to the fade to the red screen	170
8.1–8.4	The third black-out at the swimming pool	186

Acknowledgements

This book has developed from my PhD thesis on the topic of cinema and iconoclasm, which would not have been possible without the constant guidance of my doctoral supervisor, David Sorfa, whom I would like to thank in particular also for strongly encouraging me to turn the thesis into a book and for his help and support throughout. My sincere thanks also go to my second supervisor, Daniel Yacavone, for his insightful comments and his hard questions which encouraged me to broaden the research; my PhD examiners, Libby Saxton and Marion Schmid, who provided helpful insights into various ways in which I could develop my thesis into a book; and my master's supervisor, Ivelise Perniola, who was my first interlocutor on the topic of iconoclasm and cinema.

Once I set my mind to undertake the task of writing this book, I struggled with envisioning my thesis as a publishable work, and I am extremely grateful to Gillian Leslie at Edinburgh University Press for believing in my idea, even when it was not ready yet, for meeting with me and for explaining the ways in which I could have developed it for publication. Sincere thanks also go to Sam Johnson and the editorial team at EUP.

I would like to express my gratitude to Krister Collin at Svenska Filminstitutet for his help with the cover image and to Carl-Gustaf Nykvist for giving permission. Thanks to you, the cover image I had in my head is now on the cover of this book. I would also like to thank wholeheartedly Dan Harrison, Jack Walker and Nicholas Canny for their prompt help, and Davide Messina for his valuable advice on various aspects of the book.

This book has significantly benefitted from suggestions and conversations with friends and colleagues over the past few years; these include Silvia Angeli, William Brown, David Fleming, François Giraud, Pasquale Iannone and

Tyler Parks. Thank you for pushing me to question my ideas by providing feedback at conferences, or by sharing your thoughts in front of a friendly pint. I would like to thank especially Francesco Sticchi for reading drafts of some chapters and discussing ideas with me. I am also grateful to the anonymous reader whose thorough feedback has helped me deepen the argument.

Finally, I wish to express my sincere gratitude to all those persons whose support, encouragement and love have left a mark on this work. I could not have endured the stress and self-doubts of writing this book without the comfort of my dear friends, who listened to my worries and brought a smile to my face. A special thought goes to my friend Francesco Roscino, for this work is at times haunted by his memory. I am profoundly grateful to my parents, Maria Adele and Nicola, and my sister, Lavinia, without whose support and love I would not have completed this book. Last but not least, warmest thanks to my wee nephews Giulio and Davide, who have unknowingly restored my faith in this world.

Part of Chapter 1 previously appeared in a different form, as Chiara Quaranta, 'A Cinema of Boredom: Heidegger, Cinematic Time and Spectatorship' (2020), *Film-Philosophy*, 24(1): 1–21.

But certainly for the present age, which prefers the sign to the thing signified, the copy to the original, fancy to reality, the appearance to the essence, [...] *illusion* only is *sacred, truth profane*. Nay, sacredness is held to be enhanced in proportion as truth decreases and illusion increases, so that the highest degree of illusion comes to be the highest degree of sacredness.

– Ludwig Feuerbach, Preface to the Second Edition of *The Essence of Christianity*

It was no 'empty square' which I had exhibited but rather the experience of non-objectivity.

– Kazimir Malevich, *The Manifesto of Suprematism*

I am Echo, dwelling in the recesses of your ears; and if thou wouldst paint my likeness, paint sound.

– Ausonius, *In Echo Pictam*

Introduction

WE LIVE IN an age and society profoundly affected by visual images. From the screens of our phones to work computers, from advertising images scattered across towns to films and television programmes, the emphasis on sight and recorded images (both still and moving) is stronger than ever in our quotidian life. And yet, this abundance of images has not brought about a greater awareness regarding their nature. The contemporary 'iconocracy', as Marie-José Mondzain (2019, 17)[1] aptly defines it, allows anyone to become a producer of images but, at the same time, it has not made it any easier for individuals to understand the power and risk of our uses of images. What is more, and seemingly paradoxically, this extremely visible society is characterised by an unprecedented and unnoticed destruction of images on a daily basis. Hardly anybody is immune to this dichotomic situation – for instance, we easily take pictures and make videos with digital technologies, but just as easily we delete them for a variety of reasons, such as the lack of hard drive space or because a beloved face has become intolerable. Hence, the destruction of images – that is, iconoclasm (etymologically 'the breaking of images')[2] – constitutes a pervasive element of contemporary Western society and can, thus, be used as a way to investigate how we interact with and understand still and moving images.

Western Europe represents an exemplary context for exploring iconoclastic attitudes since, historically and philosophically, it has been the ground for competing interpretations regarding visual representations: bequeathed by Imperial Roman and Catholic iconophilia, it is simultaneously heir to Platonic, Biblical and Christian iconoclasm. Contradictory influences have contributed to the shaping of current European imaginary, within which a continuous production of images is accompanied by a sharp criticism and a mistrust thereof. There is indeed an omnipresence of, if not obsession with, visual images in contemporary Western societies, which has been variously addressed as 'modern ocularcentric culture' (Jay 1993, 44), 'culture of images' (Mitchell 1994, 5), 'bulimia of images' (Wunenburger 1999, 363), 'flood of modern visibility' (Mondzain 2005, 222) and 'civilization of images' (Bettetini 2006, viii; Nancy 2005, 32). And yet, imagination is often relegated to the Platonic level of inferior knowledge. As a place of daily image production, Western Europe also stands out as a site for the critique of visual representations. In such a context, the idea of the image as a faithful reproduction of a portion of reality coexists with the conception of the image as a deceitful and false copy, originating seemingly incompatible attitudes.

Catholic iconophilia, Christian and Biblical iconoclasm and the Platonic tradition are recognised as fundamental influences on contemporary stances towards images. Plato's philosophical objection to artistic mimesis and the Byzantine iconoclastic controversy, on the one hand, and the Catholic legitimation of sacred icons, on the other hand, have significantly shaped Western intellectual history about images. As consequence, contemporary society is characterised by the paradox of a constant production of images which are looked at with a suspicious eye. Jean-Luc Nancy (2005) observes,

> for the duration of the West's history, this motif [of the deceitful image] will have resulted from the alliance (and it is doubtless this that has so decisively marked the West as such) forged between the principle of monotheism and the Greek problematic of the copy or the simulation, of artifice and the absence of the original. Of course, this alliance is also the source of the mistrust toward images that continues unabated into our own time (and this in a culture that produces images in abundance), a mistrust that has, in its turn, produced a deep suspicion regarding 'appearances' or 'the spectacle', as well as a certain self-satisfied critique of the 'civilization of images'. (31–32)

The history of Western thought about images is thus the contradictory result of two extremes: always on the verge of refusing sensible representations, echoing Platonic philosophy and Christian iconoclasm, it has nonetheless welcomed the image following the Christian legitimation of sacred icons. In a culture which constantly communicates through images and in which the individual is surrounded by elements addressing sight, iconoclasm and its opposite – iconophilia – find a place in the spectrum of possible attitudes towards images. The study of iconoclastic approaches to images can therefore contribute to our understanding of current visual culture, further exploring the ambiguous nature of representations. Destructive gestures in the visual arts constitute both a way to criticise the image's illusory nature and a means for acknowledging the image's ability to provide an alternative engagement with the world when it ceases to be a mere mimetic appearance.

This book develops from the potential value of iconoclasm in the ambit of cinema. While the topic of iconoclasm has been at the centre of many scholarly works in philosophy, theology and history, it has been quite overlooked by the arts and film studies. The core of the book coils around cinematic iconoclasm and what can be termed broken images – both recalling the etymological meaning of iconoclasm and because their relationship with the referent is broken. The audio-visual images analysed throughout are literally or metaphorically broken: no longer functioning as self-evident, mimetic images of reality, these images are either broken in their physicality (the film strip is literally damaged), or broken in their ability to figuratively represent something (hence, monochromatic screens, fades to colour, disruptive sounds and altered motion). Accordingly, I have selected films characterised by an anti-mimetic aesthetics which responds to an iconoclastic understanding of the image-referent relationship; namely, Isidore Isou's *Traité de bave et d'éternité* (*Treatise on Venom and Eternity*, 1951), Guy Debord's *Hurlements en faveur de Sade* (*Howls for Sade*, 1952), *The Society of the Spectacle* (*La Société du spectacle*, 1973) and *In girum imus nocte et consumimur igni* (*We Wander in the Night and Are Consumed by Fire*, 1978), Carmelo Bene's *Our Lady of the Turks* (*Nostra signora dei turchi*, 1968), Jean-Luc Godard's *Histoire(s) du cinéma* (1988–98), Marguerite Duras's *Le Navire Night* (1979), Derek Jarman's *Blue* (1993), Ingmar Bergman's *Cries and Whispers* (*Viskningar och rop*, 1972) and Krzysztof Kieślowski's *Three Colours: Blue* (*Trois Couleurs: Bleu*, 1993).

The selected films effectively exemplify cinematic iconoclasm, which refers to the deliberate, literal or metaphorical, destruction of film images and which hinges on an interpretation of the relationship between the image and its referent in terms of alterity. That is, the image as copy is understood as inadequate for the representation of a specific model. My main contention is that the destruction of images in the cinema can be a breeding ground for an aesthetic and ethical investigation of the ways in which we understand and use moving images. Contrary to historical iconoclasm, which consists of a negation of the other's point of view through the destruction of the other's artefacts (an attitude evident in iconoclastic gestures such as the smashing of sacred icons in Byzantium in the eighth and ninth centuries and the destruction of Catholic abbeys in Scotland during the Reformation; or, more recently, in the blowing up of the Buddhas of Bamiyan and the ancient city of Palmira [Besançon 2000; Bettetini 2006, 92–104, 142; Latour and Weibel 2002; Mondzain 2019, 314]), iconoclasm in the arts has the potential to be an aesthetic as well as an ethical approach. That is, destruction as an artistic gesture within an artwork can be a way to challenge traditional canons, as well as a means to respect reality, its complexity and non-reducibility to a self-explanatory, mimetic reproduction. For example, when Kazimir Malevich creates monochromatic paintings or Robert Rauschenberg erases a de Kooning drawing, they are renewing the criteria for painting and, at the same time, reflecting on sight and mimesis. Similarly, when John Cage makes music with silence and noise or Pierre Schaeffer inaugurates concrete music, they are redefining the concept of music itself (see Belting 2002; Gamboni 1997; Weibel 2002, 570–684). In the cinema, iconoclastic approaches concretise in literal destructions of the film strip or in metaphorical negations of mimetic film images, which resonate with similar destructive gestures in the other arts. The films examined in the book display various iconoclastic gestures against the film image's ability to mimetically represent the referent, thereby echoing philosophical and historical arguments on the deceptive nature of visual images.

I develop my argument on cinematic iconoclasm from the dichotomy between two types of images, the Greek *eikōn*/εἰκών[3] and *eidōlon*/εἴδωλον. While both terms can translate as image, they nonetheless refer to two quite different conceptions of the image, and as such they are found in philosophical and theological discussions regarding the nature of visual representations. The *eikōn*, which became the icon during the Christian controversy over the representation of God in a material frame, stands for an image that references its model, whereas the *eidōlon*, which came to signify the heretic idol, consists of a deceitful image with no truthful relationship with the prototype. I have chosen to keep the Ancient Greek words rather than using the English equivalent for two main reasons. First of all, while the English 'icon' and 'idol' are strongly related to their usage in theology, where they refer to material representations of God, the Greek *eikōn* and *eidōlon* preserve their philosophical, and pagan, meaning. Secondly, the Greek terms maintain a richness of meanings which the English 'image' fails to convey. Indeed, the single term 'image' condenses a wide range of meanings, from those related to the sensible sphere to ones connected to the intelligible world. Hence, the word 'image' refers to something that can go from the extremely poor quality of appearance to the invisibility of ideas and thoughts. Any English translation of *eikōn* and *eidōlon* thus loses the etymological and philosophical meaning that the two terms contain.

Throughout the book, I rework the dichotomy between the *eikōn* and the *eidōlon* in the cinema, tracing a thread from Plato's philosophy to contemporary films. To better unfold my argument, I consider two main ways in which the opposition between the *eikōn* and the *eidōlon* can be thought of in cinema, depending on whether the attention is primarily on the *eidōlon* or on the *eikōn*. Accordingly, cinematic iconoclasm can concentrate on critiquing the image as illusory and deceptive copy (*eidōlon*), thereby bearing many similarities to the arguments made by the iconoclasts in the eighth and ninth centuries. Both theoretically and practically, cinematic iconoclasm as critique frequently occurs within the context of a Marxist criticism of commodities, mass media and capitalism's fundamental values. In the films selected for Part I, a certain type of image, that of Hollywood-like cinema, is decried insofar as it produces an illusory 'impression of reality' (Rodowick 1994, xvi), thereby concealing capitalist ideology under non-contradictory images. Particularly the exponents of leftist film theory in their arguments echoed the iconoclastic criticism of the image as a deceitful copy, which is matched practically in the audio-visually destructive works by the likes of Isidore Isou, Guy Debord, Carmelo Bene and Jean-Luc Godard.

Another way of approaching cinematic iconoclasm and its ethical potential is through what I address as iconoclastic *eikōn*. By this term I define an image which retains the character of the *eikōn* of referencing the prototype, while being reflective of an iconoclastic understanding of the image-prototype relationship. That is to say, an iconoclastic *eikōn* maintains at once the quality of being a mediator between two elements otherwise separated and an iconoclastic aspect given by the negation of mimesis; hence, the visual image is in some way insufficient to figuratively represent its model. The theme of the image's insufficiency to represent recalls the ongoing issue of mimesis, which has troubled aesthetics since its inception. How can an image, conceived as copy, represent a referent? And what if the referent lacks a phenomenal equivalent (such that it can only be thought or experienced emotionally)? Assuming that the act of looking is never neutral and that there exists specific subject matter which more forcefully entails a taking of responsibility from producers and viewers of images, iconoclastic approaches to cinema often involve the ethical significance of moving beyond mimesis. The film image as iconoclastic *eikōn* constitutes a way of showing something without making it completely visible and aurally accessible, thereby encouraging an ethics based on the fragile equilibrium between visibility and invisibility. Poignant examples are found in the work of, among others, Marguerite Duras, Derek Jarman, Ingmar Bergman and Krzysztof Kieślowski, where a need to represent audio-visually is met with a striving for an ethical film form at the limits of intelligibility.

The questions tying the book together therefore concern the ways in which iconoclastic film images establish a web of relationships with their models and the spectator. Can everything have a copy of itself? That is, can we make images of everything? This question, which is more of a quandary, also leads to interrogating the limits of our right to see and show something on a screen. Ultimately, when this right is challenged by iconoclastic gestures, we are left wondering what it is that we see when we see images of imagelessness.

Key Iconoclastic Sources and Methodology

Because of the very nature of iconoclasm and the way in which I explore it in relation to philosophy and cinema, this book is characterised by a lively interdisciplinarity, bringing together works in continental philosophy, medieval theology, history, history of art and film studies. Iconoclasm, in fact, encompasses different ambits and cannot be ascribed to one field without referring to other disciplines. It is impossible, for instance, to discuss the iconoclastic value of a monochromatic image in a film without referencing the philosophical and historical interpretations of the copy-prototype relationship. Moreover, the multidisciplinary approach is also a consequence of the scarcity of scholarly work on iconoclasm and cinema.

In a film context, only two main sources are available, and neither of them is in English. Marion Poirson-Dechonne's *Entre spiritualité et laïcité, la tentation iconoclaste du cinéma* [*Between Spirituality and Secularism, the Iconoclastic Temptation of Cinema*] (2016) represents the only monograph on the topic to date. The book establishes conceptual links between certain aspects of Christian Catholic theology and the film medium, identifying some secularised iconoclastic tendencies in the cinema, and constitutes an important source for approaching the issue of iconoclasm in film. The author discusses iconoclasm in the cinema in a broad sense, taking into account a variety of films, many of which are not iconoclastic *stricto sensu*. While also touching on two potentially iconoclastic devices (the black screen and cacophony), Poirson-Dechonne focuses more on the films' content, investigating cinematic representations of Christian themes, such as the father-son resemblance and the incarnation, in both religious and secularised terms. Her book does however contain an overview of films which directly put into crisis the relation between images and their referents, differentiating among aesthetic, political and ethical iconoclasm. It is in particular her addressing questions on our right to show and see everything on a screen that is significant to my discussion of cinematic iconoclasm. Nevertheless, my treatment of the topic considerably differs from Poirson-Dechonne's since I develop my argument from a more philosophically focused notion of iconoclasm, concentrating on the film form by means of the two opposing notions of *eidōlon* and *eikōn*. The other fundamental text on iconoclasm in cinema, to which I often turn throughout the book, is the special issue *'Cinema e iconoclastia'* [Cinema and Iconoclasm] (Perniola 2013), which collects essays ranging from iconoclastic and iconophilic interpretations of the cinematic close-up to the anti-mimetic significance of monochromatic screens. It is an extremely useful introduction to the issue of iconoclasm in the cinema and one of my main sources for discussing an iconoclastic film style.

Dario Gamboni's *The Destruction of Art: Iconoclasm and Vandalism since the French Revolution* (1997) and Bruno Latour and Peter Weibel's *Iconoclash: Beyond the Image Wars in Science, Religion and Art* (2002) constitute essential sources on iconoclastic approaches in modern and contemporary arts. While the former is a fascinating study of destructive gestures in the visual arts as opposed to vandalistic acts at historical turning points, the latter edits together essays on anti-mimetic artworks in painting, video art, music and happenings, as well as on contemporary iconoclastic attitudes in religion and science. I draw on these contributions to highlight an iconoclastic thinking running through Western arts, thus establishing a dialogue between cinema and the other arts based on their shared tendency towards image destruction. What is more, Gamboni's and Latour and Weibel's works are useful for further differentiating iconoclastic gestures within artworks from iconoclastic acts directed against cultural artefacts. Both gestures, however, attest to the political, ethical and emotional charge of images: from the literal or metaphorical dismantling of figuration in the arts to the physical destruction of sacred icons in the eighth and ninth centuries up to recent decolonisation and the BLM movements' efforts to remove statues of supporters of slavery, images rarely leave us indifferent and can often prompt visceral responses. Stacy Boldrick's recently published *Iconoclasm and the Museum* (2020) builds on this idea, expanding on Gamboni's argument and reinforcing the importance of iconoclasm – as artistic practice, institutional attitude and ethico-political approach – at the present moment, focusing on notions of loss broadly understood.

Quite contrarily, there is a wealth of sources on iconoclasm available in philosophy, theology and history. A crucial text discussing the *eikōn-eidōlon* dichotomy in ancient philosophy is Suzanne Saïd's *'Deux noms de l'image en grec ancien: idole et icône'* [Two Names of the Image in Ancient Greek: Idol and Icon] (1987), which also hints at the consequences of this opposition on contemporary interpretations of the image. Gerhart B. Ladner's 'The Concept of the Image in the Greek Fathers and the Byzantine Iconoclastic Controversy' (1953) offers a detailed analysis of the *eikōn-eidōlon* dichotomy in medieval theology, presenting the conflicting arguments of Christian iconophiles and iconoclasts. Among the essential works on philosophical and historical iconoclasm is Marie-José Mondzain's *Image, Icon, Economy: The Byzantine Origins of the Contemporary Imaginary* (2005), which effectively explains the iconoclastic and iconophilic perspectives in the eighth and ninth centuries by tracing the influence of Byzantine thought on current interpretations of images. In this work, as well as in *Le Commerce des regards* [*The Commerce of the Gazes*] (2019) and *Homo spectator* (2013), Mondzain elaborates on the constitutive relational character of the image as *eikōn*, building on its etymological meaning as well as ancient and medieval philosophy's interpretations. While my understanding of iconoclasm in an artistic context diverges from Mondzain's (because she rejects an iconoclastic interpretation of anti-mimesis), I nevertheless share her definition of the *eikōn* as relational. Other invaluable sources on which I base my understanding of iconoclasm are Alain Besançon's *The Forbidden Image: An Intellectual History of Iconoclasm* (2000), a detailed study encompassing iconoclasm from the seventh century BCE to early-twentieth-century Russian abstract art, and Maria Tilde Bettetini's *Le radici dell'iconoclastia* [*The Roots of Iconoclasm*] (2006), which thoroughly discusses iconoclasm in history and philosophy, emphasising its enduring effects on contemporary society and the entertainment industry.

As it is clear from these few titles, my approach to iconoclasm is philosophically inflected – not only because iconoclasm originated as a philosophical stance concerning the relationship between images and their models, but also because it has been overlooked by other disciplines, including film studies. Therefore, in developing and defending my argument, I have tried to maintain philosophical iconoclasm in close dialogue with the metaphorical, and at times literal, destruction of images in the cinema. The intertwining of philosophy and cinema on the issue of iconoclasm has also led me to circumscribe the scope of this book to Western European films made after World War II. The choice of Western Europe is a direct consequence of the fact that the currently available works on iconoclasm primarily investigate the topic in the philosophical and historical context of Western Europe, which is also significantly characterised by an increased emphasis on and a contradictory attitude towards the visual sphere. As such, the Western European context is particularly suitable for discussing both the pervasiveness of reproduced moving images and the potential of iconoclasm. The decision to take World War II as a temporal watershed for the book comes from its being one of the defining historical events of modern and contemporary Europe and its cinematic production, as many scholars have pointed out (among others, Aumont 2003, 145–46; Bellour 2012, 133; Daney 2004a; Deleuze 1997a, xi; Grespi 2013, 41; Sinnerbrink 2016, 56; Witt 2013, 130).

This does not mean that films made before World War II cannot be iconoclastic (for instance, there is an argument to be made about the iconoclasm of the historical avant-gardes of the 1910s and 1920s). However, I believe that the war, the Shoah and the Liberation have brought some of the already present issues of images to the limit and have accentuated the feeling of disorientation regarding reality, which find a new expression in the cinema. Moreover, the Shoah has marked an unprecedented crisis in Western representation, famously expressed in Theodor W. Adorno's (1967, 34) then retracted claim on the barbarism of writing poetry after Auschwitz. Rather than placing the Shoah under such an extreme and dangerous ban, it should be considered as one of those historical 'objects' that lack a direct image and yet demand to be made visible (see, Nancy 2005, 27–50; Saxton 2007; 2008; Wajcman 1998).

Following this thread of thought, it would seem that films on the Shoah constitute the most appropriate works for discussing iconoclasm in the cinema, and in a way they are. Nonetheless, I have chosen not to consider such films for several reasons. Firstly, the Shoah is a broad and extremely complex theme which would have taken most of the book if it were to be appropriately considered. My aim, however, is to delineate a wider notion of cinematic iconoclasm and its possible applications. Secondly, the issue of representing the Shoah in films, the absence of images of the event per se and its status beyond mimetic reproduction have already been thoroughly discussed by film scholars such as Joshua Hirsch (2004), Oleksandr Kobrynskyy and Gerd Bayer (2015) and Libby Saxton (2007; 2008). Lastly, the issue of iconoclasm in relation to the cinematic representation of the Shoah has been considered, albeit not systematically, in Ivelise Perniola's *L'immagine spezzata: Il cinema di Claude Lanzmann* [*The Broken Image: Claude Lanzmann's Cinema*] (2007) and Gérard Wajcman's *L'Objet du siècle* [*The Object of the Century*] (1998). Therefore, while my framework can be used to further discuss the problem of representation in relation to the Shoah, I have selected films which deal with a variety of topics, from self-reflexivity to others' suffering. Moreover, the initial selective criteria regarded the film form. Rather than being concerned with depictions of iconoclasm at the level of content, my exploration of the topic focuses on iconoclastic aesthetic forms in the cinema. Accordingly, the film images analysed throughout are characterised by the breaking of a mimetic audio-visual form: I look at monochromatic screens, freeze-framed shots, slow-motion sequences and scenes where sound is disruptive or disjointed from the visual element. Such stylistic devices result from an iconoclastic understanding of the copy-prototype relationship, opening up sudden audio-visual hiatuses that require spectators to fill them with meaning.

Since the book consists of an introduction to the issue of iconoclasm in the cinema, I have selected films that best epitomise deliberate destructive gestures against mimesis to bear witness to the distance existing between reality and its possible audio-visual representation. Accordingly, cinematic iconoclasm as critique of the *eidōlon* is discussed via directors who share an undermining of the film image as referential copy, short-circuiting the harmonic relation between aural and visual elements. Isidore Isou, Guy Debord, Carmelo Bene and Jean-Luc Godard have all been vocal about the film image's deceptive power, explicitly advocating for the destruction of cinema in one way or another. Their critique of artistic mimesis resonates with ancient and medieval arguments against the lure of images, establishing a connection between philosophical and historical roots of iconoclasm with modern understandings of the film medium. Isou's Lettrist film *Traité de bave et d'éternité*, Debord's oeuvre and Bene's *Our Lady of the Turks* are born out of an urgency to literally and metaphorically destroy cinema as a reproductive medium, as attested by their physically manipulating of the film strip and their metaphorically dismantling of audio-visual images as mimetic copies of reality. Godard's entire work oscillates between a critique of the capitalist image (the *eidōlon*) of Lettrist and Situationist tradition, and a liminal ethics when it comes to representing the ineffable and the invisible. Therefore, his magnum opus *Histoire(s) du cinéma* constitutes a fascinating link between the cinematic *eidōlon* and the iconoclastic *eikōn*. In considering in greater detail the ethics of cinematic iconoclasm, I have chosen films where the rejection of mimesis is inextricably bounded to ethical concerns regarding visibility. Marguerite Duras's *Le Navire Night*, Derek Jarman's *Blue*, Ingmar Bergman's *Cries and Whispers* and Krzysztof Kieślowski's *Three Colours: Blue* are exemplary of an iconoclastic approach to ethically charged topics (such as sexual desire, homosexuality, pain and death), metaphorically destroying an easy audio-visual access to the either invisible or ineffable events of the film.

Although I discuss only one woman film-maker, I believe that the selected works and directors engage with a variety of aesthetic and ethical issues that involve diversity in terms of gender, culture and language; therefore, they are conducive to an exploration of cinematic iconoclasm which transcends a patriarchal perspective. Isou, by means of iconoclastic style (*montage discrépant*, as he himself will term it), develops a critique of French foreign policy, especially of the First Indochina War (1946–54); Debord condemns the alienating society of the spectacle through a dismantling of intelligible relationships between the image track and the sound track; Bene engages with the hollowness of Catholic religion and the motherly essence that it attributes to women by way of unintelligible voices; Godard investigates a number of issues concerning cinema and history through multiple images; Duras explores sexual desire via the severing of any tie between aural and visual elements; Jarman operates a subversion of the negative representation of the person with AIDS by employing a monochromatic screen as the constitutive image track of the film, thus denouncing the status of homosexuality in 1980s UK; finally, Bergman and Kieślowski destroy female faces through fades out, recalling a long iconographic tradition concerning the face of Holy Mary and women's suffering. The films thus share not only an iconoclastic understanding of cinema and an anti-mimetic approach to film style, but also a lively interest in social, cultural and political issues, which actively contributes to making these works excellent examples of the ethical relevance of iconoclastic gestures.

Iconoclasm in Film Studies

Notwithstanding the scarcity of material on cinema and iconoclasm, there are nonetheless some works in film studies that touch on the issue. Much film scholarship on iconoclasm focuses on three core ideas: (1) the iconoclastic quality of political modernism; (2) iconoclastic and iconophilic interpretations of the face in the close-up; and (3) anti-mimesis as an iconoclastic gesture carrying ethical concerns. I build on such contributions to develop the *eikōn-eidōlon* dichotomy in cinema and explore how film can represent ethically charged topics and stimulate the viewer's imaginative capacity via a disruptive aesthetics.

The Iconoclastic Aspect of Political Modernism

Albeit never explicitly referencing iconoclasm, political modernism's critique of classical cinema resonates with Platonic and Christian arguments on the condemnation of sensible images. The exponents of political modernism, in fact, rejected cinema as a window onto the world in an attempt to 'erode identification with the image as real' (Rodowick 1994, xiii), placing classical cinema and its reproduction of the dominant (namely, capitalist) version of ideology at the core of their critique. Reiterating arguments from philosophical and religious iconoclasm, political modernism and Marxist-influenced film theory contend that the more mimetic the image is the more it lies, misleading the spectator to believe in the objective reality of what is represented on screen. Accordingly, they advocate for the destruction of the cinematic image as deceptive copy (the *eidōlon*) through images that lay bare their artificial nature.

Ann Kibbey, in *Theory of the Image: Capitalism, Contemporary Film, and Women* (2005), identifies an iconoclastic understanding of cinema in leftist film theorists' opposition between the deceptive images of classical narrative cinema and the true images of counter-cinema. She delineates similarities between the iconoclasm of Calvin's Protestantism and that of Marxism and theories akin to it. It is in particular Calvin's rejection of sacred images as false representations and his welcoming of the sacramental objects as true images which allow for a parallel with leftist film theory's opposition between false and true images in the cinema. Kibbey (2005) maintains that the theories of the image developed in the period from 1960 to 1980 are inherently iconoclastic: 'This era of film theory was fueled by an iconoclastic assault on the false images of Hollywood film, from the theorists of the cinematic apparatus to Laura Mulvey's famous essay' (2). Kibbey likens Guy Debord's spectacle, Jacques Lacan's mirror stage, Jean-Louis Baudry's cinematic apparatus and Laura Mulvey's gendered approach to the iconoclastic distrust in images. In her view, these theorists committed the sin of reiterating the Calvinist precepts of false images in their speculations, without however providing an alternative to the iconoclastic paradigm.

Drawing on Kibbey's argument, Richard Rushton's *The Reality of Film: Theories of Filmic Reality* (2011) expands on the reality-illusion dichotomy in cinema. Exponents of political modernism are understood as 'modern-day iconoclasts' (39), because of their differentiating between the deceptive (false) images of Hollywood-like cinema and the self-reflexive (true) images of counter-cinema. For Rushton, the issue lies in the oppositional logic between reality and illusion, which is grounded in a representational understanding of cinema; that is, phenomenal reality pre-exists the reality of cinema, establishing at least a chronological hierarchy between the two realities of the referent and the image. While decrying this binary logic as limited and limiting, Rushton explains the iconoclastic character of political modernism, for there is a divide between the cinematic image as a visual replica of a portion of reality which alleges to be transparent for its high mimetic potential (i.e., *eidōlon*), and the image of counter-cinema which 'denounce[s] the representation of reality and all cinematic attempts at verisimilitude' (28).

Such a perspective is reminiscent of Plato's ontological hierarchy between the world of ideas and the world of things, wherein images of art's deceptive potential hinges on their inadequacy to represent intelligible models. Rosalind Galt likens the Platonic 'denigration of the image' (2011, 180) to Marxist film theory's rejection of Hollywood cinema and defines both perspectives as iconoclastic. In discussing the Platonic *eidōlon*, she identifies the same conception of the image in the cinema, specifically in the work of post-World War II leftist theorists. As Plato distinguished between perfect, true beings and false, illusory copies, so do leftist film theorists differentiate between the illusionism of classical cinema and the reality of counter-cinema. Galt (2011) effectively claims that 'in this model of the image [i.e., the *eidōlon*], Plato lays the foundations for an iconoclasm that grounds much modern image theory' (181).

In their critical analysis of the iconoclasm of Marxist-influenced film theory, Kibbey, Rushton and Galt reject an iconoclastic perspective for its supposed reduction of cinema to an opposition between illusionistic images and self-critical images, exhibiting analogies between the Platonic and Christian suspicion of visual images and some of the arguments of leftist film theory. While I agree with their reading of leftist film theory as iconoclastic, I endorse an iconoclastic perspective in the arts, grounding my argument on a representational understanding of the cinema within which images do not stand on their own but relate to a world they re-present and re-produce. In this scenario, the *eidōlon* escapes a reduction to a simple false image. In his poetical delineating of the ancient meaning of *eidōlon*, Régis Debray (1992, 28–30) emphasises its phantasmatic status as a shadow and therefore as a double, connecting the birth of the image to death (via mortuary rites as well as the image's potential to mortify reality). Indeed, the main issue with the image as *eidōlon* is its being a double, a copy that replicates the visible features of its model, to the point of being always on the verge of replacing it, and that retains a power of influencing thought and making someone believe in a falsity. As in Plato and Christian iconoclasm, where the *eidōlon* distracts from the contemplation of intelligible ideas and God, respectively, relating itself only to the sensible realm, so in the cinema the *eidōlon* is an image which overshadows the original and aims at substituting it. In the work of Isou, Debord, Bene and Godard, the *eidōlon* is the kind of film image that hides its character of artificial copy through the naturalism of mise-en-scène and continuity editing, and this carries ethico-political consequences. The limit of this critique, however, is its trouble in overcoming the logic of self-reflexivity and bringing the discourse beyond the criticism of the image as illusory copy. As both Kibbey and Rushton observe, caught in the urge of dismantling the impression of reality of Hollywood-like cinema, some of the exponents of iconoclasm as critique risk remaining trapped in their own criticism.

Iconophilic and Iconoclastic Interpretations of the Cinematic Close-up

The cinematic close-up has been succinctly discussed as a way of exploring the distinction between iconoclasm and iconophilia, opposing the film image as revelation of a human essence and as the place of inhumanity *par excellence*. While various scholars have considered conflicting interpretations of the close-up (among others, Aumont 2003; Doane 2003; Turvey 1998), Angela Dalle

Vacche (2003) and Barbara Grespi (2013) explicitly address the issue of the face in the close-up as a field of debate between iconoclastic and iconophilic interpretations in the cinema. They dwell particularly on the iconophilic stance, identifying a sacred conception of the cinematic medium as a tool for revealing a human essence that finds its most suitable expression in the magnification of the close-up – a position exemplified by early film theorists Louis Delluc's ([1920] 1985, 34–36, 50–61) and Jean Epstein's ([1921] 1977; [1926] 2012) notion of *photogénie*, and Béla Balázs's ([1945] 1970, 52–88; [1924] 2010, 27–51) concept of physiognomy. Accordingly, Dalle Vacche's and Grespi's notion of iconoclasm suggests a disbelief in the revelatory capacity of the cinematic medium and in the close-up's viability as a mediator between a visible, exterior surface and a purported invisible, inner depth. It is 'the face in close-up and the close-up as the face of objects' (Dalle Vacche 2003, 15) that elicits a division between iconophilic and iconoclastic stances in the cinema. The opposition originates from the interpretation of the face, whether as a door to the soul or as a surface of inhumanity.

Grespi is the only scholar theorising a proper opposition between iconoclasts and iconophiles in cinema with specific reference to the face in the close-up, in her article 'L'immagine sfregiata: Il cinema e i volti del sacro' [The Scarred Image: Cinema and Sacred Faces] (2013). On the one hand, she discusses the trust in film images in the work of Epstein and Balázs, and their understanding of the facial close-up as a site for the surfacing of the soul and a manifestation of inner life; on the other hand, she considers Gilles Deleuze and Félix Guattari's concept of cinematic close-up as a dehumanising device, consequently understanding the defacement of such a close-up as an iconoclastic gesture – a controversial and imprecise perspective that does not take into account Deleuze's rejection of Platonism and duality.

In Grespi's view, the notions of *photogénie* and physiognomy bespeak an iconophilic attitude, since they hinge on the strong bond between the cinematic close-up and its phenomenal referent. Magnified by the close-up, the face intensifies its expressive power by filling up the whole screen and by connecting interiority and exteriority. In Epstein and Balázs, mystics 'of the 1920s close-up, the filmic face simply constitutes the place of interception of the sacred concealed in man'[4] (Grespi 2013, 42). The face in the close-up is therefore *eikōn* insofar as it is capable of establishing a truthful link with the phenomenal referent in a mimetic manner. This stance is corroborated by other accounts of the privileged role accorded to the face in cinema. For instance, Mary Ann Doane (2003) addresses *photogénie* as a form of cinephilia, and Jacques Aumont defines Epstein's and Balázs's perspectives as idealistic since they presuppose the very possibility of a nexus between reality and its filmic representation. Aumont (2003) remarks that *photogénie* and physiognomy 'outline an aesthetic of the face in film. Idealistic aesthetic that is, it is based on the hope of a revelation that it believes is possible because it believes fundamentally in the face as organic unit, infrangible, total. The form of this revelation is [. . .] the close-up' (139).

Grespi sets Epstein's and Balázs's iconophilic position against Deleuze and Guattari's account of the facial close-up, erroneously defining the French philosophers as iconoclasts. While sharing some of Epstein's and Balázs's arguments, Deleuze and Guattari conceive of the face as a surface, hence pure exteriority. That is, the connection between the face and interiority is severed, and the face becomes the result of a process of abstraction called 'faciality' [*visagéité*] (Deleuze and Guattari 1987, 168). This process of 'making a face' alludes to the frontal part of the head where the eyes and mouth are, but more importantly comes to signify a reference to any surface that functions as the cultural and political construct of face. The process of facialisation designates the imposition of a face onto a subject and is codified by the binary system white wall/black holes which produces the face as a politics. The facialised face is a politics because it consists in the acquisition of a standardised face, that of the 'white man' (Deleuze and Guattari 1987, 176). Deleuze and Guattari claim that 'the face is [. . .] White Man himself, with his broad white cheeks and the black holes of his eyes. The face is Christ. The face is the typical European' (176). As a socio-political construct, the face is closely linked to Christianity; however, the Christological reference acquires a political connotation rather than a religious one, in the sense of Christianity as the socio-political machine of meaning in Western Europe. Accordingly, the face in itself contains the seeds for racism since it suppresses the other's differences and aims at conforming all faces to its own. As Deleuze and Guattari explain, the face of the other than the white man 'must be Christianized, in other words, facialized' (178). Instead of establishing a relation with the other, the face produces a distance with the specific purpose of ascribing every face to the dominant face, the standardised 'white man'; the facial close-up accordingly becomes the vehicle for the revelation of inhumanity:

> *The face, what a horror.* It is naturally a lunar landscape, with its pores, planes, matts, bright colors, whiteness, and holes: there is no need for a close-up to make it inhuman; it is naturally a close-up, and naturally inhuman. (Deleuze and Guattari 1987, 190)

In the face's status as entity disconnected from reality in its *hic et nunc* lies the core of Deleuze and Guattari's interpretation of the cinematic close-up.

Complete in itself, the face does not contain the traces of its relationship with the world. Thus, the face in the close-up, far from being the site of human revelation, like in Balázs and Epstein, turns into a means for revealing 'the inhuman in human beings' (Deleuze and Guattari 1987, 171). The facial close-up is stripped of any connecting capacity and presents, instead, the very void at the core of humanity, the fact that there is nothing to be shown and revealed.

As a result, Deleuze and Guattari advocate for the dismantling of the face, making it a pockmarked face that ceases to respond to the facialisation machine – the white wall/black holes system. Indeed, if the facial close-up responds to a logic of eliminating differences in the uniqueness of the Christ-face, the defacement of this close-up would allow for a deviation from the standard and, consequently, for the expression of a face other than that of the 'white man'. However, defacing the close-up does not correspond to a return to the human head, but constitutes a politics itself. In both cases – the Christ-face and the dismantled face – Deleuze and Guattari's facial close-up ceases to configure itself as the Epsteinian and Balázsian mediator between the individual and the social life in the rising metropolis of the early twentieth century. In the view of Deleuze and Guattari, who write in the context of a globalised, post-war world, the face comes to signify the very impossibility of the encounter with the other. It is possible to trace here a specific change in the vision of the world, taking World War II as the separating event. Both the iconophilic interpretation and that of Deleuze and Guattari assign to the facial close-up a revelatory power. However, in the iconophilic perspective there is always something interior (a soul) to reveal, an invisible life of humans and things that the film medium is able to record and reproduce on the screen. Quite differently, in Deleuze and Guattari's interpretation, the cinema lays bare the absence of revelation in reality, the fact that there is nothing to be unconcealed.

Grespi (2013, 45–49) proposes an iconoclastic interpretation of the inhuman and defacement in Deleuze and Guattari, understanding the facial close-up as a de-humanising device and its defacement as an iconoclastic gesture. For Grespi, erasing the facialised face becomes the iconoclastic re-appropriation of the face, which would allow for the overcoming of the faciality process: from a facial twitch to a deformed or scarred face, the attack towards the unity of the facialised face would enable a breaking with the politics of the faciality process. That is, by interpreting Deleuze and Guattari's concept of inhumanity as something that ought to be escaped, she identifies in the defacement of the close-up an iconoclastic intent to break with a false image of a true model. However, Deleuze and Guattari never mention the possibility of a humanity in humans. Rather, it is inhumanity itself which is constituent of human beings.

Therefore, inhumanity would be the true essence instead of a false appearance. Nevertheless, it would be a mistake to discuss Deleuze using the binary opposition true-false, since he overcomes, or at least aims at overcoming, this Western dichotomy in his philosophy.

In 'Plato and the Simulacrum' (1983), Deleuze elaborates on his critique of Plato's oppositional logic between model and copy, namely between what is intelligible and what is sensible. He draws a distinction between two types of images: the *eikōn* – which he calls copy or icon – and the *eidōlon* – which he addresses as simulacrum. However, Deleuze's simulacrum does not correspond to the image as *eidōlon* in the way in which it is considered in this book. After using the term simulacrum with the Platonic meaning of *eidōlon* – namely, a false image, hence an image in a relationship of alterity with a model – he then continues his criticism of the Platonic representational system by employing the same word (simulacrum) with the meaning of an image without a model. Deleuze leaves unexplained the transition from one meaning to the other, employing the same term for two quite dissimilar conceptions of the image. More to the point, what Deleuze reproves to Plato is his representational logic, the enclosing of the image in a relationship with a model. Deleuze rejects this dualism in favour of the simulacrum without model. His overturning of Platonism, therefore, consists of the abolishment of the copy-prototype dichotomy to the exaltation of the image without prototype. Consequently, Deleuze cannot be addressed as iconoclast insofar as his philosophy positions itself beyond the representational paradigm necessary for both the iconoclastic and the iconophilic perspectives: the metaphysical requirement of a true(r) model and the binary vision of the world collapse. In Deleuze, there is no place for images referencing their model, but only for surfaces – *phantasmata*, or the exteriority of the facial close-up.

Without adopting a Deleuzian approach, I build on these contributions about the facial close-up, emphasising the significance of the face for iconoclastic gestures. Indeed, both the destruction of the cinematic *eidōlon* and the creation of iconoclastic *eikones* often involve the human face: in an attempt to break the mimetic relationship between phenomenal reality and its audiovisual representation, faces are physically or metaphorically dismantled. As during the Byzantine controversy, when icons representing the face of Christ were physically smashed, so in the cinema the face in the close-up becomes the privileged site for iconoclastic gestures – from Isou's and Bene's literally scraping of human faces to Bergman's and Kieślowski's poetic fade-outs which plunge the characters' faces into a blank screen. While I consider the significance of the Western concept of the face and its destruction throughout the book, the facial close-up is particularly relevant for the analysis of *Cries and Whispers* and *Three Colours: Blue*, where iconoclastic gestures occur on the magnified faces of the female characters. The figurative destruction of the women's faces in these films represents a clear passing from a mere rejection of the cinematic *eidōlon* (namely, a mimetic image incapable of representing interiority) to the creation of iconoclastic *eikones* (that is, anti-mimetic images which maintain a relationship with the invisible model). The human face, which is the most emotionally charged part of the body, becomes the locus for an interrogation of visibility and its limits, also developing a criticism of the mimetic representability of the female face and women's suffering – from the iconography of the Holy Mary, the quietly suffering mother, to the iconoclastic rendering of Liv Ullmann's, Ingrid Thulin's and Juliette Binoche's raw pain. Paradoxically, the destruction of the women's figurative faces becomes a way to account for a much more realistic, disorderly pain that rejects a spectacularisation of suffering.

Iconoclasm of Anti-Mimesis

Iconoclasm has been bounded to anti-mimesis since its inception – the biblical ban on any graven image and the Platonic condemnation of images of art, for instance, were fuelled by a rejection of the *eidōlon*'s excessive visual similarity with the referent. Artistic anti-mimesis does not always correspond to an iconoclastic intent, whereas the opposite is true; namely, that iconoclastic gestures within the arts are directed against mimesis. From Russian abstract art's attempts at representing the Absolute via monochromatic paintings to Lucio Fontana's cut canvases aimed at reaching the unrepresentable reality beyond the painting's surface, from avant-garde cinema's and video art's disrupting of habitual engagements with images and sounds to contemporary audio-visual media's uses of blank screens and off-screen sounds, anti-mimetic aesthetics hinge on the distance between copy and prototype, thereby implying that the image cannot truthfully reproduce the model. While intelligible models may appear to place mimetic representation more decidedly in a moral maze (how to figuratively render the invisibility at their core?), also sensible phenomena challenge a seemingly uncomplicated reproduction of reality, especially following an understanding of the visual field as ethically laden. Libby Saxton (2010c) convincingly ties the issue of mimesis to that of ethics, observing that it is from cinema's 'privileged bond with reality' (26) – namely, from its possibility to mimetically reproduce people, animals, objects (their appearance, sounds and movement) – that ethical questions arise. Similarly, Asbjørn Grønstad (2016) stresses the ethical weight deriving from the close nexus between cinematic reproduction and phenomenal reality, commenting that 'to capture images is "an ethos, a disposition, and a conduct in regard to the world"' (3). Nevertheless, if the filming of reality is thus far from being a neutral, objective recording of the world, then ethically charged models more forcefully question mimesis because mimetic reproduction potentially risks concealing the unbridgeable gap between the image and its model.

In this respect, the possibility of representing the Shoah is one of the most controversial and debated issues, opposing those in favour of its mimetic re-enactment to the advocates of more subtle ways to represent it without doubling it (Hirsch 2004; Kobrynskyy and Bayer 2015; Perniola 2007; Saxton 2008; Wajcman 1998). Gérard Wajcman (1998) and Ivelise Perniola (2007) elaborate on the issue with specific reference to Claude Lanzmann's oeuvre, understanding his refusal of archival material and re-enactment as responding to an iconoclastic ethics. The *eidōlon*'s doubling of the model is what Wajcman most vehemently condemns in discussing the role of mimesis in art after World War II. He decries and rejects figurative representations of the Shoah insofar as they constitute an 'affirmation of presence. [...] Thus, any image is a negation of death and loss. A negation of absence' (1998, 242). Wajcman is explicitly against artistic mimesis since it presupposes the very possibility of duplicating an original. While mimesis can be acceptable for some models, it becomes unethical when confronted with what does not (or should not) have a double, such as God for the Christian iconoclasts or death in the concentration camps for Wajcman. The image as figuration, hence imitation as duplication – the peculiar feature of the *eidōlon* as the double – constitutes an affirmation of presence because it implies the reproduction of the model's visual features and, consequently, the loss of the prototype's uniqueness. However, from an iconoclastic perspective, some models should be affirmations of absence: absence of images of the invisible God; absence of images of genocidal events themselves. Perniola (2007) draws from Wajcman's (1998) argument on 'militant iconoclasm' (228), analysing how Lanzmann's documentaries preserve the invisibility at the core of the Shoah by negating any access to the event per se. Through the breaking with figuration and mimesis, there is a shift from the Shoah as a spectacle for the eyes – the *eidōlon* consumed in the visible realm – to the Shoah as ethical interrogation – the *eikōn* turned to the invisible sphere.

The link between an anti-mimetic aesthetics and iconoclasm is also present in Marion Poirson-Dechonne's (2016) book on iconoclastic tendencies in the cinema, Daniele Dottorini's (2013) article on the use of black screens in art house films and Luca Venzi's (2006; 2013) work on colour and the dissolution of the film image. These scholars consider the use of black screens and cacophony as potentially ethical responses to issues regarding visibility and as ways to disrupt traditional engagements with a cinematic world. Accordingly, the black screen translates a visual impossibility – namely, something that lacks or should lack a visual equivalent, producing a halting of the spectator's look – whereas cacophony, conceived as the aural counterpart of the black screen, renders what is ineffable; that is, something that cannot be said or can only be said by means of unintelligible sounds. Via the black screen and cacophony, cinematic iconoclasm sets limits for the eyes and the ears: not everything can be clearly seen or heard.

These contributions on iconoclasm, anti-mimesis and ethics are essential for my argument on cinematic iconoclasm as an ethics of (in)visibility. Similar to some of the scholars who have delved into ethics and aesthetic forms in cinema (such as Downing and Saxton 2010; Grønstad 2016; Sinnerbrink 2016), I conceive of cinema as a potentially highly ethical medium, for not only does cinema present ethical quandaries in its content, but it can also produce an ethical form in respect to its content and can elicit the spectator's ethical imagination. It is in this perspective that the iconoclastic *eikōn* can at once embody an ethics of film-making and solicit an ethics of film-viewing by circumventing mimetic forms of representation. I propose an ethics of (in)visibility echoing Wajcman's (1998) expression 'ethics of visibility' (292). In his account, artistic iconoclasm constitutes such an ethics because it aims at '"showing" (*faire voir*) and "making present"' (219) unrepresentable and ineffable subject matter by means other than mimetic reproduction so as to preserve their uniqueness.

I have added the parenthetical (in) to underline the significance of invisibility for the ethics encouraged by iconoclastic gestures in the cinema, an ethics which is possible only insofar as what is visually accessible on the screen stretches towards invisibility, incessantly evoking it through an anti-mimetic aesthetics which overflows representation. The iconoclastic *eikōn* offers itself to sight – it is an image – and perturbs the spectator's look by presenting an absence which has become the real subject of the representation; in this way, an imaginative effort towards the unrepresentable model is aesthetically encouraged. Whether the absence with which we are presented is an absence of figurative images or the absence of our quotidian perception of movement, sound and colour, the iconoclastic *eikōn* forecloses mimetic reproduction, thus troubling our more habitual modes of consuming what is visible. Accordingly, this type of image promotes a liminal ethics that sinks its roots in what is visible while reaching out to the invisibility that inhabits, and haunts, every visible image.

Structure of the Book

The book is comprised of a prologue and two parts, which are further divided into four chapters each. The prologue provides a brief philosophical and historical background to the discussion on cinema and iconoclasm, delineating the main turning points in the iconoclastic debate, from Plato's and Plotinus's ambiguous understanding of artistic mimesis to early Christian theology of the image and the Byzantine controversy. Engaging with the *eikōn-eidōlon* dichotomy, the prologue also outlines how cinema reworks such an opposition, arguing for the aesthetic and ethical potential of artistic destruction.

Part I dwells on cinematic iconoclasm as critique of the *eidōlon* via the work of directors Isidore Isou, Guy Debord, Carmelo Bene and Jean-Luc Godard. The films analysed in this part metaphorically and literally proceed to destroy mimetic audio-visual images to counter their illusory power, thereby reiterating the criticism of the image found in philosophical iconoclasm. The first chapter looks at Isou's explicitly iconoclastic project and his avant-garde film *Traité de bave et d'éternité*, which heralds the destruction of cinema and presents several iconoclastic devices. The second chapter considers the iconoclastic use of monochromatic screens, sound-image disjunctions and freeze-frames in some of Guy Debord's films. Specifically, I take into account *Hurlements en faveur de Sade*, *The Society of the Spectacle* and *In girum imus nocte et consumimur igni*, which exacerbate Isou's iconoclastic perspective. The third chapter examines Carmelo Bene's project to destroy cinema as a medium able to communicate meaning by way of linguistic and sonic disruptions. Through an analysis of his film *Our Lady of the Turks*, I explore how the negation of intelligible images via destructive editing chimes with the elimination of intelligible speech in favour of the voice as logos-less sound. To conclude this part, the fourth chapter goes over some of Jean-Luc Godard's narrative films, specifically *Une Femme mariée* (*A Married Woman*, 1964), *Alphaville, une étrange aventure de Lemmy Caution* (*Alphaville: A Strange Adventure of Lemmy Caution*, 1965) and *Slow Motion* (*Sauve qui peut (la Vie)*, 1980), as well as the destructive works made with the Dziga Vertov Group, before engaging with *Histoire(s) du cinéma*, which constitutes the work ideally bridging Part I and Part II. In Godard's magnum opus, in fact, are found both the critique of the film image as *eidōlon* and the production of iconoclastic *eikones*, those images capable of establishing a relationship with the model by going beyond mimesis.

Part II focuses on iconoclastic *eikones* in the cinema, exploring their ethical quality, and conceptualises cinematic iconoclasm as an ethics of (in)visibility. Addressing questions concerning our right to show and see something on a screen, Part II revolves around the problematics of representing others' inner world and suffering and considers ethically charged films which are also iconoclastic in their aesthetic form. The fifth chapter centres on Marguerite Duras's subversion of the traditional hierarchy between sound track and image track in narrative cinema. I look at the contraposition between aural and visual dimensions in her film *Le Navire Night*, an imageless love story based on the impossible encounter between two lovers, arguing that such an aesthetic choice is conducive to a visually inaccessible, ethical representation of sexual desire and alterity. The sixth chapter analyses Derek Jarman's monochromatic film *Blue*, focusing on its radically iconoclastic approach to colour and sound in recounting stories of suffering, death and love, as well as its denouncing of 1980s British gender politics. The seventh chapter examines the iconoclastic use of red fade-outs and red monochromatic screens in Ingmar Bergman's *Cries and Whispers* which are iconoclastic devices to visually express what goes beyond mimetic reproduction – grief and suffering. Chapter 8 concludes with a detailed analysis of Krzysztof Kieślowski's *Three Colours: Blue*, with particular attention to the black screens that punctuate the narrative and the ethics of film-making and film-viewing that they promote.

Throughout, I trace the thread of an iconoclastic thinking which goes from Plato's suspicion about images of art, through Plotinus's theory of emanation and the Byzantine iconoclastic controversy, up to film theorists' and film-makers' investigation of the limits and ethical implications of mimesis in the cinema. Iconoclasm, as both theoretical approach and artistic practice, has proven to be a useful tool for exploring the aesthetics and the ethics of the film image. It embraces issues concerning the visible and the sayable, bringing attention to potentialities and risks of the film image, and underlines the importance of taking responsibility for the images which we decide to make, look at and share. Ultimately, the study of iconoclasm in cinema, by focusing on difficult images (namely, images which resist an easy and direct attribution of meaning), becomes an exercise in thinking about the ways in which we interact with and communicate through images. From Plato to cinema, our relationship with images is ambiguous and often conflicting: visual images are always on the verge of being considered deceitful appearances; and yet, we continue to interrogate, produce and look at them.

Prologue: The *Eikōn-Eidōlon* Dichotomy from Plato to Film

THE HISTORY OF the Western image, substantially marked by Platonic scepticism, Plotinian ambivalence and Christian iconoclasm, is the story of the human relating to the (sensible and supersensible) world and the human capacity to establish links with absence (the physical absence of God, or of the dead, but also the absence of figurative equivalents for thoughts and emotions). Up to contemporaneity, the image has been oscillating between truth (of the *eikōn*) and falsehood (of the *eidōlon*), between the ability to vivify (the dead flesh of the God-made man, for instance) and the capacity to mortify through doubling. Such an ambiguity of the status of the image, which hinges on our complexified relationship with reality and its possible representation, persists in the cinema, in which the seemingly closer relationship with reality (because of the indexical bond of mechanical recording) makes it all the more compelling to understand the relation between film image and referent.

Iconoclastic stances traverse ancient and medieval debates up to current attitudes about visuality. This prologue briefly traces some of the essential turning points in the debate on the Western image, with particular emphasis on the germinating of an iconoclastic perspective, which provides the background for destructive gestures in the cinema. In the film medium, the reality-illusion binary is significant for developing an iconoclastic rejection of artistic mimesis in an attempt to avoid the perils of the *eidōlon* and its consequent impoverishment of reality via its mimetic doubling. The political and ethical potentialities of an iconoclastic approach to cinema reside in the tension between a need to represent and a will to avoid duplication, between the extreme visibility and richness of the mimetic image and the opaque vision of the iconoclastic *eikōn*.

Main Turning Points in the Debate on Images

Platonic philosophy constitutes an essential point of reference in the debate on images and has influenced both iconoclastic and iconophilic thought (Besançon 2000, 25–37; Bettetini 2006; Halliwell 2007; Ladner 1953; Mondzain 2005; Saïd 1987). Although the more widespread interpretation is of a negative conception of images (primarily based on *The Republic*), which makes Plato a sort of forerunner of iconoclasm, there are nonetheless conflicting views on mimesis in his dialogues that challenge the over-simplified idea of Plato as utterly against images. Plato distinguishes between two separate worlds, that of intelligible ideas – the eternal and immutable beings, accessible through the intellect – and that of sensible things. The phenomenal world is a copy (mimesis) of the intelligible world, so that Plato's cosmology can be read as a descent from the perfection of ideas to the lowest copies of copies thereof. There are the ideas, eternal models; then, there are sensible things, copies of the ideas; lastly, there are images and works of art, reproductions of sensible things, images of images. Thus, everything that exists, except for intelligible ideas, is in a mimetic relation with something else.

In this context, mimesis in art tends to assume a negative connotation because it implies an act of producing a tertiary mode of being. Since the sensible world is already a reproduction of the world of ideas, or a secondary mode of being, images and works of art as mimesis of reality are reproductions of a reproduction, three times removed from truth (ideas). Plato explains this logic via the example of a bed: there are three types of bed; namely, the intelligible idea of bed, the material bed made by the artisan and the bed depicted by the painter. While the artisan directly copies the idea of bed, the painter copies the physical bed, which is a copy itself (*Republic*, 596b–598d). Therefore, the issue with images of art lies in their model: rather than imitating intelligible ideas, artworks consist of imitations of sensible things. Accordingly, art can be apprehended exclusively through the senses, and images of art are *eidōla* belonging to the phenomenal world of appearances. Art deceives insofar as it can only reproduce sensible things while claiming to imitate intelligible realities; hence, the more the image visually resembles the sensible model, the more it potentially misleads the viewer. As Suzanne Saïd (1987) remarks, '*eidōlon* appears every time that Plato wants to underline the degradation that accompanies the passage from the intelligible to the sensible or from a degree of the sensible to another thereof' (318). Plato's worries about images of art, which resonate with modern and contemporary concerns regarding visual representations, stem from their 'psychological power' (Halliwell 2002, 73); that is, images' power of influencing thought and making someone believe in a falsity. Such an attitude is a direct consequence of 'Plato's approach to the psychology of mimesis [which] is grounded in the assumption that there is continuity, even equivalence, between our relations to people and things in the real world and the people and things presented in mimetic art' (Halliwell 2002, 76). Because of this continuity, Plato maintains an ambiguous perspective on images, now repudiating them as deceptive, now granting them some dignity.

Some Platonic dialogues (especially, the *Timaeus*, the *Symposium* and the *Laws*), in fact, provide a more positive view on mimesis within which the image as *eikōn* is slightly rehabilitated insofar as it establishes a connection with what is intelligible. Although the Platonic *eikōn* does not acquire the value reserved for intelligible ideas and remains apprehensible only via the senses, it nonetheless ceases to be a mere visual replica of a physical appearance by addressing the super-sensible sphere. Stephen Halliwell (2002) unpacks some of the intricacies in Plato's thought regarding mimesis, contending that

> such complexity is connected to a characteristic tension between discrepant impulses in Plato's thinking. The first, a kind of 'negative theology', which leads sometimes in the direction of mysticism, is that reality cannot adequately be spoken of, described, or modeled, only experienced in some pure, unmediated manner (by *logos*, *nous*, *dianoia*, or whatever). The second is that all human thought *is* an attempt to speak about, describe, or model reality – to produce 'images' (whether visual, mental, or verbal) of the real. On the first of these views, mimesis, of whatever sort, is a lost cause, doomed to failure, at best a faint shadow of the truth. On the second, mimesis – representation – is all that we have, or all that we are capable of. In some of Plato's later writing this second perspective is expanded by a sense that the world itself is a mimetic creation. (70–71)

In Plato's philosophy, both the image as *eidōlon* and the image as *eikōn* coexist, paving the way for the future opposition between the Christian idol and icon. However, Plato alone is insufficient to account for the influence of Hellenic thought on the Christian theology of the image. Another essential source includes Plotinus's philosophy, which constitutes a significant link between the Platonic interpretation of the *eikōn* and the Christian understanding of the icon.

Plotinus's more positive notion of image derives from his hierarchical cosmology, within which the image becomes an intermediary between the concreteness of sensible matter and the abstraction of the intelligible sphere. For Plotinus, both the sensible and the intelligible worlds derive by emanation from the first principle of all, the One, which in a downward movement creates everything that exists (*Ennead* V.1[6]). There is therefore continuity between the intelligible realm and the sensible sphere which breaks with the immeasurable Platonic distance between the two worlds. This conception, where everything exists in a single world, shapes the overall Plotinian understanding of the image. While what is intelligible continues to form the highest level of being and sensible matter is the last thing created by the One, images nonetheless belong to, and thus are in a connection with, the same world of what is super-sensible, only at a lower ontological degree (*Ennead* V.8[1]). On the one hand, sensible matter – the lowest level of the hierarchy – corresponds to the *eidōlon* insofar as it is a formless reflection of the One; on the other hand, the image, when it is elevated to the role of intermediary between the sensible and the intelligible spheres, becomes *eikōn*; namely, the first means for carrying out the inner journey towards the One. Such partial rehabilitation of the image hinges on the continuum between the sensible and the intelligible worlds: no longer condemned to the sensible sphere only, the image as *eikōn* positions itself between the two.

However, Plotinus, too, maintains an ambiguous attitude towards mimetic art, now praising it as a means for passing from the sensible to the intelligible world, now diminishing it to a 'plaything' that 'produce[s] a simulacrum [*eidōlon*] of nature' (Halliwell 2002, 318). Art and the image as *eikōn* acquire value as the starting point for the soul's journey towards the One, mediating between sensible and intelligible realms; and yet, the representation of the point of arrival – the One – is interdicted. Christian Catholic thought about images will, however, ignore Plotinus's iconoclastic aspect, instead conceiving of the icon as a way to diminish the distance between humans and God.

The Christian theology of the image intertwines Platonic, Plotinian and Neoplatonic perspectives with the Biblical prohibition of any graven image and the Christian notion of the incarnation of God (Besançon 2000, 81–146; Halliwell 2002, 314, 334; Ladner 1953; Mondzain 2005, 73; Wunenburger 1999, 154). While early Christian theologians (second to fifth century) did not necessarily provide an aesthetics regarding sacred representations, they nonetheless offered two opposite ways of interpreting the sensible world which were to play a fundamental role in the development of iconophilic and iconoclastic arguments. There were conflicting views on the legitimacy of sacred images deriving from different interpretations of, especially, the incarnation, whether as a positive event or, at the opposite end, as an act ontologically inferior to God.[1]

In favour of icons were those theologians who interpreted the incarnation in a positive manner, for God himself had taken a visible, perishable form, and who promoted a rehabilitation of sensible matter to which the body belongs. Conversely, theologians against sacred representation had an overall distrust in sensible matter and the human body, while they highly valued the intelligible part of humans – the soul. They discredited the body in all its aspects and interpreted sensible matter as lacking being, conceiving of corporeal things as a result of human sin. Moreover, in this iconoclastic perspective, Christ was recognised as the only image of God, sharing the same divine nature, whereas man was 'in the image of the image'. Thus, following a Platonic approach, any representation of Christ would be an image having a tertiary mode of being; namely, as Alain Besançon (2000, 94) notes, sacred images would be images of an image (Christ) of the image (God). The Christian issue of 'in the image of' was thus implicated in a complex web of relations among God the father, Christ the son, humans and sensible matter. Theologians who positively interpreted the sensible world viewed sacred images as possible intermediaries between people on earth and God in heaven (*eikones*); conversely, theologians holding a negative conception of the corporeal sphere could not possibly allow the reproduction of the intelligible God in a material frame. Gradually, two main conflicting attitudes became fundamental in the Christian debate on images, that of iconophilia and iconoclasm, openly and physically clashing in the eighth century.

The iconoclastic crises taking place in Byzantium during the eighth and ninth centuries started with the destruction of an icon of Christ at the command of Emperor Leo III and a ban on sacred images in 726 CE. Existing icons were smashed, and the dispute between iconoclasts and iconophiles within Christianity began. It was to last until 843. The causes were not exclusively religious, but also political and economic (Besançon 2000, 114; Bettetini 2006, 92–93; Mondzain 2005, 76); however, it is the theological debate accompanying the Byzantine crises which concerns the relationship between image and prototype. At the core of this debate was the figurative representation of Christ, and the main points in dispute consisted of the circumscribability of the divine God in the icon and the question of consubstantiality (identity of substance between image and model).

Regarding the issue of circumscribability, the iconophiles denied that the icon circumscribes the divine essence, affirming that only Christ's human nature is depicted in the image. This is directly linked to the incarnation, which constitutes the event through which God has circumscribed himself, assuming a body of flesh. Christ is both man and God, having human nature together with divine essence; therefore, in manifesting God's human essence, the incarnation allows for the production of icons that are in relationship with the human Christ but not with his divine nature, which remains invisible and unrepresentable.

More importantly, the icon is 'not the object of a passive fascination' (Mondzain 2005, 90) but aims at taking the viewer's look beyond the visibility of the representation; that is, at transcending the materiality of the icon to reach the intellectual contemplation of God. In iconophilic thought, what differentiates the icon from the idol resides in the relationship they have with the sensible and the intelligible spheres: while the icon exists as an intermediary between the two realms, the idol purely addresses the world of corporeal things.

Conversely, in iconoclastic thought, the icon is far from diminishing the distance separating humans and God and assumes, instead, the connotations of the idol, a false god that consequently has to be destroyed. The iconoclasts rebutted the iconophilic theses, decrying them as heretic because (1) the icon cannot be consubstantial to the model since what is sensible cannot share the same nature as what is intelligible;[2] (2) the icon circumscribes both human and divine essence of Christ because the two are inseparable – God is the invisible, unlimited and un-circumscribable *par excellence*. In the iconoclasts' view, the gap between the divine model and its material image is therefore unbridgeable.

The same image was thus at once icon and idol, depending on the interpretation of the image-model relationship. Icon and idol, coming from *eikōn* and *eidōlon*, respectively, reiterate the same opposition found in Plato and Plotinus. Accordingly, the idol inherits the negative connotations of the Greek *eidōlon* as something that reproduces exclusively a sensible appearance, thereby addressing only sight, and as an image that implies the possibility of producing a visually identical double of the prototype. The image of God as idol/*eidōlon* is idolatrous because it offers itself as the direct object of adoration, without being a means for passing from the visible contemplation of the image to the intellectual contemplation of God.

While both iconophilic and iconoclastic stances rejected the idol, their conception of the icon differed. The iconophiles attributed to the icon the meaning of the *eikōn* as that which mediates between the here below and the there above, whereas for the iconoclasts the icon as conceived by the iconophiles was nothing other than an idol. The same image, therefore, was caught between two diametrically opposed interpretations.

The iconoclastic crisis of the eighth century eventually led to the second Council of Nicaea in 787 and the victory of the iconophilic thesis. The icon of Christ was legitimated and recognised as an image having a privileged link with the divine model. The sacred icon thus became the intermediary between humans and God, albeit not reproducing divine nature. To look on the visible sacredness ideally leads to the imageless contemplation of God. This legitimation was to play a key role in the future of Western thought about images: once the praise of images was detached from the religious context, any type of image began to enjoy an ever-increasing power in the social imaginary that still persists today. Therefore, it is possible to trace a pathway that goes from ancient Greek philosophy to the Byzantine controversy up to contemporary Western imaginary and cinema. As Maria T. Bettetini (2006) insightfully observes,

> there is no doubt that the second Council of Nicaea played a role in Western medieval, modern and postmodern civilization. The legitimation of sacred images drawn up in 787 by the council Fathers is universally recognised as the theoretical and political origin of our civilization of images: from Byzantium to Hollywood. (103)

The history of the Western European imaginary is marked by Platonic and Plotinian philosophy, then re-elaborated from a Christian perspective, leading to the paradoxical and ambiguous status of the image. As consequence, the image has acquired a central role, attested by the daily production of images; and yet, the status of the visual image is still often that of a secondary representation incapable of truthfully expressing reality. Such antagonistic perspectives are also present in the cinema, where both faith and distrust in the film image's ability to reproduce reality coexist.

Iconoclasm in the Cinema

My argument develops from the assumption that the binary between the *eikōn* and the *eidōlon* can be found in the cinema as well, generating conflicting stances. More specifically, different interpretations derive from a dichotomy between reality and illusion, which opposes cinema's claim to a mimetic restitution of reality and cinema's deceptive nature. Such antagonism goes back to the beginning of film theory and involves clashing views about the film image (Allen 1993; Andrew 1976; 1984, 37–56; Perniola 2013; Pezzella 2011; Rushton 2011; Thomson-Jones 2008). There are various stances in the spectrum of the reality-illusion dichotomy in the cinema, which range from a quasi-religious faith in the revelatory capacity of the film medium, such as in the writings of Louis Delluc ([1920] 1985), Jean Epstein ([1921] 1977; [1926] 2012), Béla Balázs ([1945] 1970; [1924] 2010) and Siegfried Kracauer (1960), to a fierce disdain for the cinematic image as a deceitful representation, as in the work of the exponents of political modernism (Comolli and Narboni 1971; Fargier 1971; Heath 1974; MacCabe 1974; Rodowick 1994; Wollen 1976). This picture is further complicated by the formalist position according to which the fundamental aesthetic value of cinema resides in the film image's deviation from reality (Arnheim 1958; Eisenstein 1949; 1957; Münsterberg 1916; Sesonske 1974).

As in religion and philosophy, in cinema too there is a division between a true(r) reality (phenomenal reality or the intelligible sphere of thoughts and emotions), which functions as the prototype, and a less true sensible sphere, that of film images, which stands for the copy. Following a representational understanding of the cinema, it is possible to distinguish between the proponents of cinema as a trustworthy, mimetic reproduction of phenomenal appearances and the advocates of the film image as deceptive and illusory. The first perspective, also referred to as photographic realism, finds its most influential representatives in André Bazin (1967; 1972) and Kracauer (1960), who share a positive account of the indexical relationship between film images and phenomenal referents (reminiscent of the relationship of likeness distinctive of the *eikōn*). Accordingly, the film image has a privileged bond with its model because, by mechanically recording it, it attests that something *has been there* in front of the camera. An extreme and quite negative case of photographic realism is Roger Scruton's (1981) argument on the transparency of photographic and cinematic images, which are deemed surrogates of reality and excluded from representational arts – and therefore from aesthetics. On the other side of the spectrum, the exponents of political modernism best exemplify the interpretation of a particular type of film image as an illusory copy of the real (*eidōlon*) and thus as a means for providing a seemingly objective worldview rather than granting spectators access to an augmented knowledge of reality.

Underlying these various stances there is an understanding of cinema as a re-presentational medium. That is, cinema is a medium which records a reality existing prior to and independently from it; therefore, the film image defines itself according to the relationship it establishes with its phenomenal referent. Among the possible interpretations of this relationship there are the film image that reaches a quasi-complete likeness with its referent (for instance, Scruton's utterly negative transparency of the film image) and the image that distances itself from its referent to the point of great difference. In both limit cases, as in the many stretched between them, the relationship between image and model remains fundamental, whether it is carried out in terms of similarity or alterity.

The copy-prototype relationship, in fact, constitutes the basis for both iconoclastic and iconophilic conceptions, in philosophy as in the cinema. Iconoclasm and iconophilia share the same metaphysical requirement; namely, they posit the existence of a true(r) prototype to which any copy has to be compared.

In the cinema, this metaphysical postulate can be found in the relationship between phenomenal reality and the film image, where the former functions as the prototype for the latter. What is more, the division between sensible and intelligible spheres is also present in a film ambit, although with a slightly different connotation. The sensible stands for what is visible and audible, namely what can be physically seen and heard in phenomenal experience; the super-sensible becomes that which can be shown only through metaphors because it lacks an audio-visual form in phenomenal reality (for instance, emotions and thoughts), or because it consists of something which resists mimetic doubling (for example, the Shoah). The issue of iconoclasm in cinema, then, concerns the problematic relationship between reality and its representation; it explores how emotional and intelligible contents can be transferred into audio-visual images.

What underpins cinematic iconoclasm is an understanding of the relationship between certain film images and their referents in terms of alterity, or at least inadequacy – the image being somewhat insufficient for the representation of the model. Resonating with philosophical interpretations of the *eidōlon*/idol, the cinematic *eidōlon* carries connotations of illusion and deception: it belongs to the sensible sphere only and reproduces the model following a mimetic paradigm. The image as *eidōlon* stands for a figurative image which replicates its model in such a way as to produce an impression of reality. That is, by doubling the appearance of the model, the *eidōlon* has the potential to present itself as if it were the model – which is not tantamount to say that spectators could be tricked into thinking that a moving image of a thing is the thing itself; rather, it refers to the perilous psychological power that images of art can have (see Plato's critique). The image as figuration, hence imitation as duplication – the peculiar feature of the *eidōlon* as the double – constitutes an affirmation of presence because it implies the reproduction of the model's visual features and, consequently, the loss of the prototype's uniqueness. However, from an iconoclastic perspective, some models should be affirmations of absence: absence of images of the invisible God; absence of images of genocidal events (hence, for instance, Claude Lanzmann's iconoclastic refusal of re-enacting the Shoah or using photos and materials from archives for his *Shoah* [1985]).

Moreover, the *eidōlon* in the cinema can come to signify the image of classical or mainstream entertainment cinema. Particularly in Marxist-inflected critique, the *eidōlon* corresponds to a self-evident, seemingly coherent image whose constitutive elements are reasoned (sound is in synch with the visual; the elements of the mise-en-scène are logically linked; the editing is invisible; and so on). The critique of the illusory nature of classical cinema echoes the Platonic condemnation of images of art and resonates with theological iconoclastic discourses.

The cinematic *eidōlon* is problematic, from an iconoclastic perspective, because it retains a highly psychological power and is likely to produce an impression of reality in the spectators. It does so by posing itself as objective representation of an uncomplicated reality depicted as if simply being there, beyond the screen. Thus, the cinematic *eidōlon* consists of the seemingly transparent image of the kind of cinema purported as a window into the world. Accordingly, iconoclastic leftist film-makers attack these images to dismantle the worldview they promote – for instance, in Isidore Isou's cinema, *eidōla* often correspond to images of oppressive power; in Guy Debord's films and theoretical works, *eidōlon* is any image produced by consumer society. What distinguishes the cinematic *eidōlon* is, therefore, its capacity to mimetically double the model which constitutes a threat to the uniqueness of certain prototypes and to challenging representations of reality. Everything is perfectly visible on the screen – Christ and its martyred body of flesh; the bodies and corpses in the concentration camps; the other's suffering. However, these images, the content of which is visually consumable in the clarity of figuration, are defective in evoking a relationship with the invisibility and alterity proper to their models, more often producing an unperceived distance between the viewer and the reality represented.

Quite the contrary, the iconoclastic *eikōn*, which incorporates aspects of the *eikōn* without resorting to mimesis, consists of a refusal of certain audio-visual images out of respect for reality, for its complexity and elusiveness. It thus bespeaks a withdrawal of our representational capacities before specific models. I draw the concept of iconoclastic *eikōn* from Alain Besançon's (2000, 319–82), Gérard Wajcman's (1998) and Jean-Jacques Wunenburger's (1999, 357–59) discussion of iconoclasm in non-figurative art. According to these scholars, non-figurative art reiterates the criticism of the image deriving from the arguments of religious iconoclasm. In abstract painting, for example, the image ceases to imitate nature because the representation of the Absolute, whether religious or secularised, cannot pass through the reproduction of sensible forms of reality. The status of the model as that which is beyond the sensible world determines the rejection of images as mimesis of nature. In this respect, non-figurative art recalls a conception of the image and of the copy-prototype relationship akin to that of the iconoclasts during the Byzantine controversy: the inadequacy of the material means for the reproduction of the model and the consequent rejection of any mimetic principle for representing such prototype distinctly bring to mind iconoclastic arguments against sacred images. Additionally, Wunenburger (1999) discusses how, in non-figurative art, the knowledge of the divine (whether intended in religious or agnostic-spiritual terms) is impossible by sensible means. He concludes:

Iconoclasm, religious or secularised, thus defines not so much a practice of deprivation or prohibition of images as the aspiration not to settle for an image that would claim to exhaust the being, especially when the being posits itself as absolute being. (359)

Abstract painting thus assimilates an iconoclastic component in its refusal to circumscribe an intelligible prototype in a sensible frame, thereby breaking with artistic mimesis. However, the outcome of this process (namely, the negation of the *eidōlon* as a visual double of the model) does not remain grounded in the sensible sphere only. Besançon (2000, 356) delineates the odd peculiarity of certain non-figurative art as retaining some iconoclastic aspects together with the iconophilic intent to represent the absolute being, which was strictly opposed by the iconoclasts. Similarly, Wajcman (1998, 180, 195) addresses as iconoclastic icon an image that deals with both visibility and invisibility without mimetically reproducing the model. This type of image represents something that the eyes can see without however figuratively limiting the intelligible model. While the iconophilic icon uses mimesis to represent the absolute being, reproducing features retraceable in phenomenal reality and thereby enclosing the intelligible prototype in a sensible frame, the iconoclastic *eikōn* respects the unrepresentability of certain models. It is *eikōn* because it mediates between a visual form and its intelligible model, and it is iconoclastic because it refuses mimesis insofar as it would constitute an attempt to reduce what is invisible or unrepresentable to a figurative form; the material means are inadequate for the representation of the model, and yet the model somehow needs to be shown. Hence, the iconoclastic *eikōn* comes to define an image capable of maintaining the unrepresentability and ineffability at the core of those models which lack a visible and audible equivalent in phenomenal reality.

The types of images involved – *eidōlon*, *eikōn*, iconoclastic *eikōn* – are therefore interpretations rather than fixed categories; that is, an image can be *eidōlon* for some viewers and *eikōn* for others (as in the case of Christian icons and idols). Cinematic iconoclasm does not consist in rejecting every image, but only those images deemed deceitful and illusory. The interpretation of certain images as false or inadequate depends on the prototype, on whether it can be apprehended via the physical senses or, quite differently, can only be thought through the intellect or experienced emotionally. Cinematic iconoclasm thus challenges mimetic reproduction rather than censoring images. It questions the Western obsession with mimesis and extreme visibility, contrasting them with images and sounds that undermine our capacity to represent, see and hear; in so doing, it can nurture our ethical imagination.

Concluding Remarks

There is a contradictory thinking that connects Platonic discourses about the deceptive potential of artworks, Plotinus's partial rehabilitation of images and the Byzantine iconoclastic controversy over sacred icons with cinema's dichotomy between illusion and reality. What ties together these seemingly distant arguments is the issue of mimesis, which concerns the relationship between an image as copy and its sensible or intelligible referent. Cinema addresses and reworks the *eikōn-eidōlon* dichotomy which has haunted Western understandings of the image since at least Plato: the *eikōn* is in a relationship with both the sensible world (of the image and the viewer) and the intelligible realm (of the model), whereas the *eidōlon* is exclusively grounded in the sensible sphere. Drawing on philosophical and theological accounts of the nature of images, I propose to investigate the issue of iconoclasm in the cinema using the *eikōn-eidōlon* binary, differentiating between theories and films mainly concerned with the destruction of the illusory image of mainstream entertainment cinema and others more focused on overcoming the level of critique to produce iconoclastic *eikones*. The criticism of the cinematic *eidōlon* grounds any iconoclastic gesture in the cinema and is emphatically present in the destructive works of the directors discussed in Part I. There are also iconoclastic approaches which aim at a further shift away from cinema as a spectacle for the eyes and ears – the *eidōlon* consumed in the visible and audible realm – to cinema as a sensible stimulus for actively reflecting on the object of our look – the iconoclastic *eikōn* turned to the invisible sphere – which is at the core of the films analysed in Part II. Never a rejection of images *tout court,* cinematic iconoclasm constitutes a way to critique a certain morbid fascination with extreme visibility and to probe our (ethical) relationship with the visual field.

Part I: Cinematic Iconoclasm as Critique: The Image as *Eidōlon*

| Aural Cinema: Isidore Isou's *Traité de bave et d'éternité*

PART I EXPLORES the iconoclastic criticism of the cinematic *eidōlon* – namely, a film image understood as deceptive and illusory – in Marxist-inflected works within which mainstream narrative cinema would reiterate capitalist ideology's perspective via highly mimetic images. Leftist film theorists, theoretically, and film-makers such as Isidore Isou, Guy Debord, Carmelo Bene and Jean-Luc Godard, practically, develop a criticism of the cinematic *eidōlon* which bespeaks a fundamentally iconoclastic understanding of the relationship between the film image and phenomenal reality. Echoing Plato's worries about the perceptual power of artworks and the Byzantine iconoclasts' refusal of potentially idolatrous images of God, these iconoclastic directors fiercely reject cinema's impression of reality because of the film image's inability to reproduce the model and its connivance with capitalist ideology. When the model is deceptive in itself (as in Isou's, Debord's and Bene's films), or is far too complex (as in Godard's oeuvre), iconoclastic gestures become a way to challenge habitual forms of film-making and film-viewing.

This chapter focuses on Isidore Isou, the founder of the French avant-garde movement of Lettrism, who is a neglected yet essential figure for theorising cinematic iconoclasm because of his explicit programme to destroy cinema, both literally and metaphorically. In his cinematic project, Isou grants sound a fundamental role while undermining the image as a mimetic copy. His critique of mimesis stems from the consideration that the film image has exhausted its imitative value, namely that there already exist films which have shown an effective use of mimetic images; it is now time for cinema to become something else. Accordingly, Isou proposes a cinema where sound becomes the constructive principle of the film and images acquire significance only from their opposition to the sound track. The privileging of the sonorous grounds much of Lettrist artistic practices, in which the political critique of words and images is part of a more widespread scepticism about language and representation and their ability to express reality. Thus, the criticism of artistic mimesis encompasses the aural, visual and linguistic dimensions, in an overall rejection of the sounds and images that had accompanied fascist propaganda before and during World War II. Lettrist cinema becomes one of the diverse ways through which this avant-garde expresses its attempts at overcoming the limitations imposed by figurative representation and logocentric speech.

The chapter first locates Lettrism within the broader context of twentieth-century Europe, with particular attention to the crisis of language and representation in philosophy, literature and the arts. It then delineates Isou's cinematic project, known as 'discrepant cinema' (*cinéma discrépant*), which aims at dismantling cinema as spectacle by way of breaking with mimesis and granting a privileged role to sound. Such an undermining of the visual image is also discussed through a detailed analysis of Isou's only film, *Traité de bave et d'éternité* (*Treatise on Venom and Eternity*, 1951).[1] The film's iconoclastic quality emerges from an account of the disruptive devices of discrepant editing (*montage discrépant*), which destroys synchronous sound, and the chiseled image (*image ciselante*),[2] which results from the literal scraping of and aggressions against the filmstrip.

Lettrism, or the Struggle of Ordinary Language

Lettrism is the cultural avant-garde founded in 1946 by Isou, a Romanian communist Jew who had moved to Paris a year earlier. The context is post-World War II France, a country exhausted by the Nazi invasion and the Vichy regime during the war. A general sense of meaninglessness spreads from this post-war situation through diverse areas of life and especially the arts. Isou founded Lettrism as a reaction to the existential and identity crisis that the war had provoked. The feeling of powerlessness and overall senselessness in the face of war and the Shoah manifests itself in the Lettrists' rejection of words in favour of the letter. In their view, words are always already imbued with, and thus convey, a meaning. But in a world that has lost any meaning and where language itself is found guilty of having colluded with fascist propaganda, Isou and the Lettrists rejected words and articulated speech to return to the pure aural dimension of the letter.

As the name suggests, Lettrism excludes words in favour of the letter (*lettre*) as the basis for a type of poetry founded on sounds able to transcend the limits of national boundaries (Feldman 2014, 78, 85). That is, while words are always in a specific language, letters maintain a much wider inclusive power, thereby contrasting the exclusionary quality of words. Abandoning the semantic constraints of language, the Lettrists explore the possibilities of single letters by recovering their aural dimension, creating poems made up of human noises. In such an anti-realist approach, Sami Sjöberg (2014) observes that 'language no longer names nor objectifies, neither does it separate or mediate' (222). Lettrism thus opposes the abstract sonic quality of letters to the meaning that words always bear. Immanent anti-language, Lettrist poetry allows for conveying individual experience in a manner appropriate to its fragmented and utterly subjective nature.

As both sound and visual poetry, Lettrism from its inception participated in the broader distrust of artistic mimesis which further intensified following World War II. The close bond between reality and its representation broken, post-war twentieth-century arts resorted to destructive, anti-mimetic gestures to express the inarticulated, new perception of the real. The arts withdrew into an inner dimension, where the Platonic tradition of the work of art as mimesis of the sensible world was replaced by the arbitrariness of the image/sound-model relationship as a means for expressing the intelligible, the unrepresentable and the ineffable. Although the divorce between reality and its mimetic representation had already begun at the end of the nineteenth century, World War II and the Shoah represent an essential caesura. Benjamin H. D. Buchloh (2016) discusses how certain artistic practices partially lost their *raison d'être* following

> the trauma of World War II and the Holocaust. That is one rift, a major chasm, whether explicitly or only latently expressed. Another is the realization that this historical situation needed redefinition, not only in geopolitical terms or in terms of a new national identity, but also in terms that were specifically *tragic*. [. . .] There was a sense of loss, of destruction, of utter inaccessibility to prewar culture [. . .]. (376)

Accordingly, in the aftermath of the war, visual arts further exacerbated the 'ontology of absence and lack' (Wajcman 1998, 109), as inaugurated by Wassily Kandinsky's and Kazimir Malevich's iconoclastic paintings in the first half of the century.[3] In the first decades of the twentieth century, Russian abstract art was concerned with the representation of the super-sensible (whether religious or secularised) and, in an approach reminiscent of Byzantine iconoclasm, opted for anti-mimesis to express that which is beyond the visible realm, making absence itself the subject of painting. After World War II, however, artists were not so much interested in the Spiritual/God/the Absolute but rather in the ways in which an ineffable and unrepresentable human experience could be the subject of artistic expression. The crisis of representation – namely, the loss of faith in the human ability to reproduce something audio-visually or verbally of the real in recognisable forms – involves questions regarding the spectacularisation of the model. The experience of the war and the news about the concentration camps led to enquire 'how can one, in art, respond to the Nazi reign of terror without spectacularizing it?' (Foster et al. 2016, 397). Visual arts, having lost trust in artistic mimesis, retreated into the realm of the unfigurable, the ugly and the extremely material (for example, informal art in France and Italy; the Cobra group in Denmark, Belgium and the Netherlands; Brutalism in Britain). Jean Fautrier's series of paintings *Otages* (1944–46), for instance, is paradigmatic of post-war art: inspired by the aural (the sound of bombs, rifles, cries) rather than visual dimension of the war, the paintings undermine sight to the point that only the title remains to guide the viewer to the formless lump on the canvases. 'This dichotomy between alleged theme and frustration of vision' (Foster et al. 2016, 397) would become a common trait of post-war visual and sound arts, including the Lettrist avant-garde.

The mistrust of visual representation is accompanied by a mistrust of language (Sjöberg 2013b; Weller 2018) in an understanding of the experiential as that which lies beyond the domains of the representable and the utterable. In contextualising Lettrist poetry within the broader criticism of language, Sjöberg (2013b) defines early-twentieth-century language crisis in literature and philosophy as 'in essence a crisis of representation', which was 'characterized by a distrust of language in general and skepticism about the correspondence between language and the world in particular' (53). Visual arts' slow abandonment of mimesis is matched by ordinary language's failure to express the complexity of experience in literature and philosophy. Shane Weller (2018) contends that

> The history of the West has been marked by a recurrent sense that, in the face of certain thoughts, feelings, objects, or experiences, words fail us. For Plato, the Ideas that constitute the real (of which human beings can capture only the shadows on the cave wall) may be described, but they remain in a more profound sense beyond the grasp of language, even the Greek language, considered by its possessors to be superior to all others, with non-Greek speakers falling into the category of the barbarian. Similarly, the long tradition of negative theology is shaped by a profound sense of the limited power of language, insisting, as it does, that God can be expressed linguistically only in terms of what he is not, any positive articulation of the divine essence being at best a reduction, if not an outright distortion, of that essence. [...] This skepticism

toward language becomes particularly acute, however, in the modern period, casting its long shadow over European literature and philosophy. (15)

There is a loss of faith in the ability to 'utter the world' which is at the centre of, among others, Fritz Mauthner's[4] iconoclastic critique of language.[5] Mauthner exacerbates the philosophical stance on the identity of language and thought, proposing an impossible critique of language via its own self-destruction (Pisano 2016, 95–122; Sjöberg 2013b; Weiler 1970, 269–306; Weller 2018, 23–29). Language, which is our only way to order experience, is purely metaphorical or suggestive, thereby imprisoning us in an unescapable missaying. It follows that knowledge is impossible since language is incapable of describing (our experience of) reality. Hence, as Weller (2018) remarks, 'liberation from the tyranny of language can be achieved, according to Mauthner, only through an *annihilation of language*' (27). Such a critique of language is ultimately unattainable because its goal is to utter the unsayable. Mauthner's radical approach culminates, rather logically, in a praise of mystical silence (Weiler 1970, 274, 291–96). Mysticism, in both theistic and non-theistic tradition, designates an experience characterised by an ineffable and unrepresentable component, because both language and image fail to adequately express it. Drawing from negative theology, which postulates that God can be known only negatively, by means of what God is not because of his ultimate ineffability, Mauthner adopts a secularised approach to mysticism – what he describes as '*godless mysticism*' (quoted in Weiler 1970, 294). God, like any other word, is only a metaphor (an image of), a verbal and therefore destroyable god. The outcome of Mauthner's philosophy is a mysticism without language and God: to destroy language as metaphor is also to destroy God.

Mauthner's philosophical project is thus based on an iconoclastic understanding of the world-word relationship in which language is inadequate for the expression of reality. As Libera Pisano (2016) notes, 'the main feature of Mauthner's critique of language is the unbridgeable gap between word and object' (104). Words are, at best, an approximation of reality and 'the only two available modes of language use, then, become missaying [. . .] and unsaying' (Weller 2018, 29). Accordingly, Mauthner proposes a dismantling of language through and within language itself, which is tantamount to visual and sound arts' efforts to destroy their own illusionism from within. Like visual images, words are an epistemological failure in the face of reality.

Literature similarly participates in the language crisis: Hugo von Hofmannsthal's *The Lord Chandos Letter* (1902), which Mauthner suggested was influenced by his critique of language (Nordmann 2005, 117–18),[6] attests to language's incapacity to grasp experiential reality and otherness. Symbolist poetry, in particular Stéphane Mallarmé's, rejects ordinary language to express the mystery beyond the surface of known reality by severing the relationship between the world and words' capacity to describe it; and various avant-gardes explore the limits of language and the potential of sounded words.[7] It is in this context that Lettrism originates, drawing inspiration from Dadaism's disruption between words and meaning, Surrealism's creative anarchism, Futurist poetry's use of onomatopoeia and Symbolist poetry's attention to silence and the visual arrangement of words on the page. Lettrism thus participates in the period's visual and verbal distrust, adopting a marked iconoclastic approach to reality and the arts: language first and visual images later are conceived as inadequate for conveying the experience of reality. In the impossibility to verbally, or visually, render individual experience, the Lettrists turned to iconoclastic gestures as the only way to communicate the inherent incommunicability of experience.

According to Isou (1947), Lettrism 'initiates the destruction of words through the letters' (15), finding one of its major influences in Mallarmé's negative aesthetics composed of silences, empty spaces, the arbitrariness of words and their musicality. Lettrist sound poetry further exacerbates Mallarmé's approach, destroying ordinary as well as poetic language's ability to signify, while spatialising emptiness and gaps of meaning on the page. Moreover, Lettrist poetry, because of its being an aural performance, emphasises the musical quality of letters and of bodily noises such as hiccups and deep breaths. Several Lettrist sound poems are a rewriting (that is, a destruction) of Symbolist verses by the likes of Mallarmé and Paul Verlaine, in which only the rhythm and richness in auditory sensations of the original are preserved, while words as intelligible units are destroyed.

Lettrism revolves around the aural dimension of poetry (and later cinema), placing emphasis on single letters, guttural sounds and bodily noises. But despite the focus on the sonorous quality of letters, Isou (1947) identifies art's ultimate goal as to 'concretise the silence; write the nothingness' (17). In such a mystical, iconoclastic understanding of art, which places at its core silence (ineffability) and blankness (unrepresentability), Isou was also influenced by Judaism and the Kabbalah. Sjöberg (2013a), who has extensively written on Isou's Jewish mysticism,[8] argues:

> The interdependence of divinity and unknowing is derived from Kabbalah and is crucial for the Isouian world-making, the means of which is language. Isou adopts a kabbalistic definition of God as the unknown (*l'Inconnu*), which asserts God beyond rational inquiry [. . .] Firstly, the Jewish God is invisible

and conceptually unattainable. Secondly, due to God's hidden nature, culminated in the second commandment, the role of language in Jewish exegesis, both rabbinic and mystical, is emphasised. These factors are favourable for the avant-gardist desire to 'transgress' language. (371)

Because of the strict Biblical ban on images, language is invested with a remarkable power to sustain and reinforce the relationship between God and his people. Such relationship finds its privileged means in the sense of hearing rather than sight, since God is a *Deus absconditus* [hidden God] (Isaiah 45:15) and seeing him corresponds to a death sentence (Exodus 33:20). The God of the Old Testament is not only unknowable and hidden but also jealous and vengeful. As a precaution against idolatry, the ban on sacred images (Exodus 20:4–6) was interpreted to include all images: 'Every image of a living being, even a mere ornamental motif, was strictly banned. It was prohibited to bow before a pagan statue even to drink, to pick up a fallen object, or to pull a thorn from one's foot' (Besançon 2000, 67). It is thus necessary to maintain a clear separation between the hidden God and sensible reality; the divine can never be visually represented because representation always carries the risk of idolatry. To this visual ban corresponds a verbal one; that is, 'the Jewish prohibition and grammatical impossibility to pronounce God's Name' (Bettetini 2006, 64).[9] While the spoken word is a privileged means in the relationship between God and his people (God intelligibly speaks to his people, who then take care of translating the spoken into the written word of the law), in Jewish mysticism, God's name progressively became unpronounceable, thereby sonorously matching his visual unrepresentability.

Lettrism, particularly through Isou, inherits the iconoclastic tendencies of Jewish mysticism: the Biblical ban on images and the importance of aurality in the God-man relationship, on the one hand, and mystical silence, on the other hand. While initially focused on sound poems, Lettrism turned to visual poetry (hypergraphics) in the 1950s. Here, silence progressively substituted the broken sounds of the early poems, while emptiness acquired growing importance as material visualisation of silence. The poems 'Lettrie Blanche' and 'Lettrie Vide' (Isou 1958, reproduced in Curtay 1974, 190), for instance, reject the seductive power of both figurative representation and language – something which will be present also in Lettrist cinema in the frequent use of the blank screen. The empty page and the blank page at once configure themselves as spaces of pure imaginative potentiality and attest to a total refusal of mimesis. Reduced to minimal elements, Lettrist visual poetry stresses the materiality of the text. The tension – and impossible encounter – between knowledge and expression is rendered either through blankness or excessive presence. In both cases, image and word are emptied of their capacity to provide a picture of reality and the experience thereof. This practice, based on void and extreme fullness, becomes a key feature of Lettrism, one which characterises the variety of Lettrist gestures in diverse artistic contexts, including cinema: from the empty page to the blank screen, from the letter-filled pages to aural verbosity.

Lettrist Cinema: Glory of Sound and Martyrdom of the Image

The exploration of the possibilities of sound and image continues in Lettrist cinema, although language as a constructor of meaning is reinstated as an element of the sound track. First theorised by Isou in his film and then developed more coherently in *Esthétique du cinéma* [*Aesthetics of Cinema*] ([1952] 1953), Lettrist cinema refers to a cluster of films realised in Paris in the Lettrist ambit during 1951–52. Isou's *Traité de bave et d'éternité* inaugurated it in 1951 and was followed by Maurice Lemaître's *Le Film est déjà commencé?* (*Has the Film Already Started?* 1951), Gil J. Wolman's *L'Anticoncept* (*The Anti-Concept*, 1951), François Dufrêne's *Tambours du jugement premier* (*Drums of the First Judgement*, 1952) and Guy Debord's *Hurlements en faveur de Sade* (*Howls for Sade*, 1952). The defining feature of Lettrist cinema consists of the privileged role assigned to sound and an overall depreciation of the image, which can go from Isou's physical scraping of the film celluloid to Dufrêne's complete forsaking of the film strip.

Like its poetry, Lettrist cinema grants a significant role to the sonic dimension of film. Sound ceases to be a supplement to the visual component and becomes, instead, the primary, organising element of the film. By contrast, images, condemned for their deceptive character, are physically attacked: the filmstrip is soaked in water, scratched, over- or under-exposed to light, or simply abandoned. The Lettrists thus problematise the relationship between sound and image to counter previous forms of cinema, in particular the illusionism of narrative cinema and immersive modes of film viewing. Kaira M. Cabañas (2014) observes: '[E]ach Lettrist film defie[s] cinema's established conventions (e.g., continuity editing, synchronized sound, screen), and sometimes the necessity of its image support (i.e., film), in order to generate new conditions and communities of viewing' (3). Lettrist cinema, therefore, pursues the twofold aim of destroying cinema as it had been conceived until then and promoting more critically active ways to experience film. To this end, theoretically in *Esthétique du cinéma* and practically in *Traité*, Isou formulates the notions of discrepant editing and chiseled image.

Discrepant editing is the main and most innovative feature of Isou's film and his cinematic project, and it consists of the disjunction between the sound track and the image track which are treated as independent from each other. Marion Poirson-Dechonne (2016, 181) goes over the Latin origin of the term 'discrepant' and its kinship with music vocabulary to emphasise the centrality of sound in Isou's montage. Composed of *dis-*, which indicates separation, and *crepāre*, which translates as 'to make something sound', discrepant editing points to a cinema that emits a deviant sound; namely, a sound which does not adhere to the norm. Theoretically, it invokes the breaking apart of any logical relationship between what is heard and what is seen; practically, there is a disjunction between the sound track and the image track which, however, does not always exclude a possible relation between the two. Undoubtedly, the then traditional status of sound in cinema as an addition to the image no longer exists in Lettrist films. Sound acquires an unprecedented autonomy, becoming the most significant element in Lettrist cinema and the primary tool to criticise the privileged status of the film image and the spectator's (supposed) passivity.

Isou and the Lettrists are vehemently critical of narrative cinema, for it promotes immersive spectatorship and a certain fascination with the images on screen. Accordingly, Lettrist sound does not correspond to the clearly articulated speech of narrative cinema but is built up from disjointed voices and bodily noises that do not necessarily bear any specific meaning. Moreover, Lettrist poetic practices such as '*mégapneumie*' (Cabañas 2014, 80) and '*crirhythmes*' (Feldman 2014, 92) – types of physical poetry which use breathing and cries, respectively, as their constitutive elements – are integrated in the sound tracks alongside spoken, intelligible speech. Together with the concept of discrepant editing, Isou proposes the production of a chiseled image, which results from a series of aggressive manipulations of the filmstrip. The film celluloid is, among other things, scratched, written on, immersed in water and over- or underexposed. Consequently, it is often difficult to discern what the images represent because of the tampering that they have undergone. Hanna Feldman (2014) explains the significance of such damages and their role in disrupting immersive spectatorship, contending that 'the marks made on the film's celluloid reduce its capacity to capture and register an image in its most primary quality as material ground to an imposed figure' (89). That is, the chiseling process mars the image as a reproduction or visual copy of a referent. Because of the disfigurements, the image's content becomes difficult to distinguish, and the image loses the relationship with the referent that has produced it in the first place. The chiseled image thus causes a rupture with mimesis and the idea of the image as a faithful copy of a model. It does so by exhibiting the film image in its materiality, since it is cinema's corporeality that allows the scratches and other physical manipulations to occur.

The word 'chiseled', used to define the marred images in Lettrist cinema, is reminiscent of Isou's partition of poetry first and cinema later into two phases, the *amplique* (amplifying) and the *ciselante* (chiseling), which he outlines in *Introduction à une nouvelle poésie et à une nouvelle musique* [*Introduction to a New Poetry and a New Music*] (1947, 83–148). Applied to cinema, the *amplique* phase denotes the beginning of cinema and the development of stylistic conventions, whereas the *ciselante* phase designates Lettrist cinema and its employing of the film medium to destroy cinema as it had been conceived until then. Both discrepant editing and the chiseled image are the products of a radicalisation of non-mimetic approaches to cinema and are directed towards a reconfiguration of the relationship between sound and image, in an overall assault on cinematic transparency. The Lettrist problematising of such relation also aims at disrupting any possible immersive experience of the film. These ideas about cinema assume a visible and audible form in the first Lettrist film, Isou's *Traité*.

Announcing the Destruction of Cinema

Isou's *Traité* inaugurated Lettrist cinema in 1951 and configured itself as an experimental essay-film theorising the destruction of cinema. The film explicitly aims to counter the illusionistic image of narrative cinema and the pleasure it arouses in the audience; but it also wishes to break with all previous forms of cinema, promoting a new way of making and viewing films. Accordingly, Isou employed discrepant editing and chiseled images as the constructive principles of the film. By rejecting the referentiality of images and sounds, Isou explored cinema's possibilities beyond the illusionism of mimetic reproduction.

Traité is a 120-minute film divided into three sections labelled as chapters, whose unifying thread consists of Isou's reflections about cinema. The first chapter, titled 'The Principle', is a manifesto of discrepant cinema; the second chapter, 'The Development', follows the love story between a girl named Ève (Blanchette Brunoy) and the protagonist Daniel, played by Isou himself, which leads to a reminiscence of the past love story between Daniel and another woman, Denise (Danièle Delorme); the third chapter, 'The Proof', framed by the love story with Ève, focuses on Lettrism and Isou's ideas on cinema. At the film's premiere as a fringe event of the Cannes Film Festival in 1951, the image track of the second and third chapters, which in the final version contain figurative images, consisted of a black screen. However, as Cabañas (2014, 25) explains, the absence of images in the Cannes version did not correspond to an aesthetic choice but was more simply due to Isou's running out of time to complete it.[10]

The film's most striking feature is the disjunction between image track and sound track, which not only audio-visually develops Isou's theories on cinema, but also prevents any immersive experience of the film because of the lack of connections between what is heard and what is seen. This is evident from the opening, where spectators are faced with a black screen and hear an unintelligible bodily sound, similar to a rasp intertwined with guttural choral noises, which Feldman (2014, 86) identifies as a Lettrist symphony. While the black screen lasts twenty-four seconds, the Lettrist symphony continues, like a tormenting spell, through the opening credits, the intertitles and the beginning of the first chapter, for a total duration of four minutes and thirty-four seconds. This symphony returns in intervals throughout *Traité*, punctuating the whole film obsessively. Alongside this Lettrist motif, the sound track is an intertwining of human voices and bodily noises that include the protagonist Daniel's diatribe about cinema,[11] a narrator's (Bernard Blin) monotonal voice-over commenting on Daniel's thoughts, the shouting and whistling of the audience at a ciné-club, now insulting Isou's film, now praising it, and recitals of Lettrist poems. The image track consists of a similar layering structure, composed of shots of Daniel/Isou's slow wandering in the streets of Paris, building facades, boulevards congested with traffic, texts, found footage images of soldiers, military marches in Southeast Asia, Vietnamese fishermen and temples, photographs of Ève and Denise, black screens and shots of Lettrists reciting poems.

These extremely diverse images are intentionally indifferent to both each other and the sound track. That is, almost every image is not causally or logically related to the ones preceding or following it, and images are disjointed from what is heard, according to Daniel/Isou's intention 'to make the flow of images indifferent to the sound story'. In Daniel/Isou's view, by disconnecting the image track from the sound track, words could 'reveal the limitations and the possibilities of the image'. Moreover, from the second chapter of the film onwards, the chiseled image makes its appearance. The filmstrip has been physically manipulated and defaced by literal attacks, thereby presenting deleted faces, painted figures, scraped blank screens and deformed images (Figures 1.1–3).

Isou's iconoclasm resides in the physical and metaphorical attack against images, in an 'attempt to destroy the false transparency of its [the cinema's] images' (Dottorini 2013, 54). Feldman's (2014) insightful reading of *Traité*'s chiseled images brings forth the iconoclastic quality of the film:

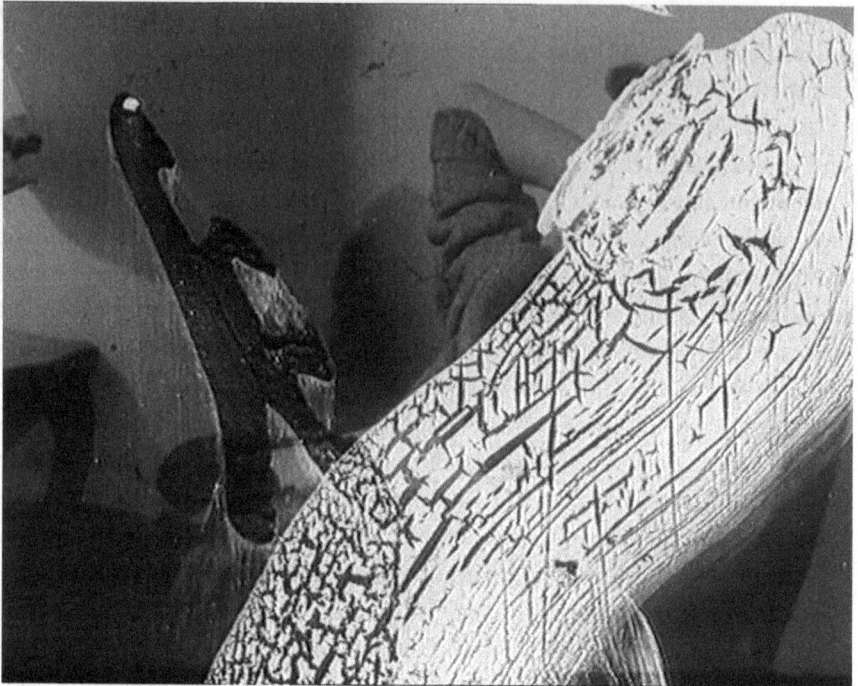

Figure 1.1 Chiseled image of Isidore Isou

> The implications of this [the chiseling process] and the multitude of marred frames that follow are crucial. First, the scratching undermines the representational function of the original image. Instead of an image of a carpenter at work, we are presented with the fragments of what had been that image. These fragments can only begin to suggest what they had stood to signify before. Indeed, the image is quite literally defaced, as the visage of the carpenter falls victim to Isou's violent scrapes. It bears repeating here that most of the scratches in *Traité de bave et d'éternité* are made over the faces of individuals. (89)

Faces of carpenters, fishermen, soldiers and officers, as well as those of some Lettrists including Isou himself, have been scratched. In a sort of democratic destruction, no face is immune from the chiseling process. These defaced images posit themselves as a both literal and metaphorical attack against the mimetic image, against its being a faithful reproduction of a phenomenal referent. But they also constitute a further impediment to an immersive engagement with the film because spectators are often deprived of the most evocative and emotionally charged image, that of the human face. In this way, Isou 'provok[es] a dismantling of realist expectations with regard to the images one sees' (Cabañas

Figure 1.2 Chiseled image of military personnel

2014, 31). Furthermore, the dismantling of faces carries out Isou's critique of French foreign policy and the First Indochina War (1946–54), which Feldman (2014, 80–108) likens to the Lettrist overall condemnation of war. The weaving of shots of Paris with that of Vietnamese temples and fishermen establishes a political link between two geographically distant places, a link which is further emphasised via the scratching of armed forces' faces. In this way, the critique of the war unfolds as a violent attack against the images of those who are responsible for political violence, who are de-individualised through the chiseling process.

Discrepant editing and chiseled images are therefore the two fundamentals of Isou's cinematic project, which he addresses throughout the film and most clearly in the first chapter. The programmatic exposition of Isou's ideas about cinema is realised, visually, via shots of Daniel/Isou's slow wandering in the streets interspersed with shots of building facades and Parisian boulevards and, aurally, through Daniel/Isou's intelligible speech, which alternates with the nervously excited outcries of the audience of the ciné-club and the monotony of the narrator's voice-over. Here Daniel/Isou condemns cinema, for it keeps repeating the same story instead of exploring new possibilities for images and

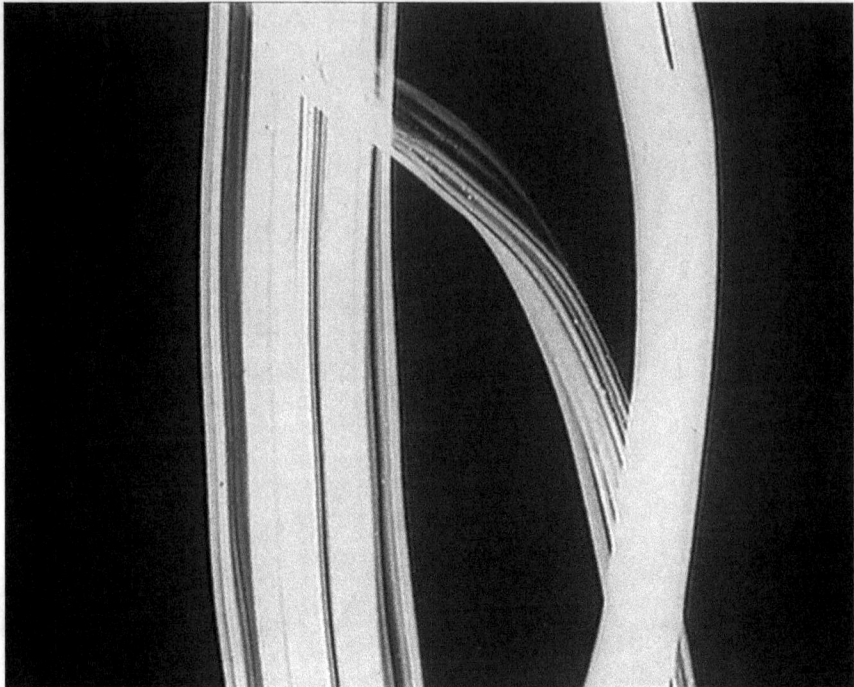

Figure 1.3 Chiseled filmstrip

sounds. While he acknowledges some films as cinematic artworks, such as that of the directors to whom the film is dedicated (D. W. Griffith, Abel Gance, Charlie Chaplin, René Clair, Sergei Eisenstein, Erich von Stroheim, Robert J. Flaherty, Luis Buñuel and Jean Cocteau), he nonetheless provides a harsh critique of imitation – both the imitation of reality and of previous films – because it prevents cinema from evolving. This evolution passes through the destruction of the cinema that had been until then and, especially, narrative cinema which is characterised by a concord between images and sounds. The voice-over asserts:

> I'd like to separate the ear from its cinematic master, the eye. [. . .] The films they make these days have a completed, perfect and calm quality. It is a result of the harmony between the components, the classic unity between the constitutive elements: word-image.

Discrepant editing and the chiseled image are manifestly in contrast with narrative cinema where shots are linked to each other via continuity editing and coupled with sound to convey an easily comprehensible story. And, indeed, Isou deliberately dismantles narrative cinema's images and sounds because he notes a fundamental problem with images; namely, that 'it is possible to make them say whatever one wants and that which they do not say'. To subvert this perceptual power of images, *Traité* mars not only the images themselves but also the relation they have with the sound track. It is no longer the image which originates sound, but sound which constructs the film: 'The word would no longer come from the screen, in order to coincide with its sequences, but would always come from an elsewhere, as if concretely and visibly it were an excess without any relationship with the organism'.

However, images still count since Isou does not entirely do away with them. He butchers the filmstrip, but these tortured images remain an essential component of discrepant cinema. Without images (namely, without a filmstrip), there would be no discrepant editing because it presupposes the presence of images with which sound can establish a disjunctive relation. Albeit devalued in comparison to sound, images therefore continue to retain significance in Isou's cinematic project. Daniel/Isou reels off his plan for the filmstrip on several occasions, claiming that 'I will blow up the filmstrip with rays of sun', 'I will take pieces of films, and I will scratch them so that unknown beauties will come into light', and 'I will engrave flowers on the filmstrip'. Discrepant cinema can be summarised as the disjunction of sound and image and the slaughtering of the filmstrip.

The Sadism of Discrepant Cinema

Besides suggesting a new mode of film-making, discrepant cinema proposes a new way of viewing films. It presents itself as most forcefully opposed to narrative cinema, not only to its film form and content, but also to the kind of spectatorship it promotes, so much so that Allyson Field (1999, 57–58) explicitly identifies a sadistic quality in Isou's cinematic project.[12] Indeed, throughout *Traité* Isou not only literally warps the filmstrip, but also recurrently voices his intention to inflict metaphorical pain on spectators. Thus, the film, and the notion of discrepant cinema as a whole, is imbued with violence and animated by a destructive thrust, which goes from the physical aggressions against the filmstrip to the metaphorical harm to spectators. Moreover, the referentiality of the image and its relationship with the sound track destroyed, *Traité* problematises the relationship between spectators and the film, making immersive reception unachievable and the audience continuously aware of their status.

Isou himself provides references to de Sade in *Traité* and contemplates physical repercussions of his film on spectators. The voice-over associated with Isou's character on screen proclaims:

> I would like a film that could really hurt the eyes. [...] One has to leave the cinema with a headache. [...] I prefer to give you neuralgias rather than nothing. [...] I prefer to ruin your eyes rather than leave them indifferent. [...] It is necessary that the spectator leaves blind, the ears destroyed, lacerated in this disjunction of the word and the image and numb in any of these distinct zones.

Isou partially appropriates de Sade's rhetoric to articulate his destructive fury against the film medium and the experience of film-viewing. As Field (1999) points out, the character of 'Daniel remarks that he would like "a film that *hurts your eyes*", connecting sadistic pain to his manifesto for the destruction of cinema. [...] Indeed, the entire concept of discrepant cinema is analogous to an aesthetic sadism' (58). It is in particular by means of black screens and voice-overs that Isou's 'aesthetic sadism' exhibits itself.

A significant instance of the film's 'aesthetic sadism' takes place in the second chapter. Unlike the first and third chapters of *Traité*, this chapter presents a loose narrative – the love story between Daniel and Ève, and the reminiscence of Daniel's past romance with Denise. However, this narrative is constantly interrupted by reflections on a variety of topics, such as politics, the communist party and religion, which prevent any immersive consumption of the love story. The sound track alone articulates this romance, which however does not find a visual correspondence in the image track, except on those rare occasions when short shots or photographs of the three characters appear on screen. The sound thus constructs a visual desire that remains unsatisfied because spectators are continuously deprived of the image that could create a harmonious unity between what is heard and what is seen.

Two black monochromatic images effectively display the sadistic quality of Isou's discrepant cinema. The frenzy of chiseled images, which have made their appearance in this chapter, comes to a halt on two occasions. The first time happens when Daniel/Isou, while recounting his romantic involvement with Ève, whom he does not love, reminisces of Denise, a woman with whom he was formerly in love. In recalling the night that he spent with Denise, the screen remains completely black, without scratches or drawings. Intimacy remains beyond the realm of visibility, and spectators are faced with blankness and the eroticism of the ear. However, this monochromatic image does not bear any ethical value, but rather consists of a direct, metaphorical attack against viewers. Unlike, for instance, Godard's use of black screens (see Chapter 4), Isou's negation of figurative images does not originate out of a respect for reality, nor a recognition of the incommensurability between an ineffable sentiment such as love and its visible reproduction on screen. Quite simply, Isou sadistically wishes to deprive spectators of visual pleasure. It is no coincidence that the black screen occurs in this moment of the narrative: the image of the pivotal event of narrative cinema – the formation of the couple, the kiss – is entirely negated to the audience and their expectations frustrated.

The second time a monochromatic black image sadistically invades the screen happens just before the end of the second chapter, when Isou directly addresses spectators as follows:

> The author knows that spectators go to the cinema to ingest their Sunday and weekly dose of tenderness and, although he does not give a damn about this [love] story, he tells it with the hope of a well-deserved success. The author doesn't love this kind of legends because it is a personal matter of taste, and the systems and forms that go beyond these stories are the only things that matter to him.

This black screen, too, qualifies as a metaphorical assault against spectators. After having deprived viewers of figurative images of the love story, Isou mocks them by condemning their taste. His statement that he has inserted a love story to please spectators seems, at first glance, a sort of kindly concession to fulfil their appetite for narrative pleasure. However, this aural flattery is visually expressed through a completely black screen. Therefore, while sound makes itself accessible to spectators, images – the figurative impressions of reality – are once again fully negated. On both occasions, by using a black screen, Isou deliberately deprives spectators of cinematic illusion. The spectators' look is twice blocked by a complete non-chiseled (or completely chiseled) blackness, which becomes emblematic of the critique of the illusory nature of film images.

There is, however, a moment in the film wherein Isou makes some concessions to the audience. In the last chapter, he introduces the spectator as an active producer of meaning, counterbalancing the more pronounced sadism of the previous chapters. Here, Ève and Daniel's love story becomes the framework for a discussion on Lettrism and cinema. Having lovingly praised Lettrism, Isou provides a succinct summary of discrepant cinema, laying out the spectators' contribution to the film's construction:

> As of today, the character turning towards the partner was shown, his gestures were seen. From now on, [spectators] will hear: 'Daniel has turned', without seeing him turning. Imagination is incorporated in the cinema because the real, the concrete, is destroyed. The spectator will be able to invent his character like he has never been allowed to do before in the history of cinema.

Viewers are encouraged to participate actively in the film production during reception, by bringing about something very personal; namely, their capacity to imagine what is not shown on the screen. Hence, Isou is invoking a thoughtful, imaginative spectatorship in which viewers cease to be exclusively receivers of images and sounds. *Traité* stimulates spectators to more critically active modes of looking at film by destabilising the mimetic relationship between sound and images and remains a most fascinating work on the disconcerting encounter with an iconoclastic aesthetics.

Concluding Remarks

Isou's cinematic project participates in the broader artistic scepticism which followed World War II, concretising in a literal and metaphorical iconoclasm. Not only does he physically attack the filmstrip, invoking its destruction, but he also metaphorically dismantles the image as illusory copy of a phenomenal referent. Reiterating the gesture proper to religious iconoclasm, the material breaking of images, Isou proceeds to destroy what cinema had been until then. Here the cinematic *eidōlon* corresponds to any image that has already been used in cinema, as well as most figurative images. Film images are stripped of any intermediary role – there is no place for the *eikōn* in Isou's cinema – and of any possible imitative value by means of the chiseling process. While invoking the destruction of cinema, *Traité* is also a love declaration to the cinema that can be and contains some of the most insightful claims on film images' potentialities – first and foremost, their power to liberate the spectator's creative imagination. Guy Debord and Jean-Luc Godard, among others, were particularly receptive to Isou's cinematic theory and its iconoclastic drive, albeit reaching quite divergent outcomes: whereas Debord developed an aesthetics of displeasure which negatively targets viewers, Godard demonstrated a profound belief in the spectators' ethical imagination.

2   An Aesthetics of Displeasure: Guy Debord's Destructive Oeuvre

GUY DEBORD IS perhaps the film-maker most associated with iconoclasm in the cinema because of his anti-cinematic aesthetics, which coils around the notion of the spectacle and its critique. His uncompromising attitude is evident throughout his turbulent intellectual history, from his enthusiastic joining of Lettrism under the wing of Isidore Isou to his breaking with it, in order to found, first, the Lettrist International in 1952 and then, the Situationist International (SI) in 1957. Such a winding artistic journey was also punctuated by harsh invectives against Jean-Luc Godard, launched via a number of articles in the SI journal.[1] The SI's iconoclastic impetus, conveyed in both their articles and aesthetic practices, partially loses Isou's poetic approach to destruction, turning into corrosive gestures against spectators.

Debord's project, further exasperated during and after the SI years, to 'undermine [...] the dominant visual order' (Jay 1993, 243) developed as harsh critique of consumer society (termed 'the society of the spectacle') following a Marxist framework. He identifies as *eidōla* those images which retain a highly seductive and alienating power affirming the values of the bourgeoisie. Accordingly, Debord's (ab)use of images and sounds stems from his political analysis of contemporary consumer society and is primarily aimed at dismantling spectatorial pleasure. However, his excessive self-reflexivity prevents the discourse on images from attaining the creation of iconoclastic *eikones*: Debord's oeuvre, heavily affected by an almost complete loss of belief in images, remains enclosed in a critique of the *eidōlon*.

The contention shaping the chapter is that Debord's iconoclasm hinges on a Marxist critique of commodity and capitalist (spectacular) society and a Lukácsian-inflected conception of consumers/spectators. It argues for an iconoclastic understanding of some cinematic devices used in his films, particularly that of blank screens, sound-image disjunctions, still images, altered motion and the destructive device of *détournement* for their breaking with an aesthetics of mimesis – conceived as that which serves dominant ideology via the illusion of realism, entrapping individuals in a contemplative state. Key films are examined, with specific attention to iconoclastic sequences which demonstrate Debord's vivid contempt for the seductive images of bourgeois society and the vision of the world they carry.

Critique of the Spectacle

The concept of the spectacle is at the basis of Debord's philosophical worldview and is developed in both films and written works. In his perspective, the spectacle does not refer to spectacular media such as cinema and television, but rather is at once the product and producer of a specific historico-economic age. In *The Society of the Spectacle* ([1967] 1994), Debord contends that 'the spectacle is not a collection of images, but a social relation among people, mediated by images' (thesis 4). The spectacle thus qualifies a society founded on appearance which has perfected the Marxist separation between producer and product: from the alienation of the proletariat from the product of their work to the alienation of citizen-spectators from the images they see. The situation further worsens, in Debord's account, because citizen-spectators are not even the producers of such images, thereby being twice separated from the objects of their sight. What is more, Debord insightfully contends that alienation in consumer society takes place most effectively in leisure time, which retains only the appearance of free time while actually having been commodified to a degree that renders alienation an all-encompassing phenomenon. The attention therefore shifts from factory workers to consumers and from Marxist devaluation of being into having to Debordian appearing. The variety of images regulating leisure time, such as advertising images and television and film images, are *eidōla* which actively contribute to modern alienation.

In his analysis of the spectacle, Debord inherits Marxist doctrine's iconoclasm in its critique of the illusionism of ideology and fetish objects. Karl Marx and Friedrich Engels ([1846] 1970) define ideology by using the metaphor of the '*camera obscura*' (47), which effectively expresses the very illusionism of the images of ideology. As in the camera obscura images appear upside-down, so the images of ideology are a distortion of reality; however, both types of images are perceived as objective representations of such a reality – in other words, they are *eidōla*, illusory doubles retaining a highly deceptive psychological power.

William J. T. Mitchell (1986) accordingly reads Marx and Engels's metaphor of the 'camera obscura as a figurative descendant of Plato's Cave' (163) since, in both cases, images are shadowy copies of phenomenal reality which, however, individuals experience as if they were objectively real. Shifting from ideas to material objects, the illusionism of ideology concretises in the fetish; namely, the commodities of capitalist society. Commodity fetishism reproposes ideology's deception insofar as the fetish objects present themselves as if they were the objects for which they are standing. As Mitchell (1986) poignantly observes, 'ideology and fetishism are both varieties of idolatry, one mental, the other material, and both emerge from an iconoclastic critique' (187). The images of ideology and fetishism are reminiscent of the notion of idol in Christian theology, which is a false, material image of God that presents itself as true god. The issue resides in the images' concealing of their status as representations, the fact that they stand for something else, deceiving believers and consumers alike.

Debord builds on the Marxist critique of commodity fetishism, thereby also appropriating its iconoclastic thrust, and identifies the spectacle as that which determines alienating relationships between individuals via a continuous mediation of images (see especially theses 35–53). Since spectacle's abode is leisure time, individuals-turned-consumers have their free time expropriated; that is, the society of the spectacle's citizen is a consumer of images (illusory appearances) which assail them during their free time, minimising any possibilities (time) for critical thinking. According to Debord, 'the real consumer has become a consumer of illusions. The commodity is this materialized illusion and the spectacle is its general expression' (thesis 47). Because it is no longer a tangible commodity, but an immaterial one – the image – which enacts spectacular separation (that is, alienation), Debord elaborates a thorough critique of sight understood as 'the most abstract and easily deceived sense' (thesis 18).

The society of the spectacle is, indeed, characterised by a privileging of anything visual – hence the term spectators in reference to citizens – and sight becomes the primary means for spectacular separation and the favoured sense in the process of knowledge. The relationship between individuals and reality is mediated by images which have been produced by a third party; therefore, the sensible world becomes known by means of abstraction, through an uninterrupted flux of spectacle-images which is 'entirely independent of what the spectator might understand or think of it' (Debord [1988] 1990, 28). Individuals are no longer responsible for their imaginative horizon, having been stripped of the capacity to produce their own images; consequently, spectacular separation impoverishes the imaginative capacity which participates in the process of alienation, so that the alienated subject of consumer society is also deprived of the ability to imagine actively and independently. A process of de-realisation of reality is also derivative of the spectacle's exploiting of sight insofar as only those events which are mediatically reproduced acquire real consistency, in an alienating process in which images construct reality itself. What is more, these spectacle-images, because they present themselves as utterly decontextualised and a-historical, talk exclusively about what is convenient to societal power, thereby actively contributing to the maintenance of the status quo in offering the (version of) reality which suits capitalist/spectacular power. In this scenario, individuals are placed in a contemplative state which qualifies them as passive consumer of appearances. Debord ([1967] 1994) emphasises:

> The alienation of the spectator, which reinforces the contemplated objects that result from his own unconscious activity, works like this: the more he contemplates, the less he lives; the more he identifies with the dominant images of need, the less he understands his own life and his own desires. The spectacle's estrangement from the acting subject is expressed by the fact that the individual's gestures are no longer his own; they are the gestures of someone else who represents them to him. (thesis 30)

There is an aspect of contemplation which involves not only the physical act of looking but also the dimension of agency and specifically, the forsaking of action. Debord (via the epigraph which opens the second chapter of *The Society of the Spectacle*) explicitly draws on György Lukács's argument in *History and Class Consciousness* (1971) on contemplation and its role in (hindering) political action (praxis). Decrying the divided state of theory and practice, Lukács invokes their unity as a 'precondition of the revolutionary function of the theory' (3); however, this unity can only occur with the emergence of class consciousness. That is, only when the class becomes conscious of itself, of its historical situation, becoming 'both the subject and object of knowledge' (2) instead of an object of contemplation, can theory and practice unite and the contemplative attitude be overcome in favour of praxis. What Debord aims to do, then, is first and foremost to awaken citizen-spectators' consciousness, to show them their misery of contemplated objects. Unable to understand their situation and their society, individuals in the society of the spectacle have abandoned themselves to a contemplation which blocks any possibility of change. Through contemplation (as both physical act and mental attitude) citizen-spectators thus experience a totalising alienation which occurs primarily in leisure time, giving rise to the illusion of personal free time which, instead, is no longer free nor intimately belongs to the individual.

Debord's critique of sight is in keeping with a long tradition in Western scepticism, particularly Marxist philosophy. He exasperates the debate on the status of images, rejecting them as possible intermediaries: the sensible world is no longer directly apprehensible through the senses because of the continuous, deceptive mediation (separation) carried out by images. Sight and visual media are at the centre of political critique because of their significance in furthering spectacular separation and preserving individuals as contemplated objects, which prompts Debord to practically carry out his criticism by means of one such media: cinema. The way in which historical materialism aims at overthrowing dominant ideology and its false images is by exhibiting its very process, which is what Marxist film theory attempts to do – show the hands at work, reconstruct the production processes and make explicit the artificial nature of cinematic images. Debord thus appropriates the film medium to articulate his critique of the spectacle and incite the awakening of citizen-spectators' consciousness, resorting to an iconoclastic approach which refutes mimetic representation insofar as it had become an effective tool for spectacular separation. Indeed, 'the cinema, too, must be destroyed', so Debord invokes in *Sur le passage de quelques personnes à travers une assez courte unité de temps* (*On the Passage of a Few Persons Through a Rather Brief Unity of Time*, 1959). But what he sets out to destroy is a certain way of making films: as spectacle, entertainment, pleasure. In his critical project against the spectacle, cinema becomes a means for dismantling the illusory unity of individual and reality by presenting images as such; namely, images as constructed representations which societal power employs to maintain the status quo. According to Benjamin Noys (2007),

> What Debord aimed to do was to put the 'unmaking' of cinema in the cause of the 'unmaking' of capitalism, and so to unmake the world. These two tasks had to be carried out simultaneously, as the history of cinema cannot be distinguished from the history of modern capitalist society. (395)

The inescapable bond between cinema and history also stems from what Giorgio Agamben (2002) identifies as 'the specific function of the image and its eminently historical character' (314). In Agamben's account, montage is that through which history can return, thereby permitting to comprehend historical past in a new light. He identifies repetition and stoppage as the two transcendentals of montage which Debord cinematically exploits: repetition, like memory, 'restores possibility to the past'; stoppage 'pulls it [the image] away from the narrative power to exhibit it as such' (Agamben 2002, 316, 317). Inseparable, repetition and stoppage allow Debord to show the image as a constructed representation; namely, 'the image as a zone of undecidability between the true and the false. [. . .] The image exhibited as such is no longer an image of anything; it is itself imageless' (Agamben 2002, 319). In Agamben's view, imagelessness refers to 'the fact that there is nothing more to be seen' (319) rather than to a figuratively empty image; contra the concealed imagelessness of pornography and advertising, Debord's cinema qualifies as ethico-political because it unconceals the ideological abuses of images. By using a variety of still and moving images produced by consumer society which he then manipulates through repetition and stoppage, Debord shows how the same image, which at the hands of dominant ideology looks like truth, if *détourned*, becomes revelatory of its deceitful usage. Thus, instead of immersive consumption, illusory narratives and transparent images, Debord's films deliberately aim at provoking constant awareness about the act of watching.

Such critical approach to cinema concretises in a rejection of mainstream films as well as auteur cinema because, in Debord's perspective, they both fail to effectively dismantle the spectacle in their preserving a pleasure of and for images. Debord's disruptive aesthetics destroys cinematic pleasure through what Thomas Y. Levin (2002) defines as *'mimesis of incoherence*: the film is unsatisfying because the world is unsatisfying; the incoherence of the film reflects that of the reality; the poverty of the film's materials serves to emphasize the poverty of its subject' (360). Similarly, Noys (2007) contends that Debord's films 'are not anti-pleasure but they are opposed to the false pleasures offered us by capital, including the false "aesthetic pleasures" of existing cinema' (397). From his first film realised in a Lettrist ambit to his last work, Debord's cinema offers an iconoclastic aesthetics which unequivocally diverges from narrative cinema in an effort to arouse political conscience in spectators. The form of this critique deliberately undermines the pleasures associated with the narrative film, whether it be mainstream entertaining cinema or auteur cinema.

Almost Nothing to See

Among the stylistic techniques used with an iconoclastic intent in the visual arts, the monochromatic image constitutes perhaps the most radical one. It is, in fact, the gesture against figuration most emblematic of the crisis of mimesis in Western arts. Like in abstract painting (Besançon 2000, 319–77; Gamboni 1997; Lowe 2002; Poirson-Dechonne 2016, 163–79; Wajcman 1998), in cinema, too, the monochromatic image consists in a rejection of mimetic representation and concretely manifests the tension between the invisible and the visually accessible. The monochromatic screen qualifies as an interruption and negation of vision, an image of imagelessness in which the look is denied entry to the world of mimetic representation. Debord extensively exploits such a device in all his films to frustrate viewers' expectations and dismantle any attempt at cinematic transparency.

In *Cinema 2* (1997a, 189–224), Gilles Deleuze considers the role of the black and white screens in contemporary cinema. Drawing on Noël Burch (1981), Deleuze emphasises the blank screen's relevance for contemporary cinema and its being a threshold between presence and absence. The white or black screen disconcerts the spectator's look, which is compelled to confront an absence of figurative images and colours. While blank screens in cinema do not necessarily acquire an iconoclastic value,[2] Debord employs them as an area in which to question the experience of film viewing and the image's status. The monochromatic screen in Debord's films thus constitutes a deliberate iconoclastic gesture which, by opening visual vacua in the cinematographic space, requires a conceptual operation to be translated into a system of meaning.

Debord structures his first film, *Hurlements en faveur de Sade* (*Howls for Sade*, 1952), based on the alternation between black screen and white screen. The film was realised within a Lettrist context and is indebted to previous Lettrist films, especially Isou's *Traité de bave et d'éternité* (1951), in its iconoclastic negation of any figurative image. Both Kaira M. Cabañas (2014, 98) and Levin (2002, 342) define *Hurlements* as a 'sound film without images'. More precisely, what is absent from the film are representational images since *Hurlements* is composed of twenty-six monochromatic screens of different lengths, thirteen white and thirteen black, for a total duration of seventy-five minutes. When the screen is black there is silence,[3] when the screen is white there is speech. Only twenty minutes of the overall running time contain human voices, with the film ending with twenty-four minutes of silent black screen.

Hurlements opens with a white screen accompanied by a wheezing and rasping sound, which is Gil J. Wolman, an exponent of Lettrism and a Lettrist filmmaker, reciting a '*mégapneumie*, what Wolman elsewhere describes as a *poésie physique* (physical poetry) that is based on breath, rather than on the letter as with Isou, and that explores the use of "all human sounds"' (Cabañas 2014, 80). Although this sound differs from that of Isou's film, it nonetheless resonates with *Traité*'s motif of the guttural, unintelligible human sound heard throughout the film. Wolman's *mégapneumie* is followed by intelligible speech in which Debord outlines his personal history of cinema, providing the cinematic influences for his film, which include Dadaism, Surrealism and Lettrism. He lists *Le Voyage dans la Lune* (Georges Méliès, 1902), *The Cabinet of Dr. Caligari* (*Das Cabinet des Dr. Caligari,* Robert Wiene, 1920), *Entr'acte* (René Clair, 1924), *Battleship Potemkin* (*Bronenosets Potëmkin,* Sergei Eisenstein, 1925), *Un Chien Andalou*

(Luis Buñuel and Salvador Dalí, 1929), *City Lights* (Charlie Chaplin, 1931), *Traité de bave et d'éternité* (Isidore Isou, 1951) and *L'Anticoncept* (*The Anti-Concept*, Gil J. Wolman, 1952) and concludes with his own film, *Hurlements*. During the remaining twelve white screens, we hear the monotonal voice-overs of Debord, Isou and other Lettrists reading bits and pieces taken from various texts, such as the civil code and James Joyce's work, together with seemingly nonsensical conversations.

In *Hurlements*, Debord applies to sound the device of *détournement*, which will become the constructive principle of all his subsequent films and a paradigmatic device of the SI (Debord and Wolman [1956] 2006; *Internationale situationniste* [1959] 2006b, 67–68). *Détournement*, meaning 'diversion' or 'hijacking', is the practice of appropriating visual or aural elements from their context – in this case that of consumer society – and investing them with a meaning often antithetical to their original one. That is, by subverting the context, the *détournement* produces anti-spectacular meanings. In *Hurlements*, *détourned* sounds intensify the overall negative aesthetics of the film already produced by the white screens: the sound track of inexpressive voices works together with the halting of figurative vision in rendering the viewing experience displeasing. Divested of their original context and pronounced almost without changes in tone, the spoken words lose the reference to their original meaning; thus, for instance, individual sentences taken from the civil code, now separated from larger paragraphs that would provide a meaningful context, 'are made ridiculous' (Field 1999, 64). It is hardly possible to feel involved in these voice-overs due to both their tone and content, and even less when faced with the double negation of images and sounds when the screen is black: it is no longer possible to see anything but blackness, it is no longer possible to hear anything but noisy silence. In Levin's (2002) passionate and at times hyperbolical reading, this film is an attack against 'the spectators [who], confronted with their *desires and expectations* for a (the) spectacle, are provoked to the point of screams (*hurlements*) when it is revealed to what extent they themselves are an integral part of this spectacular economy' (348).

Hurlements does dismantle more traditional modes of film spectatorship, testing the viewers' patience and actively promoting aesthetic displeasure to counter contemplation.[4] The complete absence of figurative images, annulled in the black and white screens, together with silence and *détourned* sounds, manifests a radical distrust in audio-visual images and a disbelief in the viewers' capacity to critically engage with cinema unless deprived of pleasure. Accounts of the first screenings of the film highlight the purposeful arousal of unpleasant reactions in spectators as a means for dismantling the spectacle.

Levin (2002) notes that 'the audience has become bored and nervous, if not violent, long before the twenty-four minute black silence that makes up the final sequence' (342), and Jay (1993) similarly comments that, 'not surprisingly, the event produced the scandal that Debord expected – those *hurlements* elicited by sadistically subjecting the audience to so mind-numbing an experience – when it was first shown to a non-Lettrist audience in London [. . .] in 1952' (245).

Debord's aesthetics of displeasure aims at countering the alienating pleasures of spectacular film images, which perpetuate the logic of the spectacle by entrapping viewers in a passive state – what Boris Groys (2002, 287) addresses as the *'vita contemplativa'* (contemplative life) of immersive cinema in opposition to the *'vita activa'* (active life) encouraged by Debord's films. According to Groys, mainstream cinema promotes active life on screen while relegating spectators to a state of (mental) immobility (namely, contemplation), whereas Debord's films would restore the spectator as an active subject. Likewise, Allyson Field contends that *Hurlements* challenges habitual modes of film viewing through the use of monochromatic screens, *détourned* sounds and long silences. In her reading, 'Debord makes the film *difficult* to watch, to hear, and to sit through, thereby making a film that aims to revolutionize the relation of spectator to film' (Field 1999, 64). It is through this difficult, potentially unpleasant watching that Debord pursues the overcoming of spectatorial contemplation, forcing viewers to face the emptiness of their alienated life which is disclosed to them once contemplation is no longer possible. While reintroducing figurative images in his subsequent films, Debord never ceased to employ the monochromatic screen as a direct attack against contemplative reception and spectacle-images, which is at the core of his last film, palindromically titled *In girum imus nocte et consumimur igni* (*We Wander in the Night and Are Consumed by Fire*, 1978).

In girum explores issues of film spectatorship as an impoverished living mode equivalent to contemplative life in the society of the spectacle, metaphorically attacking viewers for a running time of ninety minutes. Like previous Debord works, it is composed of *détourned* found footage images, film extracts, personal photos and the unusual addition of shots expressly recorded for this film, accompanied by the director's voice-over as the unifying element. From the opening, the film makes manifest its subject, that of alienated spectatorship, by presenting a static image of an audience at the cinema (Figure 2.1). Here the *détournement* disallows any possible contemplative identification between images and spectators: viewers are at once observing subject and observed object since they metaphorically watch themselves watching

Figure 2.1 Static shot of a photograph of a cinema audience

themselves. The film continues with an intermingling of photographs and shots of urban views, film spectators and citizens in their daily life to establish a parallel between living in the society of the spectacle and going to the cinema to watch films that promote a contemplative – and therefore unreceptive to contemporary alienation – experience.

The metaphorical assault on spectators manifests itself more vehemently towards the end of the film, when Debord inserts a black screen on which a white text aggressively addresses the audience as follows: 'Here the spectators, having been deprived of everything, will even be deprived of images'. Then, the screen becomes white for about two minutes, while Debord's voice-over launches into a defence of his work, emphasising his status as exiled and misunderstood. The choice of a monochromatic screen is an explicit provocation to the audience, in line with Debord's theoretical view, as it is systematically expressed in the texts *The Society of the Spectacle* ([1967] 1994) and *Comments on the Society of the Spectacle* ([1988] 1990) and is exemplary of his claimed attack against existing cinema. Moreover, the monochromatic screen also serves his denouncing of the socio-economic, historical fabric within which cinema operates; thus, dispossessing viewers of familiar images is a way to encourage an awakening from the numbness of their alienated life in consumer society. As his monotonal voice-over argues,

> It is a particular society, not a particular technology, that has made the cinema like this. It could have consisted of historical analyses, theories, essays, memoirs. It could have consisted of films like the one I am making at this moment.

While this quote most evidently expresses Debord's destructive anti-illusionism and his critique of the socio-historical context as that which determines spectacular cinema, it also interestingly affirms a separation of the technology of image-making and image-viewing from socio-cultural ideology. This conception contrasts, for instance, with Stephen Heath's (1976) argument on the ideological dimensions of Western perspective; that is, the technology of cinema, as a development of that of photography which, in its turn, reproduces the Quattrocento perspective, is ideologically coded. In Heath's view, then, it is impossible to separate the technology and the socio-cultural context/ideology. In Debord's social analysis of the contextual spectacular employment of images and in his project of awakening consciousness through a *détourning* of images of consumerism, formal interest in the medium itself is instead secondary.

To contrast the illusionism of the spectacle and to articulate its critique, Debord privileges sound over image and, specifically, speech over other sounds. Both in his first and last films, as well as in the rest of his cinematic works, 'Debord uses language to counter the purported truth of an image' (Cabañas 2014, 114). And indeed, Debord's distant and monotonal voice-over is the very foundation of all his films. The distrust in the image is compensated by a faith in the word – in its ability to communicate meaning. Such belief in the word over the image, reminiscent of Lettrist mysticism, also echoes the Biblical rejection of the eye in favour of the ear. Debord's pronounced iconoclasm stems from his considering images only in their ability to deceive rather than believing in any redemptive power. According to Levin (2002),

> Debord contends that, in fact, images as such can prove nothing, save perhaps the reigning deception. By *mis*using images however, by subjecting the cornerstones of the cinematic edifice to *détournement*, something may perhaps be revealed about the medium itself, Debord suggests, even if only negatively. (407)

Rejecting the fascination of the image, Debord has shown that the cinema 'can be reduced to this white screen, then this black screen' (Debord 1994, *Guy*

Debord, son art et son temps). The monochromatic screen is therefore symptomatic of a disbelief in the image, in its ability to represent the model veraciously. In Debord's view, there is no space for doubts about the deceptiveness of images and his conclusion on the impossibility of a true or trustworthy image (*eikōn*) is categorical.

Decomposing Cinematic Flow

Alongside the absence of figurative images of the monochromatic screen, other techniques can lead to the nullification of the referential, self-evident image without entirely renouncing figuration. This can be achieved via the intensive manipulation of figurative images and of film movement because the dissection of cinematic flow mars the nexus between images and the models that have produced them. Debord utilises visual and aural *détournements* to dispossess images of their alienating value and to show the logic of the spectacle, most effectively in the filmic rendition of *The Society of the Spectacle* (1973), which is constructed on the alternation between stasis and movement. Whether through stillness, blank screens or *détourned* images and sounds, Debord's method qualifies as negative-affirmative insofar as his anti-cinematic films make seemingly incontrovertible statements (individuals have become passive consumers of images; cinema is a tool of the spectacle; images are false; only Lettrist and Situationist cinema can make a considerable change), leaving little or nothing to the benefit of doubt.

Like the monochromatic screen, the interruption or manipulation of filmic movement is not iconoclastic per se. It acquires an iconoclastic value when used as a way to redirect the look: through stillness or slowness the attention is brought to the absence of regular motion which, in turn, should stimulate an interrogation of this stasis' meaning. The abolition or alteration of movement counters cinematic illusion and, in establishing a distance between images and viewers, allows spectators to think about cinema while at the cinema. Therefore, these images of decomposed movement aim at producing what Raymond Bellour (2012) defines 'pensive spectator' (86), inasmuch as they break the possibility of a totally immersive consumption of the film.

In his analysis of filmic movement, Bellour (2012) identifies the freeze-frame as 'the often unique, fugitive, yet perhaps decisive instant when cinema seems to be fighting against its very principle' (130); that is, movement. While Bellour remarks several times that movement is not a necessary condition for cinema, it is also undeniable that, since its origin, cinema has had close ties with it. Films have celebrated motion in multiple ways, both through the movement of the pro-filmic and via camera movements and editing. And indeed, 'moving images' is a fundamental part of the very definition of cinema, as its etymology makes clear.[5] Although it is of course possible to make films without images that move, movement is nonetheless a constant possibility for cinema, as Noël Carroll's (1996) definition of 'moving image' underlines: 'Movement in a film image is an artistic choice which is always technically available' (64). Accordingly, the interruption of motion contains an anti-cinematic quality.

Taking movement as a defining feature of cinema, Groys (2002) examines stillness as a potentially iconoclastic technique. First considering mainstream cinema, he opposes the contemplative state promoted by narrative films in spectators to the movement celebrated on screen. In mainstream films, the *vita activa* so intensively lauded on screen is negated, at least partially, to the audience who cannot directly intervene in the film and are asked to contemplate the action happening on the screen. Conversely, Groys contends, the abolition of film flow can become an iconoclastic device able to return agency to viewers. The interruption of motion on screen would thus stimulate spectators to engage with the film in more thoughtful ways. Similarly, Bellour (2012) identifies in the halting of cinematic movement the potential to provoke a more active response from the audience, claiming that, 'as soon as you stop the film, you begin to find the time to add to the image. You start to reflect differently on film, on cinema' (92). To this very end, Debord decomposes cinematic flow in his films. By deliberately thwarting the mimetic movement of images,[6] he intends to disconcert viewers so as to elicit a critical response. While it is undeniable that Debord's use of stillness and voice-over interrupts the possibility of immersive film viewing, the spectators' taking notice of their own alienation in the society of the spectacle stems primarily from his verbally and verbosely providing a meaning for this altered motion.

The Society of the Spectacle illustrates how the logic of the spectacle has permeated any social aspect of life, turning individuals into spectators. The film originates from Debord's 1967 book, a collection of theses on the concept of the spectacle in contemporary capitalist society, and is entirely composed of found footage and pre-existing material. Stylistically, it is exemplary of Debord's aesthetics of displeasure in that it prevents any contemplative viewing and exhibits the cinematic image as constructed representation through repetition and stoppage. *The Society of the Spectacle*'s anti-cinematic quality deliberately produces a 'violation of the syntax and economy of pleasure characteristic of spectacle' (Levin 2002, 396) and 'breaks with the conventional forms of aesthetic "pleasure" associated with cinema. Debord's cinema is a cinema of "unpleasure", at least in terms of what we might usually think of as the pleasures of cinema'

(Noys 2007, 396). Such an aesthetics results from visual and aural *détournements*, citations and repetitions, stillness and motion, which disclose the film image's ordinary status as a tool of the spectacle. However, in his attempt to negate the capital, and thus spectacular cinema as its integral component, Debord's dismantling of spectatorial pleasure renders his critique significantly difficult to access.

The Society of the Spectacle formally applies Debord's ([1967] 1994) understanding of 'the spectacle in its generality [. . . as] a concrete inversion of life, and, as such, [as] the autonomous movement of nonlife' (thesis 2). Film movement becomes an allegory of spectacular nonlife, whereas the paralysed film image functions as a space of re-appropriation, for spectators, of their time to think. By freezing images, Debord suppresses any possible identification between them and viewers, thereby promoting the arousal of critical thoughts on consumer society and the world of commodities. Such alternating between stasis and movement qualifies as Debord's iconoclastic method to critique the *eidōlon*, the false image produced by the spectacle which has acquired real consistency – like the religious idol worshipped as a real god, spectacular *eidōla* appear as true presence. The film thus carries out an explicit and bitter critique of capitalist society by means of its own images, which are understood as direct expressions of the spectacle.

Debord's monotonal voice-over, accompanied by a single, repeated musical motif, articulates the critique by reading some of the theses from his book together with extracts from other authors. This un-modulated voice is counterbalanced by the rhythm of the image track, which is structured on the continual alternation between movement and stasis. The images' sources range from advertising to television, film and Debord's photos of friends and his life partner Alice Becker-Ho (to whom the film is dedicated). With the exception of the personal photos, the film's images are emblematic of the consumer society and the alienating society of the spectacle: footage and pictures of naked pin-ups and models recur throughout the film, alongside that of serialised factory work, world politicians, soldiers and armies, stock market, the accumulation of waste, urbanism's devastation, concerts and ecstatic crowds. Debord also *détourns* excerpts from Hollywood films such as Josef von Sternberg's *The Shanghai Gesture* (1941), John Ford's *Rio Grande* (1950) and Nicholas Ray's *Johnny Guitar* (1954), as well as films 'from so-called socialist countries' (as the film credits them), such as Sergei Eisenstein's *Battleship Potemkin* and *October: Ten Days That Shook the World* (*Oktiabr' ili Desiat' dneĭ, kotorye potriasli mir*, 1928). De- and re-contextualised via *détournement*, the variety of images composing *The Society of the Spectacle* are unconcealed as spectacular *eidōla*. That is, the practice of *détournement* extrapolates images and sounds from their original context and provides them with a different meaning by positioning them in a new situation. Thus, for example, the extracts from the fictional films that Debord incorporates in *The Society of the Spectacle* no longer retain the meaning they might have had as part of their original film, but 'are used [. . .] to represent the rectification of the "artistic inversion of life"'. Denouncing the spectacle's 'deport[ing of] real life behind the screen', the *détournement* applied to existing fictional films constitutes a way to restore those aspects of life which the films may recall in their new context – hence, '*Johnny Guitar* evokes real memories of love, *Shanghai Gesture* [evokes] other adventurous places [. . .]. The Western *Rio Grande* can evoke all action and historical reflection' (Debord [1989] 2003, 223).

The de-/re-contextualisation which *détournement* operates also serves to unconceal the shared spectacular quality of diverse images. Debord's montage, in fact, reveals that what at first sight may have appeared as a disparate amalgam is actually the product of the same spectacular logic; therefore, the film's aesthetics expressly counters such logic. While the spectacle separates and isolates images to maintain the status quo, Debord links seemingly unrelated images to show how they all participate in the perpetuation of spectacular discourse. Accordingly, footage of the Beatles and photos of Marilyn Monroe can coexist alongside political news-reels, images of soldiers and armies, and shots of urban waste. Through the *détournement*, what may look different reveals itself as the product of the same alienating logic.

The critique of contemporary society also develops from the variation between movement and stasis of these varied images: the immobility of photos and freeze-frames constitutes the negation of the false movement of spectacular images. Cinematic flow, reiterating spectacular flow, is a reactionary movement which suppresses the time and distance necessary for viewers to reflect on the images before them; thus, illusory filmic flow, which mirrors the endless movement of the spectacle, is a paradoxical movement for the maintenance of the status quo. For instance, the critique of urbanism, which was a central motif of the SI's criticism for its reproduction of the spectacle's separation by dividing and rationalising space,[7] unfolds through the motion/stillness binary of *détourned* images. The image flux of cities, new residential neighbourhoods and building materials' waste is supplanted by the stillness of Bruegel the Elder's painting *Tower of Babel* (c. 1563). A gloomy, spiral-shaped construction dominates the space of the canvas: divine punishment has already occurred, making human communication impossible because of the lack of a shared language; the incoherence of the architecture thus reflects linguistic incomprehension. Likewise, human incommunicability governs in the society of the spectacle. Therefore, the still image of the painting and the image flux of urbanism's devastation are not set in opposition but paralleled through the sameness of their subject matter; namely, the impossible communication between individuals. The seemingly innocuous images of urban constructions are therefore nothing other than spectacle-images of human alienation.

Throughout the film, the arrest of movement restores the possibility of critical thinking without however rehabilitating the image as *eikōn*. In a sequence on the consumption of leisure time, moving images of women at the seaside are punctuated with still images of body details to articulate the critique of the commodification of female bodies and their assimilation to spectacular desire. Similarly, the criticism of the star as incarnation of the spectacle unfolds through a frenzy of moving images of the Beatles suddenly halted by still photos of Marilyn Monroe. Both moving and still images are *eidōla*, and the power of stoppage consists in extrapolating one image from the flux and exhibiting it more clearly as spectacular. Only the film's incipit provides a few instances in which Debord seems to concede a somewhat positive connotation to the image. Photos of Alice Becker-Ho (Figure 2.2), broken once by the spectacle-image of two models, are paired with a rendition of Johann Sebastian Bach's Sonata for Cello and Harpsichord in G major, *allegro moderato* and the following subtitle:

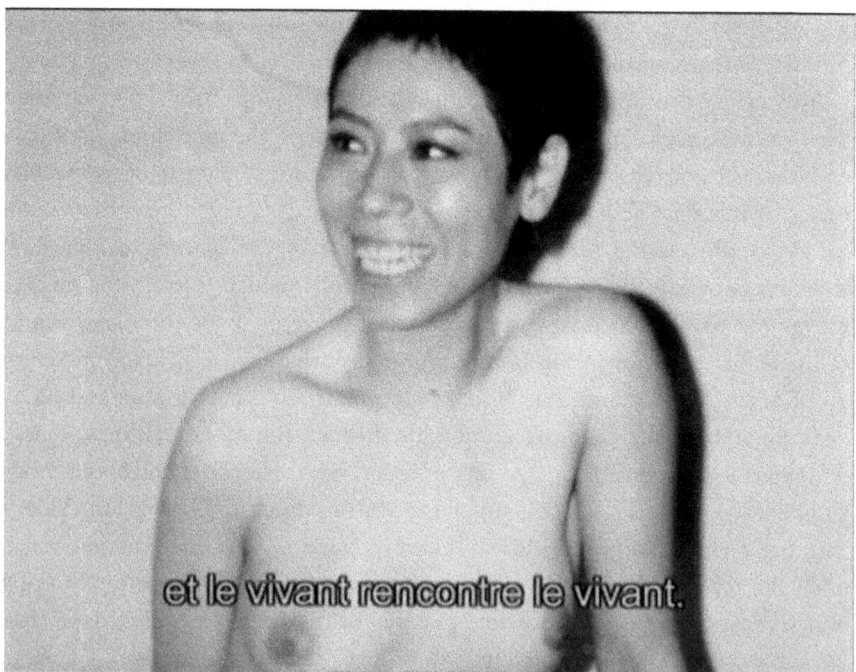

Figure 2.2 Static shot of a photograph of Alice Becker-Ho and text 'and the living re-encounters the living'

Since each particular sentiment is only a partial aspect of life and not the entirety of life, life burns to pour out through the diversity of sentiments, and thus rediscover itself in the sum of diversity. In love, the separate still exists, but not as separated, as united: and the living re-encounters the living.

The last sentence is taken from Hegel ([1798] 1971, 305),[8] according to whom love overcomes individual separation. Becker-Ho's photos configure themselves as possible locus of unity opposed to spectacular separation, which is represented through the spectacle-image of naked models. The film's incipit therefore introduces the critique of the spectacle as 'inversion of life', which is the subject of the entire film, while also leaving open for the image the unlikely possibility of being something other than *eidōlon*. Cabañas (2014) points out that, 'with the exception of the opening still images of his partner Alice Becker-Ho, the remainder of the film bespeaks the same reality: "our existence separated from ourselves, transformed by the machine of the spectacle into dead images before us, against us"' (117).

In Debord's oeuvre, the film image, whether figurative or blank, is constantly negated as truthful representation because of its belonging to the pervasive logic of the spectacle. According to Monica Dall'Asta and Marco Grosoli (2011), 'the trust in the (possible) authenticity of reproduction is that which ceases to exist in Debord's vision' (14). Via the *détournement*, Debord shows that even those images apparently closest to their phenomenal referent constitute an illusion, a false surrogate of reality. There is no belief in cinematic and photographic images' capacity of a veracious representation of reality insofar as 'in a world that has really been turned upside down, truth is a moment of falsehood' (Debord [1988] 1990, 50). Debord takes the reflection on the status of the image to its extreme, negating any possibility for the image as intermediary – as *eikōn*. The sensible world, turned into spectacle, becomes unknowable through direct experience and can be apprehended only via the continuous mediation of spectacle-images. However, this mediation establishes a nexus neither between these images and their models – since images posit themselves as if they were the models – nor between individuals and the sensible world, which is primarily lived passively through sight. Broken the *eidōlon*, Debord displays the image as a tool of the spectacle, marked by its illusory appearance.

Concluding Remarks

Debord exasperates the devices of blank screen, altered motion and sound-image disjunction, imbuing them with iconoclastic value to metaphorically attack passive spectatorship. What is more, he develops the *détournement* through which to dismantle the images of capitalist society, in an attempt to defang the alienating power that subjugates citizens and spectators alike. Thus, Debord offers a lucid critique of the film image without however providing a way forward, because he remains entrapped in an extremely self-reflexive paradigm. Following the iconoclastic tendency of Marxist critique, Debord's destruction of images derives from a distrust in the image's ability to represent the model. Spectacle-images are *eidōla* because they feign their referents with which they have severed any relationship; hence, they are reduced to pure appearances with no possible redemption. Enclosed in an absolute critique of the cinematic *eidōlon*, from *Hurlements* to *In girum* there is no place for the *eikōn* in Debord's perspective. Such a sharp critique of representation and iconoclastic approach to cinema are also present in the films of Carmelo Bene, who recuperates fiction only to further dismantle it. However, while Debord is anxious to convey his political perspective via intelligible speech, Bene embraces an absurd worldview, disrupting language through a voice which has become incomprehensible *phoné*.

3   Towards a Radical Voice: Carmelo Bene's *Our Lady of the Turks*

A LARGER-THAN-LIFE FIGURE, yet overlooked by scholars, Carmelo Bene experimented with a destructive aesthetics in a variety of media, from theatre to cinema, television and literature. (In)famous for his surly manners and narcissistic self-referentiality, he was author, director and main actor of his plays and films, which were tailored to his remarkable vocal and physical abilities. Theatre first, and cinema and television later, are beset by Bene's frenzied iconoclasm, which dismantles intelligible narrative, language and mise-en-scène. He favours a 'removing from the scene' [*togliere di scena*] (Bene ([1995] 2002b, xiii),[1] which is part of a complex aesthetics of subtraction conducive to what Gilles Deleuze (1997b) defines as Bene's 'theatre of nonrepresentation' (241). Artistic mimesis is utterly rejected in pursuit of plays and films as purely aesthetic events, in which comprehensibility is always on the verge of surrendering to nonsense.

Bene iconoclastically exploits style and content, establishing visual and aural dissonances, as well as narrative inconsistencies, in an overall refusal of cinema and theatre as mimetic representations of reality. Like Isidore Isou and Guy Debord, he privileges the sonorous dimension of cinema as a way to attack its visual lure; however – unlike the verbo-centric Debord and, to a lesser extent, Isou – Bene grounds his films in the voice as *phoné* wherein sense and communication cease to have a stable place. The voice becomes the centre around which his poetic of destruction unravels: through aural juxtapositions and disjunctions, marred elocution, neologisms and exasperated sound levels, Bene makes sonorous intelligibility often impossible to achieve while also hindering visual comprehension.

This chapter explores Bene's project to destroy theatre first and cinema later, as media able to communicate meaning by way of linguistic and sonic disruptions. It considers the significance of the voice as *phoné* for the overcoming of cinema's logo-video-centrism and for the uncoupling of a harmoniously conceived relationship between body and voice, which further dismantles cinematic mimesis. Bene's first film, *Our Lady of the Turks* (*Nostra signora dei turchi*, 1968), is exemplary of an iconoclastic understanding of cinema in its eschewing of mimetic images and intelligible narrative. Via a paradoxical use of language and sound, the film also articulates a critique of Catholic religion, and specifically of codified religious rites as opposed to the mystical experience of the sacred, well exemplified by the character of a priest incapable of intelligibly speaking, who ends up vomiting sounds, and an extremely earthly Saint Margaret obsessively repeating 'I forgive you'. This chapter thus engages with a remarkably destructive approach to cinema, through a film wherein iconic unrepresentability chimes with sonic unintelligibility.

An Aesthetics of Subtraction and Amplification

Bene's artistic project aims at negating theatre first, and cinema and television later, as meaningful representational media via an overcoming of logo- and video-centrism. Because mimesis in the visual arts often aids in the communication of an intelligible meaning, it becomes a core target in Bene's longing for a theatre and cinema that could qualify as 'inhumane refusal to express anything' (Bene [1995] 2002b, xxxv). To this end, he abolishes narrative content, dismisses comprehensible acting and relinquishes dialogue, thereby grounding his theatrical events in aphasia (the inability to communicate through language) and apraxia (the inability to execute coherent movements and gestures). Actors are forced to repeatedly fall and stagger, vocalising a text performed in spasms and broken sentences, often played-back or rendered inaudible to the audience. What is more, Bene dissects the written text through acts of subtraction which allow for minor elements to be amplified, contributing to a 'theatre of nonrepresentation' in which the spectator's identification with and understanding of what is happening on the stage is neutralised. Responding to the same iconoclastic drive, his films further exasperate incoherent bodily gestures and destructive approaches to language while also taking the mimetic image apart so that it can no longer function as (pretended) intermediary, relational entity.

In his iconoclastic approach to the arts, Bene is profoundly influenced by Christian mysticism of both the apophatic and cataphatic traditions (Chillemi 2011; Furno 2014, 206; Paiano 2020), insofar as they maintain, albeit with substantial differences (which go well beyond the scope of my argument), that the ecstatic experience of God cannot be adequately expressed in its entirety. In his written, theatrical and cinematic works, Bene extensively references cataphatic mystics such as Saint Teresa of Avila and Saint Joseph of Copertino (on whose life Bene centres his unfilmed screenplay *A boccaperta* [*With mouth wide open*] [1976] 2002a) who allow him to explore the peculiar place of the personal experience of God in positive theology and specifically, in Catholicism – the religion of icons. Cataphatic mystical experience brings to the surface a subtle tension between image and word, wherein the former seems to retain its capacity to represent while the latter reveals itself as partially deficient. Negative theology resolves this tension because of its positioning of the sacred in the domain of the ineffable and the unrepresentable, conceiving of both image and word as insufficient for the rendering of the divine and the human experience thereof. Echoes of apophatic mysticism, particularly that of Meister Eckhart, are palpable in Bene's works (explicitly in *Un dio assente: Monologo a due voci sul teatro* [*An Absent God: A Two-Voices Monologue about Theatre*] [2006], but also in his plays and films, up to the rhetorically saturated poem '*L mal de' fiori* [*The Evil of Flowers*] [2000]). Fundamental in Meister Eckhart's (2009) ruminations is the intimate relationship with God, whose most overwhelming manifestation occurs in mystical experience, which transcends the human capacity to represent (through words or images) and constitutes a breach of quotidian perception. There is no mediation between the subject experiencing mystical vision and God but only overwhelming immediacy, which is possible insofar as the subject is liberated from images. Not only does mystical experience take place without the interference of images, but also accounting for such an experience through language or image is doomed to failure (see, for instance, sermons 1, 7, 9, 14(b), 32(a), 41, 42)[2]. Much like the apophatic experience of God implies a rupture with everydayness and the human capacity to exhaustively express it, so Bene seeks an art which could sever any comprehensible communication with a given reality, attesting to the poverty of supposedly meaningful images and words in the rendering of experience; an experience, therefore, that could leave spectators with their mouth wide open in ecstatic bewilderment.

Language's failure to utter experience concretises in Bene's consistent recourse to aphasia (stammering, dis/assonances, warped elocution) and is visually paralleled with mimesis's inadequacy. In its deceptive guise of a trustworthy intermediary agent, the mimetic image corresponds to the *eidōlon*, which accordingly impoverishes the phenomenal world (which is enframed), the arts (which are reduced to a reproduction) and the artistic experience (which loses its ecstatic potential). Since there is no possibility for the image to be *eikōn* in Bene's perspective, the only available option remains the breaking of the *eidōlon*, of the image mistakenly conceived as a relational entity able to communicate, to produce instead an incommunicable artistic experience which could be tantamount to mystical ecstasy – hence, the conspicuous resorting to aphasia and apraxia, which permit the possible nearing of such an experience.

Explicitly praising the Byzantine iconoclastic emperor Leo, the destroyer of icons, Bene ([1978] 2011f) claims that 'the image is death. Leo, the iconoclast, was right. The image is death, the image is mortal, but it is not the act of dying. Dying is a continuum, agony is the crisis, the impasse' (146). Visual (and aural) mimesis configures itself as locus of immobility for its de/limiting of reality and our experience thereof. In Bene's theatre and cinema, instead, everything is set in a state of constant variation; even when something appears to be still, there is always – as imperceptible as it may be – movement (there is no death but the act of dying). The attention is brought to a-finalistic gestures and unintelligible voices which develop towards and around aphasia and apraxia. Actors are compelled to staggering movements and repeated, meaningless gestures, hampered by the objectual world and dressed in unwieldy costumes which prompt them to inexorably fall. Such bodily impediments are paired with a language which has ceased to communicate anything, since actors stutter, mumble and lose their ability to articulate speech. The voice as *phoné* becomes the vehicle for dismantling the image as relational entity because, as a logos-less voice, it constitutes an attack against language and, therefore, an attack against language's capacity to represent and communicate. Stuttering, mumbling, rumbling are placed at the forefront of the sound track for their rendering of the inability to say something clearly and intelligibly, thereby echoing the inexpressible quality of mystical experience.

What is under attack is any possible attempt at meaningful representation, which consequently involves spectatorship – what to do with the audience? How to unsettle them ecstatically and aesthetically? In a narcissistic move, Bene distances himself from traditional theatre and mainstream cinema, which elicit immersive fruition, but also from Brecht's epic theatre and avant-garde cinema for their mistaken focus on the audience. Bene, instead, claims to neglect spectators, who are 'constantly sandwiched between fatigue of the eye and frustration of the soul' (Bachmann 1972–73, 21). While Bene reiterates, in writing and interviews, his disregard for the viewers, his poetic is obsessively haunted by the recipients of his oeuvre; the will of dismantling meaning has its reason for being in the spectator, the focal point around which Bene's iconoclastic practices develop. In the theatrical version of *Our Lady of the Turks* (1966, 1973), for instance, Bene literally walls up the fourth wall with a glass panel to make it impossible for spectators to properly distinguish images or understand speech (the logos), in a move which at once rejects the illusionism of traditional theatre and shuns Brecht's destruction of the fourth wall. The iconoclastic furor against mimesis and spectatorial engagement (whether contemplative or critical) even intensifies in the cinema because of the medium's realistic pretence. In *L'orecchio mancante* [*The Missing Ear*] (1970), he enquires: 'How come that in all the other "artistic speculations" the old, realistic polemic is extinguished, crashed by well-known evidence, and only in cinema it continues in such asinine, deaf mute and blind obstinacy [. . .] on the miserable pretext of FRUITION?' (47–48). Instead of focusing on either entertaining or critically stimulating spectators, Bene frustrates audience expectations by exasperating the rupture between audio-visual images and phenomenal reality through an anti-mimetic style, and he exacerbates narrative unintelligibility via the excision of several elements.

Bene's aesthetics, indeed, proceeds from subtraction (Blau 2011; Chiesa 2012; Chillemi 2015; Deleuze 1997b; Kowsar 1986), eliminating elements of stability in favour of variations, hindering action to focus on acts. While action delineates a trajectory, thereby pointing to a (possible) meaning, acts lack purpose and sense insofar as they consist in meaningless immediacy which 'de-realises action instead of realising it' (Bene [1998] 2011b, 178). Bene's iconoclasm concretises in an oxymoronic process of amputation which leads to something else being amplified. In his theatrical adaptations, he subtracts one or more key elements from the source text while paradoxically enlarging a relatively minor component. For example, in his rendition of Shakespeare's *Romeo and Juliet*, Bene subtracts Romeo and amplifies Mercutio, who now refuses to die and demands to remain on stage until the end; similarly, in *Richard III*, Bene eliminates almost all characters and actions, amplifying the king's solitude and the female characters' ghostly presence. His 'theatre of nonrepresentation' surgically subtracts aural, visual and narrative elements in an attempt to short-circuit meaning: there is no diegetic stability or continuity, no spatio-temporal logic, no dialogue.

Such an aesthetics can be read as political insofar as the elements subtracted are those in which power incarnates. According to Deleuze (1997b), 'what is subtracted, amputated, or neutralized are the elements of power, the elements that constitute or represent a system of power: Romeo as representative of familial power, [. . .] kings and princes as representative of state power' (241). Through subtraction, major characters become powerless and their actions meaningless; hence, there is no longer consistency in the actors' gestures and voice, or in the text itself. Among the elements through which power exercises its homogenising control, such as main characters, narrative actions and teleological gestures, dialogue has a most relevant role 'because it transmits elements of power into speech and causes them to spread' (Deleuze 1997b, 245). Thus, Bene amputates power in both language and gesture, producing a theatre based on aphasia and impediments within which any meaningful action is expelled in favour of a-teleological acts of immediacy. Gestures and vocal sounds are often repeated to the point of meaninglessness, like the priest's mumbled soliloquy in *Our Lady of the Turks*, or Desdemona's continuous dying in *Othello, or the Deficiency of Women* (1979, 1985).

There is a specific interest in destroying ordinary language and, as consequence, gestures which bodily reflect language's inability to articulate meaning. To this end, Bene employs language in a paradoxical manner, which Deleuze (1997b) defines as 'be[ing] a foreigner, but in one's own tongue' (246):

> Every linguistic and sonorous component, inseparably language [*langue*] and speech [*parole*], are put in a state of continuous variation. [...] Bene brings together a work of 'aphasia' on language (whispered, stammered, and deformed diction, barely audible or deafening sounds), and a work of 'obstruction' on objects and gestures (costumes limiting movement instead of aiding it, props thwarting change of place, gestures either too stiff or excessively 'soft'). (248–49)

Bene's theatrical works unfold around the two lines of aphasia and impediments, which set everything in ceaseless variation and precarious (im)balance – of things, people and meaning. While the timbre, intensity and pitch of voices often render them unintelligible, actors walk falteringly, tripping over their cumbersome costumes. Such incessant, non-repeatable variations on gesture and voice are also at the basis of Bene's approach to cinema, wherein he exasperates the iconoclastic potential of recorded images and sounds.

His cinematic journey from 1968 to 1974, self-described as 'an "heroic" parenthesis' (Bene [1995] 2002b, 1132), allowed Bene to further his iconoclastic approach already applied to theatre. In his *Autografia* [Autography] ([1995] 2002b), he proudly lists his destructive gestures against theatre, cinema and television which include the '*tearing of language* and *sense* in the *scenic diswriting*', a '*removing from the scene*' as opposed to the logic of mise-en-scène and the '*sampling of sounds and re-conversion of the voice*' to arrive at '*cinema as acoustic image = in-con-sequence of shooting and surgical indiscipline of editing*' (xiii–xiv). Montage, performance, sound and colour sever the relationship between audiovisual images and their referents, irreparably destabilising the film medium's indexical bond with reality. In Bene's films, the recording of the phenomenal world ceases to correspond to a reproduction thereof to counter the medium's realistic pretence, which does nothing other than concealing the very unrepresentability of reality. It is not therefore a matter of finding an image that could be *eikōn*, because that consists of an impossible task; the only possible alternative is to dismantle images in their intelligible appearance. The destruction of images, since it has its starting point in the image, always engages the visual field; but while Isou and Debord privilege the blank screen to articulate their critique of the cinematic *eidōlon*, Bene proceeds towards blindness via a visual and aural excess, exploiting the aesthetic potentialities of the film medium.

Like in theatre, so in the cinema, too, speech and dialogue are abolished in favour of nonsensical, often juxtaposed soliloquies, which dissolve any possible relation and mutual understanding. Such loss of sense is further exacerbated by uncoordinated, self-harmful gestures, which nullify the actors' body as meaningful entity. Bene uses the range of stylistic devices that cinema offers to excessively multiply images and sounds – and indeed, what better way to destroy cinema than an aural and visual frenzy which incessantly disorients, neutralising any possible sense? Every formal element participates in the iconoclastic undoing of cinema: colour is used in an anti-naturalistic and often ironic manner, fragmenting bodies and gestures; out-of-focus images undermine sight; the blowing up of the film strip (Bene shoots in 16mm and then blows up to 35mm) contributes to pushing the image at the edge of the visible frame; a frenetic editing vivisects the film's body (up to *Don Giovanni*'s [1970] 4,500 cuts and *Salomè*'s [1972] 4,200 cuts); extreme close-ups, far from Epstein's and Balázs's granting access to an enhanced knowledge of reality, dissolve the face which is now so close to the point of being indecipherable. But Bene's cinematic iconoclasm is also grounded in a sonorous dimension which, similarly to its visual counterpart, erupts in a vocal, musical and noisy frenzy often abruptly interrupted by silence.

This visible and audible excess destroys the film image as meaningful unit because there are only fragments of sounds and images, which work towards neutralising spectatorial engagement. In particular, visual and aural close-ups qualify as the most effective iconoclastic means for dismantling what is heard and seen by rendering the audio-visual image unintelligible. Objects and actors are so close that it becomes difficult to discern figures and contours; likewise, the amplification of certain sounds, such as a few letters of a single word, complicates the understanding of the verbal. As a result, viewers are caught between enchanting audio-visual images and a bewildering loss of sense. This visual and aural enlargement is conducive to a sort of blindness and deafness whereby sensuous proximity is directly proportional to intelligible distance. What is more, such amplification initiates a process of de-individuation of the human through a dismantling of the unity between body and voice. That is, the human voice is set in opposition to the physical body which produces it, achieving a disconcerting effect:

> At this point, representation and meaningful words no longer exist. The logos no longer exists. Loved ones, feelings, the native land, God, grammar, the soul, spirit, no longer exist. It is the never-said [*mai-detto*] and the unsaid [*non-detto*], which speak to interiority. We are in [the realm of] perception [*sensazione*]. And finally, even the body vanishes. I have tried to achieve all this in the cinema, through the image (which I detest), butchering it via editing, working on the tilting of faces, in an attempt to find a visual melody. (Bene [1998]b 2011, 177)

Aphonia and apraxia carry out the de-individualising process, which affects the actor's body, and contribute to conjuring up the film's musicality – the entwined beautiful images and sounds that can be seen and heard but which are unable to provide access to a controllable, fixed meaning. In Bene's films, rather than voice-off, there is body-off; as Deleuze (1997a) underlines, 'it is no longer the characters who have a voice, it is the voices, or rather the vocal modes of the protagonist (whisper, breathing, shout, eructation . . .) which become the sole, true characters in the ceremony in what has become a musical setting' (191). An audio-visual, perplexing rhythm invests spectators, who are abandoned to a myriad of logos-less voices.

Against Logocentrism

Like Isou and Debord, Bene focuses on the aural/oral dimension to carry out his iconoclastic project against cinema; however, while the two French directors resort to intelligible speech in their films, what interests Bene is the voice once liberated from logos; namely, as pure *phoné*. Bene's attempt at overcoming logocentrism, which is also a refusal of its videocentrism, and privileging of the voice as *phoné* hinges on a critique of Western metaphysics. Contra a tradition in philosophy which has made speaking secondary to thinking, 'Bene seeks a primordial φωνή [*phoné*], prior to any dialectic, logical system or code, even before the mediation of rational subjectivity' (Chillemi 2015). In the sonorous and visible unrest and in the absence of a sensical narrative, the voice as *phoné* gives rhythm to films which have ceased to coherently communicate with spectators.

The relationship between *phoné* and Western logocentrism, whether developed in terms of conflict or accord, is philosophically indebted to the work of Jacques Derrida, who initiated an explicit philosophical engagement with the voice in Western metaphysics in his deconstruction of logocentrism. To put it simply (and rather simplistically), in *Speech and Phenomena* (1973), Derrida's sophisticated analysis results in an argument on metaphysical logocentrism as a phonocentrism within which the voice corresponds to 'pure auto-affection' (79). Derrida's binding of *phoné* with the history of metaphysics (as a history of ideality) is grounded in a critique of the (Husserl's) phenomenological voice which is tantamount to an inward soliloquy – and indeed, Derrida (1973) concludes that 'the voice *is* consciousness' (80). That is, logocentrism is phonocentric, inasmuch as the voice is conceived as an inner monologue, a 'hearing oneself speak' [*s'entendre parler*] (78) which necessarily implies presence and self-proximity. The peculiarity of this 'auto-affection' lies in its self-enclosedness, for in 'hearing oneself speak' there is no 'pass[ing] through what is outside of the sphere of "owness"' (78).[3] Such deconstruction of the phenomenological voice is inscribed in Derrida's work on the anti-metaphysical value of writing as *différance*; hence, accounts of *phoné* as sonorous voice with the potential to trouble metaphysics are to be found elsewhere.

Adriana Cavarero's *For More than One Voice: Toward a Philosophy of Vocal Expression* (2005), Mladen Dolar's *A Voice and Nothing More* (2006) and Slavoj Žižek's 'The Eclipse of Meaning: On Lacan and Deconstruction' (2006) position Derrida as the essential point of reference for their arguments on the voice as that which destabilises metaphysical presence, therefore rebutting his thesis on phonocentrism. Dolar's and Žižek's countering of Derrida's argument is rooted in Lacanian psychoanalysis, through which they identify a voice that withstands logos and argue for an incongruity between voice and meaning. In Žižek's (2006) words, there exists an 'excessive voice which stands for the eclipse of meaning. [. . . an] uncanny voice' (197), which is what Dolar (2006) terms 'the voice against logos, the voice as the other of logos' (52). Rather than producing (self-)presence, this voice carries an absence of subjectivity; it is structurally ambiguous: it neither fully belongs to me nor to another. Accordingly, such 'excessive voice' is also incongruous with the body. As Brian Kane (2014) comments, the Lacanian subject can never overcome 'the *acousmaticity* of the Voice' (207) – something on which Dolar extensively elaborates. Recuperating Michel Chion's (1999, 21) notion of *acousmêtre* and the disconcerting tension between sonorous voice and its non-visible, corporeal source, Dolar (2006, 60–81) concludes that de-acousmatisation is an impossible phenomenon, because the acousmatic voice is an excessive voice which can never quite match the body. According to both Žižek (2001a, 57–58) and Dolar, this occurs not only in cinema, but also characterises the status of the voice in the everyday since, even when we see the body from which the voice emanates, body and voice maintain an uncanny relationship which is fundamentally defined in terms of a gap – consequently, the voice always involves ventriloquism (*I am spoken*) (Dolar, 2006, 70; Žižek, 2001a, 58).

Quite differently, Cavarero develops an argument on the essential bond between voice and body wherein *phoné* as sonorous embodied vocality is irreducible to (exclusively) intelligible speech. She rejects Derrida's argument on the phonocentrism of Western metaphysics, claiming that Western philosophy has historically devocalised logos, rendering it a silent inner monologue, while assigning a privileged role to the visual dimension of sight, *eidos*/ideas, *theoria*; thus, logocentrism is essentially videocentric. Consequently, Cavarero proposes to overcome Western logo(video)centrism through the voice as *phoné*, advancing a fascinating ontology of plurality based on the uniqueness and relationality of the voice. She conceives of the voice as different from speech and accordingly engages with a variety of instances in which such a voice has disturbed Western metaphysics and arts. As a corporeal sound emanating from within a body to the external space, the voice refers to, and therefore identifies, a unique, physical subjectivity that produces it; moreover, the voice is inextricably relational because of its positing of an embodied subject who speaks and another embodied subject who listens (it is an invocation) – Cavarero poignantly writes that 'each voice, as it is *for* the ear, demands at the same time an ear that is *for* the voice' (170). Contra Western logocentrism which has marked metaphysics as a self-referential, fundamentally male, act of thinking, the voice is always a dialogue, even in the physical absence of a listener, because it is directed towards the exterior (of the body, thereby investing the dimension of others) and not, as in Derrida (1973, 76), towards the interior of the subject.

Cavarero's claim about the voice as that which identifies a unique corporeality is sometimes treated as a given; she does not, for instance, engage with the voice's ability to dissimulate and deceive, which is instead central for Dolar's and Žižek's complex voice-body relationship and for Chion's notion of *acousmêtre* (see Kane's [2014, 152–56] excellent critique of Cavarero). Yet, I take her work as a starting point to explore the voice as *phoné* in Bene's oeuvre because of its character of bodily sound which resists logos, the emphasis placed on the act of listening and the voice's essential relational quality, which Bene iconoclastically dismantles. In privileging *phoné* as the tool for surmounting Western logo-video-centrism, Bene's approach resonates with some of Cavarero's ideas. Like Cavarero, Bene focuses on the voice, tying it to the body and forsaking logos in favour of a pure *phoné*; however, he reaches an opposite outcome: the voice, instead of attesting to the uniqueness of the individual body which has produced it and to its relational quality, becomes the primary means for carrying out the de-individualising process through which both inter- and intra-personal communication cease to exist. That is, both Cavarero and Bene use the voice as *phoné* to critique Western metaphysics, but while the former develops an embodied ontology of intimately relational uniqueness, the latter disassociates voice and body to frustrate any possible attempt at communication and individuation. The concern with the voice implies an interest in the body which, in Bene's case, concretises in an interest in disintegrating the body; however, contra the Lacanian gap, Bene's dismantling of the body derives from the unity of body and voice.

Thus, his films display a predilection for deformed and injured bodies and an obsessive focus on the act of eating as a source of (a taste for) disgust, in an overall replacing of the heroic body of mainstream cinema with a ridiculous body which has lost any ability to purposefully move – hence, the repeated, nonsensical self-harm gestures in *Our Lady of the Turks*, Herod Antipas's (Carmelo Bene) voracious eating and dribbling of saliva in *Salomè*, or the old men's coughing up and regurgitating beer in *Capricci* (Carmelo Bene, 1969). What Bene constantly seeks is a ridiculous body in lieu of the heroic or tragic body (see, Morreale 2011, 11–15) of mainstream and auteur cinema. The actor's jerky, stumbling, injuring movements are nothing other than the bodily result of the assault against language through the voice. No longer imbued with logos, the voice as *phoné* slowly and uncannily detaches itself from the body, short-circuiting language:

> The voice is the body. But be careful: the voice does not vocalise the word; the voice is sound, not word. Therefore, it does not reproduce literary text, but elaborates on them and, more importantly, disposes of them. The voice begins with the goodbye to language. The word is always meaningful, whereas the voice is the dismantling of the word, namely the end of any meaning. (Bene [1995] 2011c, 167)

The voice no longer articulates intelligible speech; namely, it is no longer at the service of logos but becomes that through which to overcome purposeful language. Bene separates the voice from its body in multiple ways, thereby generating a disquieting effect – whose voice is this? And what is this body doing? The bewilderment caused by the voice-body dissonance is further exasperated via Bene's 'be[ing] foreigner in [. . . his] own language', as well as through the play on sound levels and the mixing of music and noise, which result in the spectator's wondering about what is being said. Bene's films thus necessitate of a hearkening and heeding to make sense of the stratified aural dimension which invests the viewer. According to Gideon Bachmann (1972–73), 'he [Bene] demands attention while refusing collaboration' (21). And Bene himself distinguishes between 'good and bad spectators' based on their ability to listen to what is being said: while bad spectators lose themselves in the visual and aural frenzy, incapable of grasping words, good spectators pay attention to the voice without turning their gaze away from distasteful or puzzling images. For instance, in *Our Lady of the Turks*, the priest who mutters while continuously eating and vomiting spaghetti provides a 'test [to distinguish] between the good and the bad spectator: the latter looks away and hears nothing, whereas the former even listens' (Bene [1968] 2011d, 26). The uncanny use of playback, de-synchronisation, dubbing and exasperated sound levels are among the devices which contribute to the splitting of voice and body, which are never harmoniously or familiarly coupled. Even though the visible body on screen is often that of Bene and the plurality of voices heard are most frequently Bene's polyphonic voice, there seems to be a gap between corporeal image and vocal sound. The grain of this multiple voice contains traces of Bene's body and yet, even in the rare instances in which the voice is in synch with the image, it creates a monstruous couple.

The voice becomes the uncontested means for abolishing the sense of what one sees and hears in Bene's ([1995] 2002b) self-declared 'anti-humanistic research on disfunctions and defects of language' (ix). Unlike Isou's focus on the letter, Bene concentrates on the word to dismantle intelligible speech through a complex play of harmony and dissonance (among others, paronomasias, alliterations, onomatopoeias and anagrammatic assonances). Thus, the word is complexified through dis-/as-sonances (see Bachmann 1972–73; Martin 2010) and rendered an indecipherable or meaningless sound by the voice uttering it. Adrian Martin (2010), commenting on the 'be[ing] foreigner in one's own language' which permeates Bene's films, tentatively suggests that word and voice used in this way could 'liberate [. . .] from [a text . . .] a *chora*, perhaps'. Like the Platonic *chora*, which withstands logos and therefore qualifies as that about which it is difficult to talk, Bene's use of language resists intelligibility not only through the words he selects but also via deliberate phonetic errors, repetitions and dis-/as-sonances. If, on the one hand, the voice as *phoné* tampers language, on the other hand, it generates a rhythm which is also modulated by other aural elements of film – music, silence, noise. Above all other sounds, one competes more forcefully with the voice to dominate: music.

What interests Bene is rhythm, musicality, of every cinematic component which also allows for subtracting what is superfluous. It is no coincidence that the only two film-makers whom Bene defends (not without mercilessly critiquing them) are Sergei Eisenstein and Jean-Luc Godard (Bene [1968] 2011d, 27), who placed rhythm at the core of their cinematic oeuvre. Bene, however, is far more radical in his approach because he yearns for neither the political nor the ethical, but rather the purely aesthetic:

The cinema is a matter of ears [...]. One has to hear things. Whether it is opera, theatre or cinema, seeing is not enough; what counts is rhythm. When we look at things, we never really see them. [...] When montage occurs at the same time as the shooting, it is then possible to obtain a film-music. [...] One needs to be as much as possible in harmony with the event and not with the understanding of a meaning that this event has. [...] Cinema should be destroyed. (Bene [1970] 2011e, 59–60)

Opera music, in particular, recurs throughout his films, imbuing them with a perplexing erotism and exoticism.[4] The musicality of amorous songs jarringly encounters the musicality of images which have nothing to do with sexuality, thereby producing a new kind of erotism, a becoming erotic of what is usually foreign (*exotikos*/ἐξωτικός) to its dimension; at the same time, what is ordinarily conceived as erotic is rendered exotic; that is, alien to erotism. And indeed, in Bene's films, there is nothing less erotic than naked bodies, which are frequently ridiculed through the full range of stylistic devices to comment on cinema's obsession with the eroticisation of bodies. At the core of the inverse process – namely, the becoming erotic of the exotic (that is, what is foreign to erotism) – there is often the sacred, whose Christian link with love as caritas or *agapē* strikingly intertwines with love as eros. It is no longer humans who attempt to elevate themselves above earthly love to a wholly spiritual one, but it is saints and Madonnas who become incarnated and experience eros.

Such a process of turning the erotic into the exotic and vice versa contributes to the othering of the representation; that is, it precludes images, even in the case of figurative images, from constituting themselves as doubles; namely, as *eidōla*. Bene decisively eliminates the mimesis of reality: what we see is no longer ascribable to a reproduction of the phenomenal world because images are frequently underlit or overexposed, scratched, extremely blurred or opaque; but even when the image is figuratively clear, the absurdism of the narrative acts and gestures, paired with an inconceivable voice, destroys any possibility for the audio-visual image to be a double. Bene's cinema thus upsets quotidian understanding (of film and language) and perception (of images and sounds). Shared cultural references and cinematic canons are subverted, thereby rendering the film an alien object (perhaps an exoticisation of cinema) wherein elements of content and style lose their traditional meaning. Intelligibility ceases to have something to cling on, and the film becomes an utterly aesthetic experience. According to Bene ([1995] 2002b), his 'cinematic parenthesis' produced five films in which *silence* reigns and *logos* is decisively expelled. [...] Instead of a narrative, [there is] this *bricolage* of sounds and images destined to cite a narrative; [there is] this myriad of signs drifting away on the sound wave, which dictates movement. Everything [is] played in a perfectly asynchronous manner, in the idiosyncrasy between 'musicality' and 'music', which do not always coincide. Therefore, if you like, *Our Lady of the Turks*. (1133)

Erotism of the Sacred and Exoticism of Sense

Bene began his brief cinematic career in 1968 with *Our Lady of the Turks*, which was preceded by a homonymous novel (1966) and theatrical play (1966, 1973) and which is deliberately iconoclastic in style and content. The diegesis eschews a simple, fully intelligible summary and could be vaguely described, in Bene's ([1995] 2002b) words, as 'amused and cruel parody of "inner life"' (5). There are continuous variations on onerous gestures, aborted actions and stratified 'foreign' voices in the absence of any spatial, temporal, logical, or narrative continuity. Bene's attack against cinema and subjectivity unfolds via the parody of what ordinarily contributes to give life a meaning; namely, love and religion. Throughout the film, a desecrating taste for distaste invests the audio-visual representation of the sacred, the erotic and the heroic, at last achieving Bene's longed-for absurd sense of ridiculousness.

Set in a temporally short-circuited Otranto, a small town in southern Italy which was invaded by the Ottomans between the fifteenth and sixteenth centuries (Devereux 2016) and which Bene introduces via the retelling of the Ottoman massacre of over 800 Christian in 1480, the film has a nameless male protagonist (Carmelo Bene) who is visited by Saint Margaret (Lydia Mancinelli). Throughout, Bene gives life to a ridiculous anti-hero who carries out a variety of non-sensical gestures via body and voice, multiplying his identity only to destroy it. At the end of the film, while the saint turns into a statue over an altar, the male character finally dies at her feet. This loose plot unfolds in a disconcerting yet spellbinding orgy of colour, movement and sound. According to Emiliano Morreale (2011), in *Our Lady of the Turks*, 'traditional mise-en-scène is broken apart in a violent conflict between words and images, between music and voice, by means of a montage which recreates and destroys every shot, underlining the artificiality and physical presence of the film' (13). Bene's iconoclastic fury encompasses everything visible and audible, in an audio-visual ecstatic and aesthetic excess that allows for the vanishing of any easily accessible sense.

Both stylistically and content-wise, the film plays with variations on repetition: some sequences are played twice with differences in either the image track or the sound track (for instance, the opening monologue is repeated towards the end of the film but on a different sequence of images; similarly, an amorous sequence is visually repeated twice, however with a different sound track), and characters repeat gestures and sentences with phonetic changes (the most evident being Saint Margaret's obsessive 'I forgive you'). Moreover, the audiovisual tumult provides no aid to comprehension because images and sounds become undecipherable via the exploiting of the anti-mimetic potential of style. The film celluloid is blown up to 35 mm and burnt, stepped on, cut and crumpled, thereby producing tactile plays of light which also deface figurative images (Figure 3.1); camera movements and shots are extremely jarring, creating a vertiginous effect which is further enhanced by the numerous close-ups and extreme close-ups (Figure 3.2); colour is employed in an anti-mimetic manner which privileges bright red in both colour filters and mise-en-scène; mirrors are positioned in front of the camera or within the mise-en-scène to distort the pro-filmic, which appears as if fluctuating; superimpositions abound, rendering the image difficult to grasp and, even when in focus, images retain an estranging quality because of their sometimes unnaturally geometric composition. The

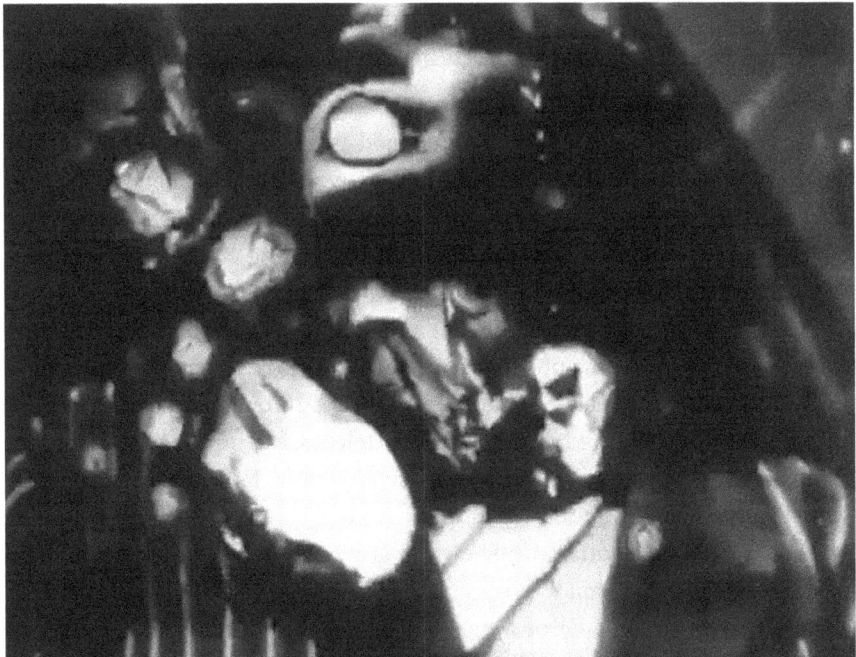

Figure 3.1 Burnt medium close-up of Carmelo Bene

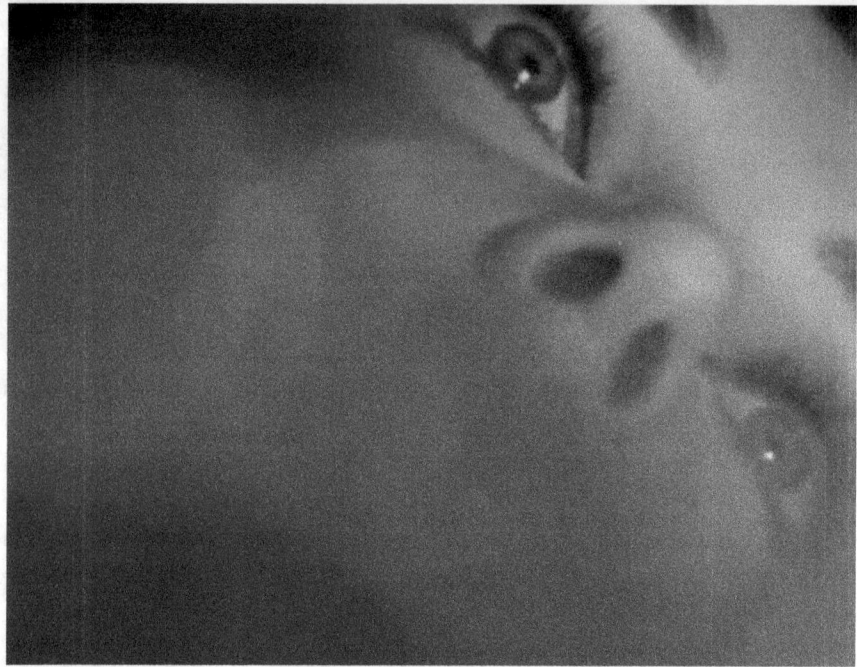

Figure 3.2 Extreme close-up of Lydia Mancinelli and red filters

aural counterpart heightens such visual unrest through incomprehensible words and sentences, which are frequently layered with extremely loud opera music and exasperated ambient and bodily noises, thereby producing a rich sonorous dimension which silence uncannily interrupts every so often. Through such an iconoclastic approach, the audio-visual image no longer accessibly doubles the phenomenal referent with which is constantly at war; nonetheless, there is no beyond, no invisibility evoked through this dismantling of the *eidōlon* (that is, there is no place for the *eikōn*).

The non-sensical content of the film intensifies the stylistic iconoclasm, contributing to the cancelling of cinema as a medium of (meaningful) communication. Particularly the male protagonist articulates through body and voice the demolition of a narrative by carrying out a-teleological or a-logical gestures – for instance, wrapped in bandages in a burning room, he clumsily grabs books with his mouth and throws them into a fire to fuel it; having duplicated himself, one double shoots the other, who however is unable to die (or perhaps continuously dies); half naked, mildly covered with bandages and casts, he gives himself an injection in the middle of a busy public square. Throughout the film, he continuously falls and repeatedly hurts himself in a series of attempts to tear the body apart, reducing it to a de-individualised body whose voice and movements are defective. In keeping with this, the protagonist's multiplications into various characters (the priest, a Renaissance clown, a suited gentleman, to name a few) work towards subjective annihilation: he changes costumes, make-up and roles, deforming his face through grimaces and clownish look; only his voice remains. However, the voice also pursues the dismantling of the subject since Bene speaks asynchronously, whispers, regurgitates mumbled sounds, emits disturbing bodily noises and obsessively repeats nonsensical sentences at varying sound levels. Alessandro Cappabianca (2012) pointedly notes that

> here, Bene ultimately secures for himself an inglorious body, an unhealthy body, which is deliberately fractured. Since he cannot realise his dream of becoming one of the Christian martyrs of the Otranto massacre, since that opportunity is forever lost, since he cannot achieve martyrdom, he searches at least for injury.

Although haunted by a fascination with mystical experience, with an existence whose most fundamental sense is achieved only via a paradoxical suspension of sense – or better, via a renouncing to intelligibly grasp this sense with images or words – Bene forsakes the search for a 'beyond' characteristic of mysticism. But if there is no divinity which could bring about salvation (that is, meaning) to our existence, if, in other words, there is no mystical experience of God, the ecstatic overcoming of understanding reality is entirely located in the human. Francesco Chillemi (2011) accordingly argues that, in Bene's poetic, 'between man and the human existential wound there is the defective man' (265). Such 'defective man', who endlessly 'searches [. . .] for injury', is the vehicle for attaining an absurd sense of ridiculousness which could provide something tantamount to mystical experience contra the pretence of meaning of codified religious rites.

The mocking of religious inner life and the desecrating critique of Christianity are a leitmotif throughout *Our Lady of the Turks*. This is notably evident not only in the continuous verbal references to martyrs and visual images of their skulls, in the beseeching appeals and in the character of a priest, but also in the sensuous character of Saint Margaret who, among other things, abandons herself to the pleasures of the flesh, prays to the human instead of God and smokes, undressed, while reading a pop magazine, in an extremely earthly imagery. Less manifestly, Bene's parody of religion concretises in his character's deliberate falls and self-harm acts which qualify as (failed) attempts at becoming like a saint. The monologue of the imbeciles (*cretini*) in the first half of the film provides such an explanation. Bene's soothing, slow-paced voice-over comments:

There are imbeciles who have seen the Madonna and there are imbeciles who have never seen the Madonna. I am an imbecile who has never seen the Madonna. Everything consists in this, to see or not to see the Madonna. [...]

The imbeciles who see the Madonna have sudden wings, can also fly and return back to land like a feather. The imbeciles who don't see the Madonna do not have wings, are denied flying and yet they fly nonetheless but, instead of landing, they fall down like someone who, wanting to get rid of lead weights around the ankles, decides to cut his [*sic*] feet and drags himself towards salvation, in the midst of the swineherds' scorn who are sure about the imminent haemorrhage that will stop him. But those who see do not see what they see, those who fly are they themselves the flying. One does not know who flies. This miracle destroys them: rather than seeing the Madonna, they are themselves the Madonna they see.

The scene's opening close-up shot of Bene's face staring at the camera (Figure 3.3) is slowly replaced by a poorly lit space wherein the character, with casts on his legs and bandages around the body, painfully drags himself. This imagery represents the male protagonist's failure at becoming like the saints

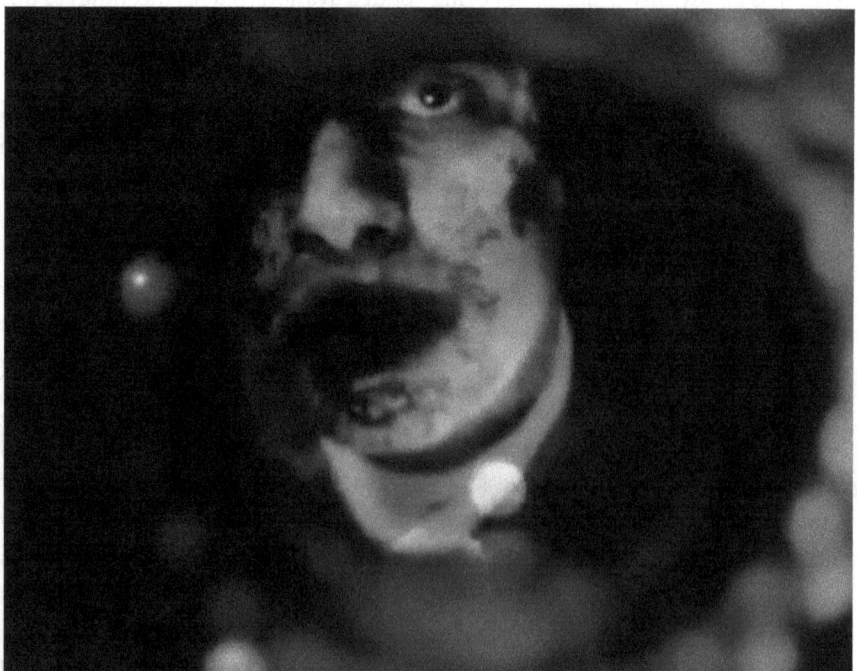

Figure 3.3 Partially out-of-focus close-up of Carmelo Bene

about which he talks, because there is no holy flying but only human falling. Darkness progressively consumes the image to construct the act of seeing (of both the saints and the spectator) as an empty look, while Bene's voice continues: 'But the imbeciles who see the Madonna do not see her, like two eyes which stare at two eyes through a wall'. What follows is a list of some of the ways in which Catholic believers and Saints delude themselves into adulatory self-perceptions instigated by faith. The parody of Christianity (the religion of the turning of the other cheek) thus begins with Bene's representation of religion as a remarkably subjective experience which can easily become a narcissistic mirroring and continues throughout the rest of the film with the eroticisation of the sacred.

According to Jean-Luc Nancy (2005), 'religion is the observance of a rite that forms and maintains a bond [. . .]. The sacred is what, of itself, remains set apart, at a distance, and with which one forms no bond (or only a very paradoxical one). It is what one cannot touch (or only by a touch without contact)' (1). While Bene ridicules religion by severing the bond, which is rendered as a self-referential delusion, he eroticises the sacred as the exotic par excellence through a touch with contact. In the film, there is no privileged, religious bond but a variety of sensuous bonds with the sacred, primarily expressed via the protagonist's amorous encounters with Saint Margaret – a sacrilegious violation of the sacred through an extremely carnal touch. However, even the physical bond with the sacred is undermined by the male character's equally flirting with the saint, a man dressed up as an early-twentieth-century explorer (Salvatore Siniscalchi) and a young woman (Ornella Ferrari). Bene eroticises the exotic via the intercourse with the sacred (Saint Margaret); but he also exoticises the erotic in multiple instances as a further way through which to increase the loss of sense and the film's unintelligibility.

One poignant example occurs in the second half of the film and consists of the love-making between two young lovers in a luxuriant garden. The sequence is twice replayed and variously de-eroticised to accomplish its exoticisation. The first time, amidst an uncanny silence, the camera jerkily moves behind colourful flowers and verdant leaves, repeatedly tilts and frames the lovers obliquely and from below, making it difficult to distinguish human bodies from their surroundings – a breast among plants can easily be mistaken for a flower (Figure 3.4); a light, pink dress fluttering on the vegetation seems like an enlarged, delicate petal. Sex becomes a purely aesthetic matter with no narrative, erotic or ethico-political function. The scene is then replayed from the beginning with an altered sound track, which carries out the becoming exotic of what is ordinarily erotic. Sound is reintroduced; however, it is not synchronous with the images, with which it

Figure 3.4 A breast disguised amidst the vegetation

has no coherent relation. Ambient noises seem to be loosely emanating from the absurd content of Bene's voice-over: when he talks about a priest who has a passion for eating, the banging of pots and pans emerges together with the sound of heavy rain and occasional thunder; when he bursts into sudden, furious screams and guttural noises intermittently intertwined with incomprehensible words, the sound of plates being crashed to the floor can be heard. It will become clear only later that this sound track is actually a partial sound flash-forward to the following sequence of a priest cooking spaghetti. Such screeching sonorous, which brings together religious references (the priest) and a sensuous imagery (the young lovers), decisively removes any remaining erotism from the scene, which is now an indecipherable audio-visual melody.

The exoticisation of the erotic through visual and aural elements is also at the core of a sequence close to the film's end in which the erotic and the heroic become explicitly ridiculous. The male protagonist, now dressed as a medieval knight, enters on horseback into the priest's kitchen where a young woman is cleaning the spaghetti mess caused by the priest. The dish-washing slowly turns into love-making, while the air *'Salut, demeure chaste et pure'* (*I Greet You, Home Chaste and Pure*) from Charles Gounod's opera *Faust* permeates the scene. Instead of creating an atmosphere of grandeur, the music contributes to the scene's ridiculousness, welcoming the protagonist's unheroic entrance and accompanying the beginning of the intercourse, which is de-eroticised also via the sound of clashing plates. While he slowly undresses the woman, who continues to unabatedly clean the dishes, the tomato sauce spreads from the dirty plates to the characters' bodies. Here the erotic is rendered exotic by means of the bright red tomato sauce and the leftovers, which stain surfaces and bodies, as well as by the presence of the horse in a modern kitchen, and by the armour, which clashes both visually and aurally with the love-making act. No kisses, sighs, or words that the characters seem to exchange can be heard, only the extremely loud metallic sounds of the armour. The erotic, becoming exotic, trespasses into the ridiculous, which is Bene's ultimate goal: instead of the hero's return and a dramatic love encounter, there is their absurd parody. This scene, and the film as a whole, exhibit the audio-visual image's rupture with a graspable reality; images, sounds and gestures deliberately work against signification, destroying the *eidōlon* – of what, in fact, are these film images the shadow/double? Bene exoticises the tragic, the heroic and the erotic, at last reaching an ecstatic sense of ridiculousness beyond any fully intelligible meaning.

Concluding Remarks

Bene's longing for a secularly mystical blindness is achieved through a paradoxical visual over-abundance paired with aural excess. The voice as logos-less *phoné* constitutes the primary way through which to trouble Western metaphysics and to overcome its logo-video-centrism. If logos has historically developed as deaf, inner monologue with a coherent narrative and intelligible images (even Plato, while often mistrustful about images, could not forsake them), Bene's critique develops through a logos-less voice which consumes any coherent sense, favouring a disharmonic rhythm of things, bodies and sounds. Dismissing the idea that the audio-visual image could be a trustworthy representation of reality, Bene strives to break the *eidōlon* while never acknowledging that the image could be *eikōn*. Hence, ridiculous bodies and phantasmatic voices inhabit his films, where an iconoclastic aesthetics purposefully dissolves intelligibility. At the core of the cinematic critique of the *eidōlon*, the voice/word is extremely significant also in Jean-Luc Godard's work, in which logos is reinstated to elaborate on the image's struggle between insufficiency and salvific potential.

4   In Search of a True Image: Jean-Luc Godard's *Histoire(s) du cinéma*

JEAN-LUC GODARD'S ICONOCLASM, too, takes the form of a critique, his initial experimentations largely concerned with film aesthetics. But he is also committed to creating iconoclastic *eikones*, those images capable of establishing more truthful relationships – between each other as well as with spectators – which will become the core elements of his magnum opus *Histoire(s) du cinéma* (1988–98). Much like Isidore Isou, Guy Debord and Carmelo Bene, Godard puts into crisis the mimetic image, but he does so to favour relationships between images. His films call into question the cinematic and phenomenal world, giving visibility to the space in between images via primarily the blank screen and the interruption of mimetic film flow. While in his earlier films these devices are more symptomatic of an aesthetic renewal of cinema, in his later films, above all in *Histoire(s)*, they constitute an explicit gesture against the plenitude of the image.

A belief in images as relational, and redemptive, entities is paradoxically sustained through a suspicious attitude about mimesis since it entails a relationship between an image and a model rather than relationships between images. This results in the coexistence of diverse and at times conflicting tendencies in Godard's cinema. In *Histoire(s)*, as in other films of his, there is a sharp critique of consumer society and a desire to destroy its illusory images, which reiterate capitalist ideology; but there is also a sheer, mystical love for cinema and its images, and a belief in their redemptive power. Such contradictory leanings prevent a fixed categorisation of Godard's cinematic perspective. Neither radically iconoclastic nor fully iconophilic, Godard, like his images, is in-between: between destruction and creation, between iconoclasm and iconophilia, between the breaking of *eidōla* and the search for iconoclastic *eikones*.

This chapter investigates Godard's intricate iconoclasm, discussing the ethical significance of his aesthetic choices. It emphasises the complexity of his approach to cinema within which a criticism of the insufficiency of film images to represent specific models exists alongside a belief in the image's ability to convey something about reality, albeit in an iconoclastic manner. While briefly considering various Godard films, the following pages concentrate on *Histoire(s) du cinéma*, where he puts into crisis the mimetic image to favour relationships between multiple images.

A Faltering Belief in the Image

Godard's paradoxical positioning as iconophilic iconoclast hinges on the coexistence of a belief in film images, together with the urgency to destroy certain images. His films often exhibit the image as in some ways insufficient for representation, which has led to conceiving of his oeuvre as iconoclastic (Bergala 1986, 58; Brenez 1998; Poirson-Dechonne 2016, 151–63); and yet, moving and still images, once manipulated and entangled, can be adequate for representation, thereby permitting an iconophilic interpretation of Godard's cinema (Rancière 2002, 118; 2007, 41; Williams 2016, 13). Such competing understandings of Godard's films revolve around the issue of belief, which is a central notion for any argument on iconoclasm or iconophilia.

A belief in a truthful relationship between copy and prototype or a lack thereof is, indeed, what leads towards either iconophilia or iconoclasm. Given that generally 'beliefs are "truth-directed"' (Lengbeyer 2009, 75), 'to believe' concerns the act of understanding something as being true. This act occurs between a subject who believes and an object that is believed to be true. Contrary to knowledge, belief does not necessarily require tangible proofs; thus, while belief is objectively located in the sphere of possibility – for the lack of proof – it is subjectively situated in the domain of certainty by the social actors who experience it as true. As an example, we may consider belief in God. Belief in a religious context is faith (although faith is not necessarily a belief).[1] People believing in God consider God as a true existing entity, even though they cannot physically and incontrovertibly prove his existence. Accordingly, while objectively impossible to demonstrate, God's existence is experienced as subjectively true by believers.

By something being true I refer to the correspondence theory of truth and, specifically, Thomas Aquinas's metaphysical version. This theory entails 'the idea that truth consists in a relation to reality, i.e., that truth is a relational property involving a characteristic relation (to be specified) to some portion of reality (to be specified)' (David 2016). Thomas Aquinas (1923) defines truth as '*adaequatio rei et intellectus*' [equation of thing and intellect] (126), which points to an accordance between a given reality and one's thought about that portion of reality. More precisely, as Fabrizio Amerini (2009) explains, this accordance occurs between a copy and its ideal model:

> According to Thomas Aquinas, a true thing is a thing that exists; but a thing exists inasmuch as it exemplifies an ideal form, that is, inasmuch as it complies with the model. Being true, for a thing, expresses exactly the relation of conformity that that thing establishes with its ideal model. [...] Hence, for Aquinas, something is true when it is related to an ideal model, whether that model is the divine intellect (which is thought as anterior to and cause of the being of a thing) or the human intellect (which is thought as subsequent and subdued to the causality that the thing exercises on it). (38)

Truth is a relational concept and not a quality of the thing itself. In the case of images (understood as images *of*), belief concerns the image's capacity to reference its model; namely, to posit itself as *eikōn* rather than *eidōlon*. Such belief originates different attitudes towards images, including that of iconophilia and iconoclasm. The iconophiles believe that the image is true – that it represents the human essence of God, referencing his divine nature (it is *eikōn*) – whereas the iconoclasts believe that the image is not true (it is *eidōlon*). In cinema, this belief deals with the film image's relational capacity;[2] namely, it involves believing in the image as a relational entity capable of establishing a link with its model, be it sensible or intelligible. In iconoclastic directors of the likes of Isou, Debord, Bene and Godard, the confidence in the possibility for the image to be a truthful representation of the referent is lost, not only because of the status of the model itself, but also because of the cultural and socio-economic context within which cinema operates (that is, bourgeois capitalist society). What becomes of primary importance, instead, is the relationship that images can establish with each other. But while for Isou, Debord and Bene almost any link between images also qualifies as deceitful, with only rare instances of feeble truth persisting in a beloved face or a blank screen, Godard maintains that belief in the film image can be restored via truthful relationships between images. Single images may be *eidōla*, but there remains the possibility of redemption in the superimposition of images or in the in-between images, those invisible zones that make it possible for images to become visible.[3]

Godard shifts the focus from the impossible relationship between image and model, which is doomed to incur in the deficiencies of the *eidōlon*, to the relationship between an image and another image as that which can convey a sense of the real. In this context, spectators are encouraged to identify these image relationships – a task which also involves the becoming aware of an invisible space that permits the existence of any visibility. This invisibility made visible is the in-between images; namely, the editing cut that glues images together and that entails a number of consequences which shall be discussed later in the chapter. Godard's spectators, like Isou's, Debord's and Bene's, are called upon to recognise the illusory nature of film images. But they are also challenged to confront themselves with a small lump of invisibility which is more than just what remains of the destroyed *eidōlon*. There is, in fact, a delicate interplay of visibility and invisibility at work in Godard's oeuvre which has the potential to renew our relationship with the world.

Such an interplay concretises in Godard's use of blank screens, sound-image disjunctions and altered motion. The blank screen takes on two functions that Godard himself develops theoretically in *Scénario du Film 'Passion'* (1982) through the metaphors of the white page (*page blanche*) and the white beach (*plage blanche*). Ágnes Pethő (2011) suggests that 'both metaphors emphasise the underlying, "primordial" emptiness of the screen' (269). The screen as a white or blank page functions as a blackboard (Deleuze 1997a, 185; Pethő 2011, 271–76), or 'a page for writing' (Bellour 2012, 387). That is, as a surface where the director can unfold the relation between image and text – a method that resonates with a Lettrist quality, as Pethő (2011, 272) notes. Accordingly, the screen as a white page is a way to develop the aesthetic possibilities of cinema in relation to the dynamic between image and text.

The screen as a metaphorical white beach points instead to the interstitial space between images. This liminality consists of the space between the shots, which is usually hidden by the movement of the film (Bellour 2012, 168–73; Deleuze 1997a, 179–81; Pethő 2011, 276). It is the editing cut which, sealing images together, conceals the process of editing through the flow of images. However, as Deleuze (1997a) observes, 'if the cut [. . .] grows larger, if it absorbs all the images, then it becomes the screen' (215). Godard's in-between, what Deleuze (1997a) describes as 'Godard's intersticial [*sic*] method' (214), is this enlargement of the cut which becomes visually and temporally present. As such, it opens hiatuses in the film space, hinting at something that resists figuration and yet seems to battle for some visibility. Thus, Godard's black screen as in-between, by undermining the completeness of mimetic representation, bespeaks a constitutive deficiency, namely the impossibility of seeing and saying everything; equally, it allows invisibility to surface on the visible screen via an image of imagelessness.

Nicole Brenez (2004) terms Godard's black screen 'the ultimate Question-Image', attributing to it four possible meanings:

> Firstly, a black image is an image that one does not want to make; secondly, a black image is an image that one must not accept [...]; thirdly, a black image takes the place of a just image; and fourthly, a black image indicates what is outside the film. (174)

The black screen, in its apparent simplicity, harbours the evocative, imaginative power, as well as the unsettling potential of a visual blockage. In Godard's cinema, so Brenez (2004) continues, 'the dialogue between different kinds of images accords an essential place to the virtual, to the conditional, to the absent, to the negative, to the unacceptable – in a word, to the problematic' (174). The monochromatic image, and specifically the dark void of the black screen, is the most evident visual rendering of that which is uncertain, questionable, difficult; it functions as a tool to stimulate spectators' ethical imagination while also maintaining the complexity of reality, its non-reducibility to a single, mimetically accessible image.

Godard employs the black screen in this way in various films throughout his career. In *Une Femme mariée* (1964), for instance, the dissolution of a love affair is developed also through the visual decomposition of the lovers' bodies via black screens. The opening sequence introduces the female protagonist, Charlotte (Macha Méril), the married woman of the title, and her lover, Robert (Bernard Noël), during one of their encounters. In a hotel room we see fragmentary shots of the two lovers tenderly getting dressed. However, the bodies seem unable to reach for each other for a prolonged amount of time, because soon after every time they touch one another, their image fades to a black screen. In this way, the human body is twice fragmented: by the framing which shows only pieces of hands, legs and faces, and by the enlarged cut between the shots. This black screen, while also foreboding the final break-up between the characters, references the cinematic process since it gives visibility to the editing cut, thus bearing witness to the space between film images. Moreover, the black screen in between the shots of the protagonists' piece-meal bodies hints at the irreducibility of this love affair through the surfacing of a zone of invisibility and ineffability.

A similar use of the black screen is also present in *Alphaville* (1965), a film set in a dystopian society where emotions and illogicality have been banned. An agent from another planet, Lemmy Caution (Eddie Constantine), encounters and falls in love with Natacha von Braun (Anna Karina), an inhabitant of Alphaville unaccustomed to emotions. Natacha's unawareness of emotions is particularly evident in a sequence in which Lemmy Caution questions her about the definition of love. Her mellow voice-over, almost a sibylline whisper, tries to give an oral form to love; however, language fails to express the complexity and mystery of such a sentiment. While chunks of sentences – a lyrical collage of verses from different Paul Éluard poems – evoke the irreducibility of love, Anna Karina's face intermittently plunges into and emerges from a black screen. The fragmentary nature of love and, as consequence, of any discourse on love is thus conveyed through the incompleteness of visual and aural elements.

Both in *Une Femme mariée* and *Alphaville*, Godard does not entirely negate a figurative depiction of sentimental relationships but, by enlarging the editing cut between the figurative images, renders them highly partial. What is denied, then, is an exhaustive representation insofar as the visual and aural completeness would remove, or at least undercut, love's ungraspable nature. As Deleuze (1997a) puts it in discussing Godard's black screen, 'that void [. . .] is the radical calling into question of the image' (180). By fragmenting the figurative representation via black screens, Godard is alluding to something that cannot be said or seen. That is, the monochromatic screens punctuating the interaction between characters show that not everything can have a fully visible or expressible form. There remains a portion of reality which is unrepresentable and to which the black screen respectfully alludes. Hence, the bodies in *Une Femme mariée* seem to be constantly prevented from encountering each other, and the protagonists in *Alphaville* oscillate between figuration and blankness.

Godard progressively radicalises the use of the black/blank screen as a locus whereby invisibility takes visible form, gradually pairing it with a disruptive sound. While in his New Wave films the monochromatic screen has a primarily poetic function, in his later films, such as those realised with the Dziga Vertov Group, the blank screen assumes an explicitly political meaning. *Le Vent d'est* (1970), for example, separates the sound track (history lesson on proletariat; critique of Hollywood cinema) from the image track (parody of a spaghetti western) and further frustrates spectatorial engagement via sixteen red monochromatic screens, which have been scratched in a reference to Isou's chiseling process. Over these red screens, a female voice discusses communism and Marxism; towards the end of the film, the same voice-over continues her political account on a series of black monochromatic screens. A consistent use of black screens also recurs in *Vladimir et Rosa* (1971) and *Lotte in Italia* (1971) as a way to counter bourgeois cinema. Such disruptive aesthetics is enhanced via asynchronous sound, dubbing and layering of voices, as in *Un Film comme les Autres* (1968), in which various voices of characters not frontally framed are stratified to the point of unintelligibility, or in *Lotte in Italia*, where an actress

(Cristiana Tullio-Altan) speaks in Italian while being simultaneously overdubbed in French, thereby complicating the understanding of what is being said.

The exploitation of the creative potential of the aural dimension in its divorce from the visual image reaches one of its peaks in Godard's later film *Sauve qui peut (la Vie)* (*Slow Motion*, 1980), where the director iconoclastically plays also with cinematic movement. What manifestly characterises *Slow Motion*, from its English title to its film form, is the sudden yet recurrent alteration of motion, to the point that the film breaks 'the pact that links its movement to the spectator' (Bellour 2012, 147). Viewers usually expect to see film images moving at the velocity that mimics the way in which we perceive movement in phenomenal reality; here, instead, Godard makes repetitive use of slow motion as a tool for investigating and breaking down film movement. Instead of the recourse to the black screen, *Slow Motion* proceeds to dismantle cinematic images via disorderly movement and sound, which produces at once fascination and unsettlement.

Composed of five parts, each introduced by a title – 'Life', 'The Imaginary', 'Fear', 'Commerce' and 'Music' – the film is centred on an incestuous fantasy shared by almost all the male characters. In terms of style, the film frequently opposes the jamming of the visual elements to the naturalism of sound. While the image track is slowed down or intermittently freeze-framed, the sound continues naturalistically, producing an estranging effect, as if something was hampering vision. In the progressively slow-motioned sequence of Denise (Nathalie Baye) cycling through the Swiss countryside, the altered movement, paired with a naturalistic sound track, causes a certain bewilderment. In other cases, the effect of combining slow motion with natural velocity is disturbing, such as in a slap scene where a man is slapping a woman now in slow motion – 'at the same speed of a kiss' (Stam 1981–82, 196) – now at a natural pace, which releases an even harsher violence by directly and suddenly following the slowed-down caressing slap.

The relationship between stasis and movement, as well as that between sound and image, is problematised throughout the film, but one sequence epitomises it. It takes place towards the end of the film and revolves around the secondary plot of Denise and Paul's (Jacques Dutronc) break-up. Denise and Paul are sitting in front of each other at the kitchen table in the apartment which they once shared and which is now up for rent. Suddenly, in slow motion, Paul throws himself onto Denise and, entwined, they fall to the floor. While the image track shows the anti-naturalistic slow-motioned fall, the sound progressively dissociates itself from the visuals. The first part of the scene is characterised by an alienating electronic music and the realistic noise produced by objects breaking – those on the table that Paul crushes in his lunge at Denise. The co-presence of these two elements produces a highly disturbing effect, heightened by the slow-motioned images; nonetheless, the first part of the scene maintains an overall legibility because of the domestic and naturalistic sound of broken objects. Conversely, the second part of the scene undergoes a process of abstraction provoked by the vanishing of ambient noise and the resulting dominance of the music. Denise's and Paul's interlaced bodies slowly and jerkily fall to the ground. No diegetic sound accompanies this fall which, through slow motion, assumes the proportion of a true and proper crash. Only the obsessive electronic music remains, and for an instant the spectator loses awareness of what is happening in and to the image.

What is constantly invalidated here is the completeness of the representation, even in the presence of figurative images. Raymond Bellour (2012), in his poetic analysis of the film, comments on the creation of an impossible image through the decomposition of movement:

> The images seem to hit each other, musically, pictorially, striking each other admirably and thus making impossible any continuity of movement which would produce – when it becomes a matter of bodies and sexes – an imaginary ideality that has simply ceased to exist. (125)

The fragmentation of cinematic movement, like the monochromatic screen, interrupts an immersive consumption of the film – every time the spectator might yield to the temptation to contemplate, a new disjunction occurs to prevent it. The temporal and spatial discontinuance produced by freeze-frames and slow motion alludes to something that escapes mimetic reproduction, or something whose complexity would be partially downplayed by mimesis. Rather than in single images, meaning resides in these 'halts on the image in *Slow Motion* (Where does the caress end and the slap begin? Where does the embrace end and the struggle begin?)' (Deleuze 1997a, 195). These interrupted images hint at an in-between zone, which progressively acquires more and more importance in Godard's films, to the point of becoming the locus where meaning is at stake.

The Redemptive Potential of Film Images

Godard dedicates 266 minutes to his own, highly personal cinematic historiography in *Histoire(s) du cinéma*, wherein a criticism of the insufficiency of images to represent certain models coexists alongside a belief in the image's ability to establish a relationship with its prototype, albeit in an iconoclastic manner. *Histoire(s)* is an enigmatic opus realised over a period of ten years and represents a *summa* of Godard's thinking about cinema, the world and their intertwined history. The film condenses the stylistic devices used in his narrative and experimental films which here work towards a further investigation of the status of images.

The film is composed of eight chapters of different length which, while reverberating (especially stylistically) with one another, nevertheless differ in their themes. Chapter 1A, 'Toutes les histoires' [All the Histories], constitutes an introduction to the audio-visual history of cinema and the twentieth century that is *Histore(s)*, with particular emphasis on World War II and Hollywood cinema, and contains the main ideas developed in the other sections. Chapter 1B, 'Une histoire seule' [A Single History], focuses on cinema's main features and explores sex and death as the two spectacular themes that have taken over cinema's documentary potential since its inception. Chapter 2A, 'Seul le cinéma' [Only Cinema], opens on Godard in conversation with Serge Daney; they discuss the many histories contained in *Histoire(s)* and draw attention to cinema's peculiarity and superiority in comparison to other art forms because films are projected. Chapter 2B, 'Fatale beauté' [Fatal Beauty], examines the cinematic representation of beauty and its most frequent expression through female beauty. Chapter 3A, 'La monnaie de l'absolu' [The Currency of the Absolute], centres on the ways in which cinema has dealt with the topic of war, with specific attention to Italian Neorealism and its influence on the French New Wave, which is the main subject of Chapter 3B, 'Une vague nouvelle' [A New Wave]. Chapter 4A, 'Le contrôle de l'univers' [The Control of the Universe], is a reflection on the nature of power, which then progresses into observations on cinema by means of Alfred Hitchcock's mastery of the film medium. Chapter 4B, 'Les signes parmi nous' [The Signs among Us], briefly and fragmentarily overviews the main themes of *Histoire(s)*, discussing notions of ineffability and unrepresentability.

Except for Michael Witt's 2013 monograph, which thoroughly examines *Histoire(s)*, analyses primarily focus on one or two fragments, or a specific topic. One of the most examined fragments is taken from Chapter 1A and presents in the same frame shots of Elizabeth Taylor's serene face in *A Place in the Sun* (George Stevens, 1951), juxtaposed with footage shot by the same director at concentration camps in 1945[4] and Giotto's *Noli me tangere* rotated ninety degrees. This fragment has been variously used to discuss the seminal idea of *Histoire(s)* as an audio-visual account of the entwined relationship between cinema's stories (*histoires*) and twentieth-century history (*Histoire*) (MacCabe 2003, 299; Rancière 2002, 113–19), as well as cinema's potential to redeem the traumatic past (Rancière 2004, 225–26; Saxton 2004, 366–79; 2008, 49–51; Witt 2013, 130–34). The film image's redemptive potential is *Histoire(s)*'s leitmotif, which this fragment exhibits in the clashing juxtaposition of the concentration camps and Elizabeth Taylor, whose image is later superimposed onto Giotto's fresco. Libby Saxton (2004) observes how 'an image of separation, absence, an empty tomb, is transfigured, becoming an act of resurrection' (366). Cinema 'resurrects' historical reality by projecting the past in a disjunctive, layered montage, allowing for the image to become *eikōn*:

> Sequences such as the Auschwitz/Taylor/Giotto encounter, where the falsity of the *eidōlon* recruits to itself the truth of the *eikōn*, testify to a faith in the 'bleeding', intrinsically multiple 'Image' (with a capital 'I') produced at the interstice as a vehicle not only of resurrection but also of truth and redemption: 'I believe in images', the director proclaims quite simply. (Saxton 2004, 366–67)

Multiple images such as the Taylor/camps/Giotto sequence can thus redeem cinema from the crime that Godard assigns to it – namely, its failure to record the Shoah – by projecting the past in the present while maintaining the absence that is at its very core. However, Godard's *j'accuse* is somewhat problematic, because it is not so much a sin of omission (we could have filmed the Shoah but failed to do so), but one that is systemic (we could never have adequately filmed it).[5]

Cinema's redemptive potential is also linked to Christianity, which takes on an allegorical function (Hori 2004, 334–49; Rancière 2002, 113–19; Williams 2004, 288–311). In Godard's oeuvre, the significance of the sacred shifts from religion to aesthetics, to arrive at *Histoire(s)*' conceiving of cinema as a secularised mystery whose images transcend our most habitual experience of film (Daney 2004a, 71; Poirson-Dechonne 2016, 151–57; Witt 2013, 133). In *Histoire(s)*, in fact, we are presented with diverse still and moving images coexisting in a single frame rather than a serial succession of moving images. Such multiple images, which result from superimpositions and layering, aesthetically and ethically concretise Godard's iconoclasm.

No Image for Itself

Among other things, *Histoire(s)* is a reflection on images, on their nature and power. Ironically, it is also a demonstration of Isidore Isou's claim against images, for 'it is possible to make them say whatever one wants and that which they do not say' (*Traité de bave et d'éternité*). Indeed, Godard makes images do whatever he wants so that his history of cinema consists of a collision of disparate visual and aural elements. The multitude of images that compose the visual track comes from different sources, such as films, paintings, books, photographs and lithographs, which are repeatedly manipulated and reassembled. Still and moving images are superimposed on one another, as if lacerating the screen, frozen in stills, framed in close-ups, slowed down or speeded up, obsessively replayed and covered with text. Likewise, the sound track results from the layering of aural elements coming from a variety of sources. Godard's own voice-over, which is the dominant and unifying element of the sound track, is accompanied by excerpts from films' sound tracks and dialogue, music, popular songs, ambient noises and silence. As a result of this collage, images and sounds are removed from their original context, and their meaning becomes increasingly ambiguous.

Histoire(s) thus proceeds by tearing apart a variety of disparate images and simultaneously layering them in a single frame, thereby emphasising the importance of the audio-visual image as a relational construct. While taken individually, images cannot disclose any truth about the world (namely, they cannot 'resurrect' the traumatic past), they acquire a possible redemptive power when entangled in multifarious relationships with each other. The generative power of images, so Brenez (1998, 348) observes, is a constant feature of Godard's oeuvre and constitutes the supreme principle at work in this film. In *Histoire(s)*, no image exists for itself, but only in relation to other images and sounds. A single frame can reach a denseness of meaning due to the superimpositions of different images and sounds which precariously coexist, thus giving life to an image made up of many images. Interviewed, Godard (1996) explained his layering of images and his use of 'very fast superimpositions so that there is only one image, but we understand there are two'. Instead of a serial succession of images, which is nonetheless present in *Histoire(s)*, Godard creates stratified images composed of different images, both still and moving, thereby 'constructing the world of "images" as a world of general co-belonging and inter-expression' (Rancière 2007, 63). Saxton (2008) contends that 'the images establish disruptive new relationships which begin to produce a compelling logic of their own' (50). It is the logic of 'no image for itself'; namely, the logic of superimposition which allows Godard to create a profound entanglement among cinema, the other arts and the history of the twentieth century, which all coexist in the space of a single frame.

Consequently, it is possible to claim with Jacques Rancière (2004) that, in *Histoire(s)*, 'being an image still means being a link' (224). But an image as a link is *eikōn* – an intermediary between two elements. In this sense, Godard's film images, and especially those in *Histoire(s)*, can be addressed as *eikones*; however, they are iconoclastic because in their entanglement, they break their mimetic bond with the reality that has produced them in the first place. Isolated from one another, *Histoire(s)*' images are appearances unable to convey a truthful sense about the world and its past because reality is irreducible to a single image. Conversely, in the superimposition of diverse images, reality's ambiguity can transpire. The iconoclastic interaction among images is that which makes possible for a true image to surface (namely, an image capable of expressing something true about cinematic and phenomenal world). Witt (2013) argues that 'a true image [...] is always the result of the combination, tension, and dynamic interplay among a number of component elements' (180). Similarly, Godard himself defines the relational status of images as follows:

> The image is a relationship. It's either two distant things that we bring together, or two things that are close together that we separate. 'As thin as a hair, as vast as the dawn'. A hair is not an image; dawn is not an image; it's their relationship that creates an image. (quoted in Witt 2013, 180)

Accordingly, in Godard's films a true image is not a single image; it is always at least two entangled images. Moreover, the enlarged cut already present in Godard's previous films here acquires the status of image in its own right. It is the image of cinematic editing, which is the constitutive principle of *Histoire(s)*, but it also becomes an image of blindness which punctuates the film and remarks cinema's limits: film cannot record or show everything. The expanded cut is therefore fundamental to the making of *Histoire(s)* as a work between the audio-visual frenzy of the superimpositions and the blind ecstasy of the black screen which at once contains all images and none.

The relational status of images is evident throughout *Histoire(s)*. I will focus on two fragments which explicitly deal with the nature of images and their close connection with Christianity in the West. The reference to Christianity is of particular importance for discussing the status of Godard's use of images because of the redemptive power that the film-maker attributes to them. Like Christ in the theology of the image is *eikōn tou Theou/εἰκών τοῦ Θεοῦ* – that is, *eikōn* [i.e., true image] of God (2 Cor. 4:4c) – and thus the mediator who has redeemed humanity, so the film image as *eikōn* is that which contains the potential to redeem the past. In *Histoire(s)*, redemption can be attained via a continual superimposition of sounds as well as still and moving images. On these composite film images, the director spells out his comparing of cinema with Christianity through the concept of belief. According to *Histoire(s)*, belief in the image and, specifically, in the images of cinema, like belief in God, requires something akin to religious faith on the part of the spectator. Mingling the sacred and the profane, Godard's montage is reflective of both cinema's general suspension of disbelief and the faith in the revelatory power of images for which *Histoire(s)* calls.

'That the Image Is in the Domain of Redemption – That of Reality'

As the title 'Une vague nouvelle' suggests, Chapter 3B is both a lyrical evocation of the New Wave (*nouvelle vague*) and a vague short story (*une vague nouvelle*) on cinema's creative power. The disquisition on cinema is developed through the persona of Henri Langlois, founder of the Cinémathèque Française and a key figure for many directors of the French New Wave. The fragment that I have chosen takes place roughly at two-thirds of the section and lasts seven seconds. It opens with a black screen over which Godard's voice-over begins the sentence: 'That the image . . .' This blank screen almost immediately cuts to a shot of Godard in his study room finishing the sentence in synch: '. . . is in the domain of redemption'. Superimposed over this shot of Godard is the text 'CINÉMA HISTOIRE(S)' and a still image which begins its superimposition from the centre of the frame and radially takes over the whole frame (Figure 4.1). This still image is a detail from Fra Angelico's fresco *The Mocking of Christ* (ca. 1438–40). Godard frames Christ's blindfolded face in an extreme close-up, while his voice-over specifies that the domain of redemption is 'that of reality' (Figure 4.2). The image remains still for two seconds, before it, too,

Figure 4.1 Text superimposed on a detail from Fra Angelico's *The Mocking of Christ* superimposed on Godard in his study room

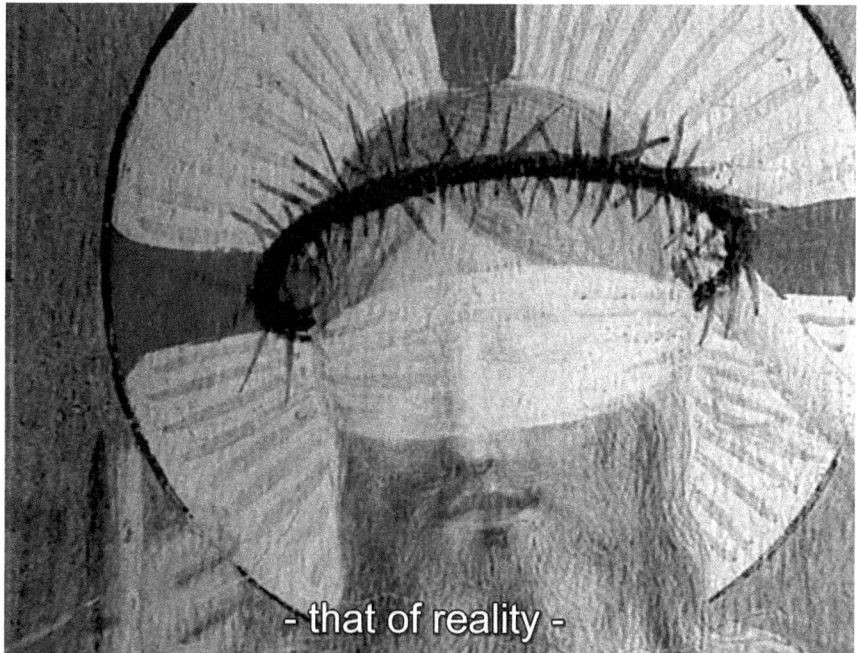

Figure 4.2 Detail from Fra Angelico's *The Mocking of Christ*

is lacerated by the superimposition of the following image, a still frame of an ecstatic Brunella Bovo from Vittorio De Sica's *Miracle in Milan* (*Miracolo a Milano*, 1951) (Figure 4.3).

The superimpositions in this fragment convey the sense of generative power that the images in *Histoire(s)* have. Every image, whether moving or still, opens up like a wound from the centre of the frame and promptly expands itself to fill the entire frame: the still detail of Christ's face is generated from and covers the moving image of Godard in his study room; the still image from *Miracle in Milan*, in its turn, is generated from the fresco and ends up taking its place. This editing method continues throughout *Histoire(s)*, giving life to an interplay of images which at once are generated from and destroy each other, thereby communicating the idea of a multiple and composite film image. At the same time, this montage carries a somewhat violent component given by the continuous lacerating of images – the images momentarily coexisting in a single frame seem to be literally tearing each other apart, like an open wound lacerates the skin, showing the flesh beneath. These continually superimposed images, which exist in a reciprocal entanglement, are however forced to metaphorically destroy one another in their competing for some visibility in the frame.

Figure 4.3 Still frame of Brunella Bovo superimposing on the shot of Fra Angelico's *The Mocking of Christ*

In terms of content, everything in this fragment is rife with Christian references, from the visual elements to the spoken words. The face of Christ from the fresco refers to both the incarnation, which has legitimised sacred images in iconophilic understanding, and his martyrdom, which, according to Christian theology, together with the Resurrection has led to human salvation (redemption). While linking the nature of images to Christianity, thereby acknowledging the influence of Christian thought over Western interpretations of images, Godard also explicitly indicates that redemption should be pursued in the terrestrial world rather than in a distant celestial sphere ('the domain of redemption [is] that of reality'). This fragment's mixing of references to the sacred and phenomenal reality well expresses Godard's atheistic mysticism, which exudes everywhere from *Histoire(s)*. The idea of a magic or sacred aspect of reality is also skilfully conveyed via the superimposition of the still frame from De Sica's film on Christ's face: on the one hand, the reference to one of the most eminent exponents of neorealism remarks that 'the domain of redemption [is] that of reality', which is also expressed through the contrast between a painted Christ and a photographic image of the Piazza; on the other hand, the choice of using a still frame from *Miracle in Milan,* a magic neo-realist fable where the fantastic element is quite predominant, is a way of acknowledging the presence of a mystical aspect inherent in phenomenal reality.

'The image is in the domain of redemption – that of reality', Godard enigmatically affirms. The world incarnates in an image which, in turn, has the potential to redeem. However, a single moving or still image cannot bring about this redemption; it is in the intertwining of images that some solace can be found, as the continuous superimpositions reveal.[6] In this fragment, as in a good part of *Histoire(s)*, there is little or no time to arrest the look on a single image in the frame, because diverse still and moving images are so profoundly entwined with each other. Meaning, thus, resides in the interrelationship between these fleeting, multifarious images.

'Cinema, like Christianity . . .'

Links between cinema and Christianity abound in *Histoire(s)*, so much so that some religious notions can be used as tools for an understanding of Godard's conception of cinema. A fragment from Chapter 1B, 'Une histoire seule', is particularly significant for discussing his likening of cinema and Christianity via the concept of belief. In a rapid montage which alternates and juxtaposes a variety of images, we see the shot of a train cutting to a black screen, a white screen with the text 'L'IMAGE' appearing and disappearing in the blink of an eye, the black screen cutting to the still image of a detail from Giotto's *Flight into Egypt* (ca. 1303–5) which then cuts back to the black screen, a still image of Ingrid Bergman in absorbed prayer from Roberto Rossellini's *Joan of Arc at the Stake* (*Giovanna d'Arco al rogo*, 1954) intermittently superimposed on a blue-tinted still frame of Birger Malmsten and Doris Svedlund from Ingmar Bergman's *Prison* (*Fängelse*, 1949) (Figure 4.4), then the same still image from *Prison*, now tinted in green, intermittently superimposed on a shot of Godard in his study room, to which the still image of the text 'L'IMAGE' on a white background is continuously superimposed; that is, various still and moving images compete for their visibility in the frame (Figure 4.5); however, they all succumb to the black screen upon which the text 'I CONFESS' rapidly appears. Such a bewildering montage is aurally accompanied by Arthur Honegger's symphonic movement *Pacific 231* (1923) and Godard's voice-over declaring twice 'cinema, like Christianity, is not founded on historical truth', then repeating for two times 'cinema, like Christianity' and finally concluding with 'it [cinema] supplies us with a story and says: Now, believe!'

Here Godard's generative-destructive montage articulates a reflection on belief that both cinema and Christianity entail. It does so by alternating the

Figure 4.4 Ingrid Bergman absorbed in prayer, superimposed on a blue-tinted still frame of Birger Malmsten and Doris Svedlund

various superimposed images, which all contain explicit or hidden references to Christian religion, with eight black screens, as if remarking that for everything that we see there is always also something else which remains hidden. Cinema demands that viewers believe in something which does not exist (such as the fictitious cinematic world), or something which is not tangible or physically accessible. As such, cinema, like Christianity, requires a belief in an absence, be it the terrestrial absence of God or the characters, the physical absence of the pro-filmic during reception (images of absents), or the absence of figurative images (the blank screen as an image of imagelessness). Belief in film images thus acquires a religious, yet secularised, connotation. Following Godard's argument on images in *Histoire(s)*, cinema has the potential to redeem historical reality by resurrecting the past and projecting it into the present on the screen. However, redemption and resurrection necessitate faith – if one does not believe in resurrection, one will fail to recognise it. Witt (2013) highlights the 'leap of faith required in religious (and, for Godard, cinematic) belief' (132). Godard's belief thus results from two seemingly clashing perspectives: the metaphysical one of Christianity and the immanent one of atheism. A secularised, mystical faith in

Figure 4.5 Layered superimposition of green-tinted still frame of Birger Malmsten and Doris Svedlund, Godard in his study room and text

film images can re-establish a relationship between spectators and reality; that is, cinema can restore belief in this world and in what happens to us in it.

The Christian, specifically mystical, yet atheist quality of Godard's belief in film images is also evident in the recurrent statement of cinema as mystery. In Christian theology, mystery is a supernatural truth which can be grasped neither through sensible experience nor via the intellect. It is, however, revealed to humans who can accept it by means of an act of faith (see First Vatican Council 1868, Sess. III, *De fide et ratione*; Pohle 1912, 194–95). If we apply the Christian understanding of mystery to Godard's claim, cinema would be that which cannot be grasped in its entirety and whose images require from viewers something akin to Christian faith. That is, it requires to believe in entities or events – the incarnation, the Holy Trinity, historical reality, film images – the meaning of which cannot be visually or verbally exhausted.[7] Junji Hori (2004) aptly observes:

> It is not a question, therefore, of any religious doctrine but of having faith in the invisible image and in the cinema that cannot be seen. [. . .] [W]hat enables

Godard to redeem reality through the image is precisely his secular faith in images. (2004, 341)

Godard manipulates images and sounds, stratifying them, to transcend the limits of mimetic reproduction since it cannot account for the complexity of reality. Hence, he destroys the single image as a copy *of*, articulating an elegant critique of mimesis. In *Histoire(s)*, destruction and creation precariously cohabit with one another: a love for images, evident in the density of the image track, coexists alongside a montage that breaks them into pieces. Irreparably distancing the image from its model, Godard creates multiple images which, by challenging mimesis via a complexified figuration, have the potential to restore belief in the sensible world.

Concluding Remarks

Godard's is a cinema of secularised faith – faith in cinema's capacity to disclose something about the real; faith in the film image's potential to preserve the memory of what has been. However, such faith also testifies to the image's insufficiency to directly represent reality – at least if one wants to avoid falling into the *eidōlon*. Thus, a disruptive audio-visual aesthetics underpins Godard's oeuvre, politically and ethically commenting on the power and limitations of mimetic images and intelligible sounds. The investigating of the visible and the sayable and their respective limits grounds much of *Histoire(s)*, manifesting the struggle between a belief in images and a need to overcome the ethico-political constraints of mimesis. The composite images that Godard creates break with the Christian tradition of the icon, in which the copy figuratively encloses the model, thereby responding to an iconoclastic understanding of the copy-prototype relationship; they are reminiscent of mystical tradition in that they comprise an ineffable and unrepresentable quality. There is no true image, but only more or less truthful relationships between images which make it possible to approach the complexity of reality. But a zone of unseen and unsaid underlays these transient images, constituting the premise for their existence.

# Part II: Cinematic Iconoclasm as an Ethics of (In)visibility: The *Eikōn* as Iconoclastic

5 Impossible Encounters: Marguerite Duras's *Le Navire Night*

PART II FOCUSES on the ethics of cinematic iconoclasm, illustrating how an iconoclastic aesthetics can carry ethical concerns (on the part of film-makers) and promote an ethics of looking (among spectators). The premise for my argument is that the acts of making and looking at images are never neutral, but ethically implicate both image-makers and viewers. Mimesis is, once again, the central issue for investigating the ways in which contents at the verge of the unrepresentable and the unsayable can be shown cinematically. The films discussed in this part share a disquieted attitude about mimetic representation, which goes from Marguerite Duras's separation between sound and image, over Derek Jarman's absolute negation of figuration, to Ingmar Bergman's and Krzysztof Kieślowski's anti-mimetic use of colour and fades. An iconoclastic perspective subtends these films' rejection of mimesis without however renouncing the reference to the image's model; thus, the iconoclastic *eikones* inhabiting the films stretch towards the invisible and the ineffable, audio-visually acknowledging the image's insufficiency to reproduce everything mimetically.

Chapter 5 first considers the ethical turn in film studies, with an emphasis on Emmanuel Levinas's ethics and its import for film-philosophical approaches to morality, and it engages with the relationship between ethics and aesthetics in cinema. It then elaborates on Marguerite Duras's disruptive aesthetics, through which the sonic quality of desire emerges while alterity is preserved as mimetically irrecoverable. In her cinematic oeuvre, there is an interplay of an aurally possible and visually impossible representation of the other('s desire) which is carried out through a privileging of the vocal dimension, particularly the disembodied female voice, which also provides a means of expression for the director's feminist and anti-colonialist stance. Albeit heavily relying on the aural/oral aspect of film, Duras's is nevertheless an extremely corporeal cinema which solicits an embodied spectatorship while also continually frustrating the viewer's desire to see.

Such a frustration of spectatorial desire is achieved by subverting the traditional hierarchy between sound track and image track, and by irreparably disjoining them. *Le Navire Night* (1979), which develops as an imageless love story based on the impossible encounter between two lovers, exemplarily illustrates the separation between sound and image, in which visibility cannot account for the unrepresentable nature of desire without running the risk of rendering it obscene. The chapter's main contention is that the contraposition between aural and visual dimensions, in which the protagonists' bodies become invisible containers of desiring voices, is conducive to a visually inaccessible, ethical representation of (the other's) sexual desire and love.

A Liminal Ethics

In *The Ethics of Visuality: Levinas and the Contemporary Gaze* (2013), Hagi Kenaan provides an engaging link between ethics and vision by means of Emmanuel Levinas, introducing his argument via a well-known biblical image: the aftermath of Adam and Eve's eating of the fruit from the tree of knowledge. Knowledge opens their eyes and makes their gaze reflective; indeed, for the first time they notice their nudeness and feel shame. Kenaan (2013) writes:

> After eating from the tree of knowledge, good and evil have turned into the essential poles, the actual coordinates of the visual field. Henceforth, the visual field can no longer be understood as a neutral, transparent, formal domain that simply contains the totality of what encounters the eye. (xi)

Thus conceived, the visual field, which we share with others and in which we establish relationships, carries ethical implications for both producers and consumers of images: what we let in and partake in the visual field provides ethical perspectives and involves ethical judgements. Like an ever-present mist, images surround us in the everydayness, often presenting themselves as unproblematic representations through which, however, the alterity of the other tends to be reduced to a consumable image. Kenaan explores how Levinas's inseparableness between vision and ethics offers a fruitful framework for reflecting on images in contemporaneity; the idea of ethics as optics can also be conducive to approaching alterity in cinema – to the extent, however, that one is willing to consider films against the iconoclasm of Levinas's work, which is significantly affected by Judaism and the notions of the divine and transcendence.

Succinctly, Levinas conceives of the image as *eidōlon* because it doubles the thing represented and, far from establishing a closer bond with reality, it distances itself from the represented object (of which it is only a shadow), thereby producing a distance between viewers and reality. In *Existence and Existents* ([1974] 2001), Levinas claims that 'this way of interposing an image of the things between us and the thing has the effect of extracting the thing from the perspective of the world' (45–46). The image thus understood not only degrades the thing represented but also impoverishes our relationship with the world, because it consists in an enclosing which interrupts any possibility of transcendence. Notwithstanding Levinas's negative account of the image as idolatrous copy and of art as a degradation of the infinite in texts like *Existence and Existents* and 'Reality and Its Shadow' (1989), his philosophy, specifically the notion of the face-to-face, has become a point of reference for many of the studies in film ethics (to name a few, Cooper 2006; 2007; Girgus 2010; Grønstad 2016; Lamberti 2020; Saxton 2010a, 95–106).

The concept of the face-to-face is developed in *Totality and Infinity: An Essay on Exteriority* (1969) as part of Levinas's conceptualisation of being and of ethics as first philosophy. To be is essentially to be exterior (290–91), and to exist is a proper *ex-sistere*, from *ex* which denotes 'out of' and *sistere* which means 'to be placed', thus translating as 'to step out or forth' and 'to come forth'. Exteriority is infinity in the sense of that which is exterior to totality, otherwise it would be finite. According to Levinas, 'being is exteriority, and exteriority is produced in its truth in a subjective field, for the separated being' (299). There is only exteriority, which significantly emerges in the face-to-face; namely, in the ethical encounter between the same[1] and the other. However, the face of the other cannot be directly thought or seen because that would be tantamount to reducing the other to the same, to enclose infinity. In Levinas's words, 'the face is present in its refusal to be contained' (194); that is, the face of the other is the manifestation of an infinite exteriority, of something that is and remains exterior to the subject, without the possibility of being reduced to the same, otherwise it would be contained and become finite. To reduce the other to the same would correspond to negating the uniqueness of the other by means of a mental image or a thought about the other person – a sort of cognitive copy of the other. Levinas continues:

> To manifest oneself as a face is to *impose oneself* above and beyond the manifested and purely phenomenal form, to present oneself in a mode irreducible

to manifestation, the very straightforwardness of the face to face, without the intermediary of any image, in one's nudity, that is, in one's destitution and hunger. (200)

The face-to-face relationship configures itself as imageless and as that which is beyond thought since thought can think only of the same. It is an irreducible epiphany (from *epiphaneia/ἐπιφάνεια*, 'appearance', 'coming into view', 'manifestation', often referred to deities) that in manifesting itself somehow also conceals itself. Because Levinas situates meaning in the responsibility towards the other, knowledge (and ontology) is secondary to the ethical appeal which grounds the relation with the other. As Seán Hand (1989) aptly explains, 'the communication which must be established in order to enter into relation with the being of the Other means that this relation is not ontology, but rather religion, a place where knowledge cannot take precedence over sociality' (4). And indeed, Levinas (1969) writes: 'Man as Other comes to us from the outside, a separated – or holy – face' (291). The term 'separated', while also indicating that the two entities involved in the relationship are maintained as irreducible to sameness, references the Latin etymology of 'sacred' as the separate (see Nancy 2005, 1–14). The Levinasian other as separated/sacred is an entity independent from that of the same, an irreducible, infinite entity, and an encounter with it is reminiscent of the epiphanic manifestation of the sacred – to encounter the face of the other is to establish a paradoxical bond which eschews conceptualisation. The face-to-face relation is thus transcendence for it is impossible to reduce the other to a thought or an image. And in this impossibility of fully grasping the other lies the foundation for a relationship in which both terms – the same and the other – are respected. Levinas (1969) remarks: 'Expression, or the face, overflows images, which are always immanent to my thought, as though they came from me. [. . .] Because it is the presence of exteriority the face never becomes an image or an intuition' (297).

The transcendental conception of the face-to-face belongs to Levinas's broader argument on ethics as first philosophy. The face of the other transcends any prior knowledge and appeals instead to my endless responsibility towards the other, marking a relationship that exceeds any totalising effort: 'the epiphany of the face is ethical' (Levinas 1969, 199). The imageless encounter with the other calls for personal responsibility towards the other because the other's face, in its vulnerability and nudity, corresponds to the commandment 'you shall not commit murder' (Levinas 1969, 199). That is, in Levinas's philosophy, the other's right to exist and the other's ethically summoning me take precedence, in an overall conceiving of being as being for the other ('to be oneself is to be for the other' [Hand 1989, 5]).

Levinas's philosophy resonates with Biblical iconoclasm in its account of the face-to-face and its praise of speech as that which 'refuses vision' (Levinas 1969, 296) and is superior to the image. While speech respects the exteriority of the face-to-face, the image is always on the verge of reducing exteriority to the interiority of the same because 'vision is essentially an adequation of exteriority with interiority' (Levinas 1969, 295). Jean-Luc Nancy (2005), commenting on the iconoclastic connotation of Levinas's account, affirms: 'Levinas gives a striking example of a thinking that is mostly inspired by iconoclasm [. . .], even if it is dominated by a motif of the *face*' (146 [note 17]). Indeed, in Levinas's argument, images – visual or mental – would reduce the alterity of the other in much the same way as religious iconoclasm has understood the enclosing of God's infinity and the consequent loss of his uniqueness in the image. *À propos* of this Françoise Armengaud (2004) observes that 'the face is essentially non duplicable; it has no double', for otherwise it would glide into the idol (*eidōlon*). However, since perception already involves a commencing of duplication – namely, the temptation of rendering the face of the other an image – 'it is not by abstaining from "making" images that we will escape idolatry' but through an 'ethical attitude towards others' (Armengaud 2004). The face of the other – irreducible and non-duplicable – stretches 'at the limit of holiness and caricature' (Levinas 1969, 198). Thus, Levinasian ethics seems to open to either an idolatrous aesthetics (the caricature of the other's face) or to an aesthetics of the invisible (the holiness of the face) in which the face of the other can be *eikōn* only via a renouncing of representation.

How then can Levinas's philosophy be conducive to an ethical reflection on film images? It can be a starting point to discuss films wherein form maintains the other and our encounter with alterity as irreducible to indifferent consumption; that is, films whose form encourages a non-indifferent participation to difference. Libby Saxton (2010a) cogently argues:

> Viewing films *with* Levinas always involves a degree of viewing *against* the iconoclastic thrust of his writings. This negotiation is essential if we are to avoid downplaying the specificity of the medium in the service of an autonomous and in some ways conflicting theoretical agenda. Levinas's denigration of vision, so intimately bound up with his conception of the ethical, provokes us to look differently at the images on the screen, to seek out those fissures in their being through which alterity intrudes. (105)

Thus, in film scholarship which explicitly draws on Levinasian ethics – such as Sarah Cooper's *Selfless Cinema? Ethics and French Documentary* (2006),

Asbjørn Grønstad's *Film and the Ethical Imagination* (2016) and Edward Lamberti's *Performing Ethics Through Film Style* (2020) – as well as in works which incorporate Levinas's thinking in broader film-philosophical approaches to ethics – such as Lisa Downing and Libby Saxton's *Film and Ethics: Foreclosed Encounters* (2010) and Robert Sinnerbrink's *Cinematic Ethics: Exploring Ethical Experience through Film* (2016) – the attention is brought on the ways in which aesthetic choices can be conducive to an ethics of film-making and film-viewing based on the irreducible alterity of the other. Such contributions place the accent on *how* certain contents could be responsibly represented in cinema, reframing the debate on the limits of the film image and also reading Levinas against the grain of his iconoclastic conception of images – it is not a matter of censoring contents, but of recognising and imaginatively exploiting the ethical weight of form.

These works are part of a wider interest in film and ethics which has resulted in a considerable increase in scholarship on the topic in recent years, in what has been termed the ethical turn in cinema. The relationship between film and moral issues has been variably discussed as regarding narrative and characters, style and spectatorship, stretching from film as a medium through which to understand ethical systems to film as a medium of ethical experience. In addition to numerous contributions which primarily focus on the ethical significance of characters, plot and the narrative-viewership relationship (among others, Choi and Frey 2014; Jones and Vice 2011; Kupfer 2012) and scholarship which thoroughly examines style by means of Levinas, there are works that unequivocally reject binary-based perspectives and ethical approaches grounded in alterity in their engagement with film. Overtly opposing a Levinasian ethics, Lúcia Nagib's *World Cinema and the Ethics of Realism* (2011) is attentive to a realist ethics encompassing film style and 'modes of production and address' (3); David Martin-Jones's *Cinema Against Doublethink: Ethical Encounters with the Lost Pasts of World History* (2018), also distancing itself from Levinas, adopts a Deleuzian approach combined with Enrique Dussel's transmodern ethics of liberation to explore the tension between forgetting (the many lost histories) and remembering, maintaining the time-image's capacity to resist double-think and to produce a hesitant ethics; engaging with, among others, Dussel's account of 'barbarian philosophy' and his notion of non-being, William Brown's *Non-Cinema: Global Digital Film-Making and the Multitude* (2018) theorises non-cinema in reference to aesthetically and geo-politically peripheral films, carefully emphasising their ethical potential, their involving a 'becoming otherwise' (3); and David H. Fleming's *Unbecoming Cinema: Unsettling Encounters with Ethical Event Films* (2017) employs a Deleuzian approach to probe the significance of negative affects and sad passions in and through narratively and aesthetically unsettling films, from whose encounter an ethics of becoming can thrive.

Despite the diversity of approaches and cinemas involved, these titles, which are in no way comprehensive of the burgeoning scholarship on ethics and film, attest to the growing interest in issues of responsibility regarding our capacity to audio-visually represent and consume, inextricably linking ethics with optics. My own approach to the topic is affected by Levinas's ethics of alterity and shares with some of the above-mentioned scholarship a focus on ethical film forms; that is, aesthetic forms which carry ethical value. Much like Downing and Saxton (2010), whose premise is that 'every aesthetic decision has an ethical dimension' (18), and Grønstad (2016), who claims that 'film [. . .] provides an ethical experience not primarily on the level of narrative but on the level of form' (85), I argue that the iconoclastic *eikōn* is an image (that is, an aesthetic form) resulting from an ethical choice: a figurative image is negated out of respect for its model – for its non-reducibility to mimetic reproduction. Also drawing on Sinnerbrink's (2016) notion of cinematic ethics as 'the idea of cinema as a medium of ethical experience with the power to provoke emotional understanding and philosophical thinking' (x), the contention which shapes the remaining chapters is that the iconoclastic *eikōn* founds an ethics of (in)visibility which involves both producers and consumers of images. Throughout, I use ethics/ethical interchangeably with morality/moral – not to be confused with moralism – and conceive of ethics in cinema as 'a process of questioning' and 'a way of responding to the encounter between the self and other/s' (Downing and Saxton 2010, 3). Thus, cinematic ethics involves issues of responsibility and desire in regard to the images one decides to show and look at; following Sinnerbrink, cinema can provoke ethical experience, thereby eliciting from spectators a challenging of their moral beliefs.

While research on ethics and aesthetics in a film ambit has flourished more recently, accounts on the ethical charge of formal choices have been traversing film criticism since its inception. Particularly, two articles critiquing a now (in)famous shot in *Kapò* (Gillo Pontecorvo, 1960) have significantly contributed to reconceptualising the notion of beauty in its relationship to ethics. Jacques Rivette's 'De l'abjection' [On Abjection] (1961) and Serge Daney's 'The Tracking Shot in *Kapò*' ([1992] 2004b) argue against the binding of the good and the beautiful (a philosophical ideal found, among others, in the Ancient Greek concept of *kalokagathia*/καλοκαγαθία, 'the beautiful and the good', Plato [*Republic*] and Kant [CJ 225–230]), claiming that the aestheticisation of atrocities is unethical. *Kapò*, a film about the concentration camps, includes a highly aestheticised tracking shot of Emmanuelle Riva's suicide which abjectly lingers on her dead body on the camp's barbed wire. Commenting on this shot, Rivette (1961) insists on the immorality of realism regarding death in concentration camps (which echoes Gérard Wajcman's [1998] critique): 'Total realism, or what serves as realism in cinema, is impossible here; any attempt in this direction is necessarily *unachieved* (therefore immoral), any attempt at re-enactment or derisory and grotesque make-up, every traditional approach to "spectacle" partakes in voyeurism and pornography' (54). The issue with a realistic and beautiful representation derives from the model, which resists mimetic doubling insofar as the spectacle of realism, in this case, would render the intolerable (death in the concentration camp) tolerable. There can be ugly forms which are morally good, and contra *Kapò*'s extreme visibility, impossible contents can be rendered via gaps and holes in the representation. Daney ([1992] 2004b) also remarks on the immorality of *Kapò*'s tracking shot because 'one should never put himself [*sic*] where one isn't nor should he speak for others'. Therefore, both critics put forward the idea that certain ethically problematic contents should determine a film form which could maintain them as at least partially inaccessible.

This is valid not only for a content such as death (and specifically death in the concentration camps), but also for some representations of pain, intimacy and desire to avoid their becoming obscene. Of uncertain etymology, obscene here refers to a representation that makes what pertains to the intimate, invisible sphere utterly mimetically accessible. In this regard, Slavoj Žižek (2001b) discusses representations which constitute 'obscene violations of the "No trespass!" sign; the only proper thing to do is to maintain a distance towards the intimate, idiosyncratic, fantasy domain – one can only circumscribe, hint at, these fragile elements that bear witness to a human personality' (73). For its very nature of being visible, the film image always runs the risk of trespassing into the obscenity of the showing it all. The boundary between hinting at and exhibiting something is thin, and yet ethically and aesthetically immense. As André Bazin (1972) reminds us, 'the cinema can say everything, but not show everything' (174). However, cinematic iconoclasm challenges even the medium's ability to say (clearly and intelligibly), as it will become clear throughout the remaining chapters.

While at first sight producing images may seem more ethically implicated, the choice of keeping our eyes open in front of certain images bears a similar ethical weight. In *Spectatorship: The Power of Looking On* (2007), Michele Aaron contends that 'spectatorship is ethically loaded' (88), because it is not solely the act of image-making, but also the act of looking that implies responsibility for what one decides to look at. The terms and methods within which what is audible and visible are produced and consumed, especially in a society where sight and images have acquired a fundamental role in the everyday, call into question the ethical dimension. As in Christian iconoclasm, also in the cinema, it is the content which raises ethical concerns regarding form; therefore, the form needs to be adequate to the content. The Christian iconoclastic ban on images occurred because of the model – the content of the image – and was not extended to other types of representation; similarly, iconoclasm in the cinema does not target every type of image. Iconoclastic *eikones* originate from ethically charged models that not only the physical senses but also thought has a hard time processing and that can never be fully cognised. The others' suffering, loss, grief, death and desire are some of the contents at the edge of representability that I will discuss in the following chapters. I will look at film images which, by rejecting mimesis and the idea of the film's content as figuratively accessible, open audio-visual gaps that spectators are called upon to fill with meaning; namely, images whose form can grant viewers the freedom to imagine and make ethical judgements.

What I have termed iconoclastic *eikōn* is thus a coalescing of apparently conflicting features. On the one hand, it retains the philosophical meaning of the *eikōn* as that which mediates between the sensible and the intelligible sphere – in other words, between a visual form and its model. On the other hand, it attains so by breaking with mimesis. This anti-mimetic aesthetics, which hinges on the distance between copy and prototype, is iconoclastic because it implies that the image cannot truthfully reproduce the model. There are models, in fact, that transcend physical reality and can thus be represented only metaphorically. For instance, love can be thought or felt, but we lack a specific phenomenal prototype of love per se; therefore, love can be visually reproduced only metaphorically, for example, through images of people kissing or holding hands. Some models, however, question mimesis itself because mimetic reproduction – whether metaphorical or not – potentially risks concealing the unbridgeable gap between the image and its model. My contention is that the iconoclastic *eikōn* constitutes a way to represent intelligible and ethically problematic subject matter without spectacularising them. What changes is the relationship between the cinematic world and phenomenal reality: to preserve the complexity of the latter, the former ceases to have a mimetic relation with it.

In addition to interrogating the limits of our right to show everything, iconoclastic *eikones* also question our right to look at every image. What, indeed, does it mean for spectators to look at extremely intimate or painful events in the lives of others? Do we have the right, just because we have the technology, to entomologically scrutinise the lives of others? Iconoclastic *eikones* destabilise this right from both a film-making and spectatorial perspective; as such, they configure themselves as ethical, appealing as much to reflection as to emotion. An emotional response alone would be insufficient for spectators to make sense of the audio-visual aporia produced by these images and to take responsibility for what they see and hear. Aaron emphasises the necessity of a reasoning response regarding ethical spectatorship when it comes to the representation of others' suffering. According to Aaron (2007), who draws on Susan Sontag's (2003) argument on being moved by photographs of others' pain, 'being moved [. . .] marks the experience as moral but not ethical: involuntary emotion is the opposite of reflection and implication' (116).[2] Aaron continues by pointing out that an emotional response alone, such as crying in front of scenes of others' suffering, does not imply a conscientious act of responsibility from the spectator because 'these involuntary or visceral reactions symbolise a requisite, defensive denial of the profundity or implications of the representation. [. . .] we are denying our part in what we are watching' (116–17); eventually, 'when we are moved [. . .] we are not taking responsibility for' (117) what we are watching. Saxton (2010b, 62–75) also considers reflective responses to images of others' suffering. Engaging with Aaron's reading, as well as with that of Sontag, Lilie Chouliaraki (2006) and Luc Boltanski (1999), she stresses the idea that an emotional response alone is insufficient to stimulate viewers towards actively questioning the meaning and implications of what they are looking at. What is more, Saxton (2010b) explores spectatorial responsibility in regard to images of others' real or fictional suffering in films, concluding that 'what and how we view has consequences, [. . .] spectators are not isolated from the spheres of ethical action and accountability, but [. . .] our privileges – including the privilege of looking – are linked to others' suffering in ways we need to actively interrogate' (74).

Although iconoclastic *eikones* are not limited to the representation of others' suffering, they nevertheless deal with similarly complex issues which pose ethical challenges to mimetic representation. Like the real or fictional images of others' pain that Aaron and Saxton discuss, iconoclastic *eikones* require a reflective response from the spectator to become fully intelligible. Reasoning is essential for the constitution of a pensive, ethical spectatorship and for reflecting on the questions opened by iconoclastic *eikones*. Spectators, in fact, are invited to fill the visual and aural gaps on screen if they are to make any sense of what they (do not) see and hear. Therefore, the iconoclastic *eikōn* assumes an additional relational character: not only does it establish a relation with its model – it is *eikōn* following philosophical tradition – but also mediates with the spectator. That is, it configures itself as a relational entity.[3] Meaning resides in the encounter between spectators and iconoclastic *eikones*, in the relation which they can potentially establish together. What I set out to explore, then, is the web of relationships that the iconoclastic *eikōn* has the potential to encourage and that concern the ethics of producing, looking at and sharing images.

A Desire Beyond Mimesis

Marguerite Duras's work on desire, displacement and intimacy (intended not solely as sexual intimacy but also as intimacy of affections, thoughts and emotional states) is apt for exploring the ethical limits of filmic representation and the spectator's troublesome place, thanks to her disruptive aesthetics. Duras articulates desire – both the desire experienced by the characters within the diegesis and the spectator's desire – and maintains it as irretrievable through a consistent use of de-synchronisation and an increased undermining of figuration. A questioning of representation, already evident in her early films, progressively turns into a destruction thereof via a radical use of the black screen. The later films display a disillusionment with the film medium which unfolds in terms of separation – of actor and character; of image and sound; of body and voice. Concomitantly, moments of imagelessness augment following a progressive mistrust about cinema's representational capacity.

Le Camion (1977) initiates, in Duras's cinema, 'the end of representation as we know it' (Günther 2002, 77) because instead of the film, we watch Duras and Gérard Depardieu reading a draft of the script of the film that will never be shot, which further develops a separation between actors and characters already present in previous works such as *India Song* (1975). *Le Camion* manifests a radicalisation of Duras's approach to cinema also through its concluding sixteen-second black screen, the use of which becomes more prominent in subsequent films, from *Le Navire Night* to *Les Mains négatives* (1978) and *L'Homme atlantique* (1981). *Les Mains négatives*, whose image track consists of unused shots from *Le Navire Night* and an opening black screen, expands on issues of race, colonialism and sexuality through a visually marginal aesthetics that rests on the evocative power of the aural dimension while undermining that of the visual. *L'Homme atlantique* further exacerbates some of her aesthetic and thematic concerns, subjecting viewers to a final fourteen-minute black screen on which Duras reads from her text *L'Homme atlantique*. The black/blank screen – a favourite image in Duras's later production – is 'a reminder of a longer-standing anti-spectacular and non-representational drive' (Cooper 2019, 144) and functions as a means for encouraging the spectator's imaginative possibilities through its halting of the spectator's look. Emptiness, blankness and sound-image disjunctions can in fact elicit the viewer's imagination by nurturing a continually frustrated desire to see. Elaborating on the imaginative potential of Duras's aesthetics, Jean Cléder (2014) contends:

> To say that the image is emptied in Duras's films (up to *L'Homme atlantique*'s black screen) is true to some extent, beyond which we can still sing the refrain of the unrepresentable [. . .], but certainly not account for the spectator's experience: freed by the dispositifs designed by the film-maker, the exercise of the gaze is suddenly mobilised towards 'a space of clairvoyance [*voyance*]' which multiplies the ways to see and the possibilities of the narrative. (10)

If, on the one hand, the overcoming of figuration and synchronisation comments on mimesis's problems of representation and truth, of image as truth, on the other hand, it potentially liberates spectatorial imagination: faced with a considerably empty image, the viewer is often encouraged to sustain an ethically charged imaginative effort. In *Film and the Imagined Image* (2019), Sarah Cooper develops a compelling argument on mental image-making, exploring the capacity of non-representational images to engage the spectator's imagination and trigger the formation of imagined images. Duras's films are thoroughly discussed as exemplary for stimulating spectatorial imagination via a disruptive relationship between voice and image (Cooper 2019, 140–55). Indeed, her films appeal to the imagination not solely through the more jarring black screen, but also by means of figurative images which no longer offer a mimetic rendering of the story that the voice-over articulates. Thus, characters visually disappear, and empty rooms accumulate throughout Duras's cinematic oeuvre, to the point of becoming the film itself: the ghostly spaces of the palace in *India Song*, the deserted rooms in *Son nom de Venise dans Calcutta désert* (1976), the places emptied of bodies in *Le Navire Night*.

In such context, sound, and specifically the voice, qualifies as that which constructs and sustains desire, preserving alterity as irreducible to sameness. The voice in *Le Navire Night*, for example, is conducive to the expression of diegetic desire while also producing spectatorial desire – there is the lovers' desire for each other, which lies exclusively in the aural dimension, and there is the spectator's (unachievable) desire to match the voices heard together with their bodies. De-synchronised sound, therefore, becomes a vehicle for expressing the unrepresentable, and more specifically issues of desire and sexual difference, via the interplay of absence and presence. But it also serves a critique of colonialism and Western (French) foreign policy, which intersects with Duras's feminist politics through her work on language and speech. There is a work against the French language which signifies a work against patriarchal, colonising language via elliptical sentences, a scarcity of verbs paired with an abundance of nouns, an ambiguous use of feminine and masculine pronouns, the adoption of languages other than French without the aid of subtitles and the exploitation of noise. Thus, Duras not only employs the voice as a means for intelligible speech, but she also uses it beyond semantic signification.

Such aurally disruptive aesthetics is particularly apt for a feminist politics and the portrayal of non-hegemonic subjectivities, exemplified in the voice-off of the Laotian beggarwoman in *India Song*, whose singing, laughing and screaming at once literally give a voice to the colonised woman and refuse to make her visually accessible and therefore controllable. According to Laura McMahon (2012), 'in ocular terms, the beggarwoman's exclusion from the image signifies her marginalization by colonial society, yet in acoustic terms, she exceeds the spectacle, gesturing to a disruption of both visual mastery and political control' (88). The lack of a visual image of the beggarwoman runs the risk of reinforcing her lack of societal visibility and agency; however, it can also be read as a move to provide her with a politically disruptive agency through a voice which is maintained as semantically irrecoverable. Moreover, the non-becoming image of the beggarwoman complicates a reduction of alterity to sameness (to what I know or may think of the other), framing the spectatorial encounter with this woman in terms of a listening (and openness) to difference. In this way, instead of an *eidōlon* which would visually enclose alterity via mimetic reproduction and therefore degrade the holiness/infinity of the other in such visual containment, we are faced with an imageless, aurally unsettling other who exposes us to confront alterity affectively and reflectively; in other words, we are presented with an iconoclastic *eikōn* which evokes alterity through an aesthetic foreclosing of clarity and, in so doing, may disturb our ethical stances. What we hear are bodily noises and, except for spectators who understand Laotian, a speech which deliberately remains a noise because of the absence of any translation. Used in this way, noise also relates to rejection, interruption, resistance and transgression, and it configures itself as politically disruptive.[4]

In *Noise: An Essay on the Political Economy of Music* (1985), Jacques Attali illustrates noise's subversiveness, thereby contending that society's repression of noise corresponds to a political repression of social bodies. If, in fact, noise is culturally perceived as something that disturbs and therefore needs to be regulated, it qualifies as a potentially effective tool to critique the power system which sustains a harmonious sonority purified of noise. Attali (1985) observes that 'the entire history of tonal music, like that of classical political economy, amounts to an attempt to make people believe in a consensual representation of the world' (46). Accordingly, societal control of noise is a de facto control exercised upon individuals for the maintenance of the status quo – thus, the political primacy of 'the right to make noise' (123). Paul Hegarty, in *Noise/Music: A History* (2008), advances a fascinating, and in some respects similar, argument. Because '*noise is cultural*' (3), the understanding of a sound as noise varies according to the context and intersects with power dynamics: 'Certain types of noise are to do with the sounds of "other people", and these are the ones that are most complicit with power, and lead to noise control regulations' (4). Noise is something that disturbs our hearing and resists meaning; in so doing, however, noise can lead to an uncontrolled listening within which the sonorous outweighs (a fixed, accessible) meaning, thereby upsetting the regulatory containment of sound. That is, if a comprehensible sound or a sound which at least does not disturb is implicated in dominant power dynamics, then noise as a negatively accented sound can be a means for criticising that very same dynamics. Thus, the beggarwoman's voice-off maintained as noise in *India Song* emphasises her oppression at the hands of colonial and patriarchal powers (the 'double colonization' of women [Tyagi 2014, 45]) while also expressing her 'right to make noise'; namely, her right to be listened to and therefore exist as a subject.

The disembodied female voice thus serves to challenge Western representations of colonised women in the use of noise as a vehicle for the expression of non-hegemonic identities. Duras exploits the ambiguous gap between sounds and their source images (bodies and places) to comment on power structures and subjectivities excluded from hegemonic discourse. Such a voice also provides a feminist perspective insofar as it defies a tradition in Western visual arts wherein woman is a beautiful image with no voice (Cavarero 2005, 107; Karpf 2017, 27–28), as well as mainstream cinema's convention of 'join[ing] image and sound together in a relation of hierarchical mimetic unity' (Hill 1993, 113). Although the disembodied female voice is very much an essential component of Duras's critique of patriarchal and colonising powers, there is also a feminist exploitation of silence. The coupling of woman and silence has a long history in Western thought (Cavarero 2005; Karpf 2017) and consequently cinema, where the silent woman can both attest to a lack of agency and bespeak a strategy of resistance (Dalton and Fatzinger 2003; Kaplan 2009). In Duras's films, silence, in the cultural form of female silence, is used dialectically in relation to male speech to explore and articulate issues of sexual difference (see, for example, Heathcote's [2000] and Kaplan's [2009] analyses of silence and violence in *Nathalie Granger* [Marguerite Duras, 1972]). A criticism of patriarchal and colonising language thus emerges from the aural tension between female voice and female silence, between articulated speech and noise, and between female silence and male speech.

This feminist critique is carried out through a criticism of Western mainstream cinema since this has frequently been used for perpetuating a patriarchal and colonising perspective. Duras does so by exploiting blankness and the disembodied female voice, thereby dismantling synchronisation, through which sound's transgressive potential is tamed and the viewer reassured. Michelle Royer (2019) explains:

> Duras thought the conventions of mainstream cinema, with its hierarchical divisions and oppositions between sound and image, represented the filmic equivalent of Western power and patriarchal structures that had to be totally abolished before a new, egalitarian society and culture could exist. Hence her films had to be experimental and innovatory, create new forms of expression and provide a different experience for her spectators by replacing the focus of Western cinema on the explicit and the visible with a cinema that privileges sounds and gives a larger place to viewers' imagination. (3)

The sonorous dissonances which dominate her films are purposefully developed in opposition to mainstream cinema's sound techniques through which the illusory harmonious coupling of sound and image is made possible. The aural dimension as developed by Duras appeals to senses other than sight, in particular touch, eliciting an embodied spectatorship (see McMahon 2012, 74–113), while also fostering the viewer's imagination. Duras uses the full gamut of sound-image disjunctions, as well as sounds themselves and silence to create a sense of corporeal intimacy, both among characters within the diegesis and between spectators and the film. Far from being immaterial or de-individualised, the visually body-less voices are always referring to the embodied singularities which have originated them (most often that of Duras herself), thereby evoking the sensuous sphere of the carnal. Moreover, in contrast to mainstream cinema's impression of reality, Duras's voices, bodily noises, music and silence, now separated from their source images, increase the spectator's imaginative capacity which is called upon to actively produce meaning. *Le Navire Night* builds on these premises, unfolding desire as a lovers' dialogue while maintaining it visually inaccessible.

An Imageless Love Story

Le Navire Night is a 'love story' and, more specifically, a 'story without images' and a 'story of black images', as Duras's voice-over makes clear early in the film. As an impossible love story between two lovers who never meet, the film explores issues of desire through a disjunctive aesthetics which heavily relies on listening as the possibility of being with another. The film's narrative verbally unfolds on an image track comprised of empty places, black screens and shots of the actors (Dominique Sanda, Bulle Ogier and Mathieu Carrière) silently sitting at a table or undergoing make-up. This stylistic choice recalls and continues a tradition of negative aesthetics in French cinema, from Isidore Isou to Guy Debord and Jean-Luc Godard; however, in Duras's work, the effacing of characters and the irreconcilable separation between body and voice is far from dismantling individuality or from a nihilistic intent, evoking instead the carnality of the unseen bodies, also and especially because the female voice we hear is distinctly the director's own voice. While the image can no longer produce and sustain desire, a disembodied yet sensuous voice becomes the vehicle to overcome such visual impasse.

Duras's disillusionment with cinema forcefully erupted in the early days of *Le Navire Night*'s shooting, leading her to abandon the making of the film which would resume, albeit dramatically changed, after a sleepless night. Instead of shooting the film that was supposed to be, Duras decided to 'shoot the disaster of the film. [. . .] Little by little, the film came out of death. [. . .] We turned the camera backwards and we filmed what entered of the night, the air, the projectors, the roads, the faces too' (Duras 1979, quoted in Alazet 1992, 146). Slow, wandering travelling shots of empty places and film equipment, fixed shots of the stone-faced actors, black screens and a blue sky caught between mimesis and abstraction provide the visual substratum for an aural love story which however never finds a correlative in the image track. The narrative develops exclusively through Duras's and Benoît Jacquot's voices off-screen, alternating direct and indirect discourse and switching between genders.

One night a man, J. M., who works for a telecommunication company in Paris, dials a random number out of boredom and begins to talk with a woman, F. The two initiate an aural love story lasting several years, during which they never physically meet. Duras's and Jacquot's voices provide the only access to the story, since we hear about J. M. and F. but never see them; in fact, we see no character from the narrative but only the three actors. McMahon (2012) observes that, 'in *Le Navire Night*, Duras thus makes invisible what would normally be visible (the story of J. M. and F.) and makes visible what would conventionally remain invisible (the technical workings of film)' (99). Such extreme disjunction between sound track and image track is conducive to the expression of sexual desire as that which can only be sustained by a work of the imagination. To the exception of rare shots in which some sounds are visually embodied in their sources, specifically that of a man playing the piano and the sound of the piano, the film maintains the gap between sound and image as insurmountable for both characters and spectators. A few times, the places to which the voices refer find a visual correspondence in the images of the Père Lachaise cemetery and the villa in Neuilly, but for the most part there is a dialectical tension between what is heard and what is seen.

The separation between voice and image is further reinforced through the separation between actors and characters. Actors, who are no longer characters, move slowly and stare at each other or at something in front of them, which is precluded to viewers, without ever uttering a word (Figure 5.1). The characters – F., J. M., the father, the two mothers, the priest – exist exclusively in the aural dimension, in the story recounted by Duras's and Jacquot's voices. Thus, *Le Navire Night* continues a process of 'suppressing the actors, and the very presence of bodies, of the characters' incarnation in the image' (Coureau 2014, 132) already at work in Duras's previous films. Marion Poirson-Dechonne (2016) talks about an 'aesthetics of de-incarnation' (194) in regard to Duras's cinema and this film in particular, where 'in the absence of bodies, the impression of de-incarnation manifests itself but, paradoxically, absence imbues the characters with extraordinary force' (195). While in some of Duras's previous films, imagination could rejoin voice and body since actors were also characters, in *Le Navire Night* it is no longer possible to reconcile the voices heard with their source images, because Duras and Jacquot are never visually present and because Sanda, Ogier and Carrière are never aurally available. And yet,

Figure 5.1 Actors in *Le Navire Night* (Marguerite Duras, 1979)

the unseen characters acquire consistency through their sensuous sonorous presence, even though they never incarnate in bodies visually accessible to the spectator.

Le Navire Night is a film on desire (the desire of the other and the desire for the other), which the voice elicits, and its destruction, which the image produces: desire emerges in darkness (at night; on a black screen; without faces or reciprocal touch), maintained by disembodied voices which appeal to the imagination; it will succumb to images mimetically depicting F. Halfway into the film, F. sends two photographs of herself to J. M., who reacts in startled disgust at such a sight.'Desire is dead. Killed by an image', the voices pronounce. The coupling of a lover's sight and death has been present in Western arts since ancient times and finds one of its most popular examples in the myth of Orpheus and Eurydice. In the traditional interpretation of the myth (from Ovid's *Metamorphoses*), Orpheus's desire to see his beloved literally kills Eurydice; in *Le Navire Night*, the sight of F. kills J. M.'s desire for her. Throughout the film, desire is steeped in death – the death hovering over F., who suffers from leukaemia; the recurring shots of tombs at the Père Lachaise cemetery. A mortiferous atmosphere is also evoked stylistically, via the stillness of objects and empty spaces which contrasts with the mobility of desire and the voice.

There is a tension between the liveliness of the sonorous (articulating desire) and the deathliness of the mimetic image (depicting the desired subject). From the film's inception, the mimetic image of reality – shots of a metropolis which the voice-over identifies as Athens – is broken by black screens. The dark blankness not only violates figuration but also stimulates the imagination, which is further enticed by an utterly desynchronised sound. While images (de)limit – physically, the visual field; metaphorically, the imaginative capacity – sound enfolds and pervades the whole body while also appealing to imagination. In his work on listening, Jean-Luc Nancy (2007) argues that 'the visual is tendentially mimetic, and the sonorous tendentially methexic' (25); that is, sound can more easily establish a relationship of (co-)participation for it is characterised by contemporaneity – of things which *are happening* at the same time (see Nancy 2007, 31). Moreover, sound's experiential duration outweighs the physical hearing of a sound, as Steven Connor (2003) contends: 'The nature of sound is to occupy a passage rather than an instant of time, a duration rather than a moment. To hear a sound, one must have already heard it start to decay, or come to an end; one must already have started finishing hearing it. One hears very largely analeptically' (112).

Accordingly, the aural dimension is particularly significant for the arousal and maintenance of desire because it corporeally envelops the subject, appeals to the imagination and lingers long after the physical sound has ceased. Through the withholding of visual images of the other and the dominance of the dialogical voices, the film is also addressing us, first and foremost, as listeners. In *The Other Side of Language: A Philosophy of Listening* (1990), Gemma Corradi Fiumara advocates for a recovering of logos's aural dimension as essential for listening as being-with. In her critique, Western philosophy has halved logos into speaking and listening wherein only the former has a philosophical right, thereby rendering logos a 'saying-without-listening' (3). However, if the two halves are rejoined, the relational valence of aurality powerfully emerges, and we can become aware that 'there could be no saying without hearing, no speaking which is not also an integral part of listening, no speech which is not somehow received' (1). The resulting saying-with-listening has an ethical import since it points to a relation which can expose us to a being-with others in terms not reducible to possession. Corradi Fiumara emphasises the significance of a 'germinative listening' (60) in the construction of a communal, transformative culture which, by being able to listen and therefore being open to the other, is capable of change. Authentic listening is always interactive because it presupposes an openness towards the other and is thus defined in terms of reciprocity and co-existence.

Via the voice, *Le Navire Night* engages with listening as the possibility of being-with another, which the mimetic image shatters. The sound-image separation which grounds the film is apt for the creation of iconoclastic *eikones* which prevent alterity to become a consumable, controllable image. While the *eidōlon* impoverishes the content of the image as much as the viewer of such image, Duras's iconoclastic *eikones* permit the accessing of alterity in manners which attest to the irreducible quality of the other person and their desire, constantly stimulating the ethical potential of spectatorial imagination. Alterity overflows visual representation and is indirectly evoked via the voices in their disjunctive relation with the images, through a style which marks the encounter with the other in ways irreducible to figuration, clarity, possession – in a word, irreducible to sameness. Even when the voices seem to encourage us to imagine the faces, the bodies and the carnal pleasure of this desire, the possible resulting mental images are likely to remain opaque, blurred by the lack of any visual rendering of the characters, thereby making the figurative containment of the other impossible also at an imaginative level. Duras's iconoclastic style thus preserves the other person as intractable to mimetic representation, shielding them from the control of the gaze. Equally, this aesthetic form, which shapes an incomplete, ambiguous representation of love and desire, insistently urges the spectator to an imaginative effort.

The voice's evocative power incites imagination, setting it free in the absence of figurative images of the other person; thus, F. can assume any physical appearance in the freedom that the disembodied voice and listening accord to individual imagination (that of J. M. as well as the spectator). However, this imaginative liberty collapses in the face of figurative images. Duras maintains the spectator's imagination free while disappointing J. M.'s: the two photographs which kill J. M.'s desire by providing an image of F. devoid of imagination (that is, by pulling F. away from the multifarious possibilities of the virtual) are never shown to the viewer, who is therefore able to continue imagining F., albeit fragmentarily. Conversely, J. M. finds himself experiencing the gap between the imagined woman (F.'s disembodied voice) and the actual woman (the two photographs); a gap so unbridgeable that, at first, he is even unable to recognise F.'s voice. Her voice no longer belongs to the body imagined by desire; thus, desire itself crumbles in the face of two mimetic images which remain beyond the possibilities offered to the spectator: we never participate in the sight of the photographs but instead see slow pans of a park, while Jacquot's voice remarks: 'It is too late for her to have a face'. This iconoclastic interdiction against looking (which involves the characters, who cannot see each other, and the spectators, who cannot see the characters) and the primacy of the voices are conducive to evoke the experience of alterity, leading to iconoclastic *eikones* of the other('s desire). And thus, when this prohibition is violated, when the face of the other becomes a figurative image accessible to the gaze and imagination has little left to cling on to, something is broken: J. M. no longer encounters – existentially, desirously – F.

Differently, viewers are kept safe from the face of F. in the film's privileging of voice over image and in its interpellating us as listeners. The love story to which we are aurally granted access is imageless throughout, and the film demands that we listen to the sounds of a desire which can never be assimilated to sameness. Hence, the voices unfold the amorous relationship; yet, the carnal intimacy of the characters remains inaudible, protecting (the other's) intimacy from the obscenity of the showing it all. Thus, for instance, the orgasm that Duras offers to her characters is aurally inaccessible to spectators – we hear *of* it, but we do not hear it. Throughout the film, a listening beyond visual mimesis opens up the possibility of being-with, the sharing of a desirous experience – whether for a prolonged amount of time or only an instant. The imaginative and evocative potential of this aesthetics, in which the other is irreparably located beyond the image, offers an experience of alterity (of the individual and of desire) which encourages an ethical encounter between us spectators and the film, also compelling us to confront our desire to see (the other) at the moment in which such a vision is invariably frustrated.

Concluding Remarks

Duras's cinema bestows value on the voice as that which is capable of expressing what is forbidden to the image; thus, the voice becomes the constructor of meaning amidst the loss of faith in the image's representational capacity. Such a preference for sound, and specifically the sound of the voice, to the detriment of the visual image resonates with ancient iconoclastic discourses which also built on the Biblical account of God as that who cannot be seen but can be heard. The voice in Duras's films compensates for the figurative image's insufficiency which degrades alterity and interrupts the spectator's imaginative possibilities – if everything is plainly visible on the screen, what is left to spectatorial imagination? Instead, the audio-visual hiatus produced by separating voice and body creates the conditions of possibility for the spectator's imaginative and ethical engagement with the film. Based on such potential of the voice and the sonorous, Derek Jarman constructs his testament-film *Blue*, within which the voice is at once a means to communicate meaning and an irrecoverable echo.

6 Blind Vision, Aural Resonances: Derek Jarman's *Blue*

DEREK JARMAN THROUGHOUT his career maintained a consistent distrust in images which reached its apex in his last feature film, *Blue* (1993) – an intimate, lyrical sound-story of the director's experience of living with AIDS. While he worked with highly visual media such as painting and cinema, realising visually mesmerising films, there remains in his oeuvre a search for something beyond the mimetic surface of the image. A visual pleasure for images, in fact, accompanies a taste for anti-mimetic aesthetics, which ranges from the poetic superimpositions in *The Tempest* (1979) to the more pronounced sound-image disharmonies in *The Angelic Conversation* (1985), the angry montage and aural collage in *The Last of England* (1987) and the consistent, disruptive use of the black screen in *Edward II* (1991).

Such ambivalent attitude towards images was also fuelled by Jarman's interest in Renaissance occult philosophy, which brought together ideas from the Hellenic, Christian and Jewish traditions (see Wymer 2005). The Neoplatonic trust in sensible beauty as a means for reaching intelligible beauty is relentlessly bedevilled by Plato's condemnation of images of art and the Biblical ban on graven images. *Blue* abounds with verbal admonitions about visual images and literally visualises the second commandment by completely rejecting figuration. In this film, Jarman's enduring scepticism about the mimetic image intersects with the ethics and politics of representing the person with AIDS (PWA). Characterised by a negative over-determination, the portrayal of the PWA consists of a spectacular image of the suffering body which bears no similarity to the actual experiences of the disease. In a fierce subversion of such representational code, Jarman employs a blue monochromatic screen as the constitutive image track of the film, thereby placing great emphasis on the significance of abstract colour while rejecting stereotypical depictions of the PWA. What is more, the highly evocative, queer sound track, which alternates clarity with unintelligibility, further intensifies the irreducible quality of Jarman's account of AIDS. This chapter thus considers a radically iconoclastic approach to cinema whereby mimetic, self-explanatory film images are conceived as unethical means for trespassing into obscene representation. It argues that *Blue*'s lack of figurative, easily understandable images and its acousmatic aurality between sound and sense are conducive to the rendering of the experience of AIDS, while also stimulating the viewer's imaginative and empathic capacity.

The Issues of Representing AIDS

After his HIV diagnosis in 1986 and the slow worsening of his condition, including his vision, Jarman 'yearned to make a film about the illness, [. . .] but according to biographer Tony Peake, he was held back, in part, by "the impossibility of visualizing an unseen virus". But Jarman began to realize that the film could embody that very impossibility' (Remes 2015, 112). In addition to the virus's invisibility, other issues became inextricably implicated in the problematic representation of AIDS: the negative portrayal of the PWA, mediatic misinformation and Thatcherism's homophobic moralism. How, then, could the personal experience of AIDS be audio-visually rendered without, however, reiterating its spectacular representational mode? Jarman's thoughtful approach to the topic eventually led to a monochromatic film which consists of a lyrical meditation encompassing the politics of vision and the ethics of representation.

In the 1980s and 1990s, when HIV was often a death sentence, the PWA was the object of a stereotypical mode of representation: the subjects were de-sexualised and stripped of their personal identity, with no reference to the actual politics of AIDS (Ellis 2009, 242–44; Lawrence 1997). The overall image of the PWA that emerged not only in the media and politics, but also in the works of those artists who claimed to support the AIDS cause, was negative and tended to equate HIV/AIDS inescapably with white male homosexuality, implying that the virus was a punishment for moral depravity (Crimp 2002, 83–107; Higginson 2008, 78; Watney 1987). Accordingly, AIDS was culturally mediated and represented as a metaphor (see Sontag 2002, 89–180). The perception of AIDS as a single disease, which results from the merging of the range of illnesses consequent to the infection, and the identification of a group to blame stem from the 'the language of political paranoia, with its characteristic distrust of a pluralistic world' (Sontag 2002, 103). As Susan Sontag (2002) highlights, 'authoritarian political ideologies have a vested interest in promoting fear, a sense of the imminence of takeover by aliens – and real diseases are useful material' (147). In a British context, Thatcherism used a moralistic rhetoric of fear regarding AIDS, which factually promoted the social construction of homosexuality as alien to society. And the visual representation of the PWA built on this negative mythology.

In mediatic representation, the PWA is usually male, white and portrayed as the living dead, his body carrying the visible marks of a life sexually active outside the heterosexual paradigm. Simon Watney (1987) calls such images *'the spectacle of AIDS'* (78), the function of which is to erase the plurality of experiences of people with AIDS and to hinder empathic engagement. These images are aimed to induce both fear and relief in their target audience (heterosoc)[1] via the equation of the disease and homosexuality; that is, AIDS and the sexuality – mediatically, politically, popularly – associated with it are frightening and, yet, heterosexuality is safely removed from the picture. This 'slippage from corruption theories of homosexuality to contagion theories of AIDS' (Watney 1987, 77) determines the exclusionary aesthetics of the mediatic representation of AIDS as well as the political rhetoric of fear surrounding the disease. Ellis Hanson, writing in 1991, decries:

> Typically, in media representations of AIDS, I find neither people who are living with AIDS nor people who have died with AIDS. What I find, rather, are spectacular images of the abject, the dead who dare to speak and sin and walk abroad, the undead with AIDS. I find a late Victorian vampirism at work, not only in media constructions of AIDS now, but in the various archaic conceptions of same-sex desire which inform the present 'Face of AIDS'. (324)

'Spectacular images of the abject' well renders the main issue with the representation of the PWA; that is, the effacement of reality in favour of a depiction that could at once maintain the PWA as abject (namely, homosexual and bodily disfigured), therefore producing a reassuring gap with heterosoc, and that could at the same time tame homosexuality, rendering it 'harmless' through the de-sexualisation of the subject. The representation of the PWA is thus characterised by a euphemistic approach which attenuates the unpleasant reality of the disease. By concealing the reality of AIDS (for instance, by distancing AIDS from heterosexuality) and the identity of people with AIDS, such a mode of representation reinforces the negative stereotypical images which Watney (1987) aptly defines as *'tableaux mourants'* (79). Only the body spectacularly consumed by the disease remains visible, while the PWA is de-sexualised and de-subjectivised. Douglas Crimp (2002), commenting on such images, remarks:

> Certainly we can say that these representations do not help us, and that they probably hinder us, in our struggle, because the best they can do is elicit pity, and pity is not solidarity. We must continue to demand and create our own counter-images, images of PWA self-empowerment, of the organized PWA movement and of larger AIDS activist movement [. . .]. But we must also recognize that every image of a PWA is a *representation*, and formulate our activist demands not in relation to the 'truth' of the image, but in relation to the conditions of its construction and to its social effects. (100)

The issue with images eliciting pity but not a reflective response is at the core of several works on the ethics of visual representation (see Chapter 5), which criticise spectacular images aimed at provoking an immediate yet fleeting emotional reaction without prompting a taking of responsibility from viewers or an unsettling challenging of their moral beliefs. Hence, there is a need for counter-images, which could give visibility to the PWA without falling into the category of the tragically spectacular. Such representations were particularly advocated for in the West in the 1980s and 1990s to oppose mediatic misinformation, which reinforced the identification of the PWA with white, male homosexuality and spread alarmist, homophobic messages, as evidenced by some of the headlines that Jarman (1992) cites in his autobiography:

AIDS BLOOD IN M&S PIES PLOT
[. . .]
18 VICE BOYS IN AIDS REVENGE
PULPIT POOFS CAN STAY
VILE BOOK IN SCHOOL – PUPILS SEE PICTURES OF GAY LOVERS
[. . .]
AIDS MENACE: HE CARRIES KILLER VIRUS YET WORKS WITH SICK KIDS
POLL VERDICT ON GAY VICARS: KILL 'EM OUT
[. . .]
HOLIDAY ISLE IN AIDS TERROR
[. . .]
GAY SENATOR SHAME
[. . .]

MORE CHANNEL 4 SHOCKERS: THEY BUY TWO GAY FILMS FOR
SHOWING UNCUT
[...]
I'D SHOOT MY SON IF HE HAD AIDS, SAYS VICAR
(91–97)

These headlines illustrate how the British press contributed to the spreading of misinformation about the virus transmission, on the one hand, and promoted discrimination and hatred, on the other hand. In their over-emphasis on exclusively spectacular images of AIDS, in which the physical degradation corresponded to moral corruption, the media diverted the attention from real norms of prevention and transmission. A lack of information about AIDS thus accompanies 'a medicalized dream of the prevention of gay bodies' (Sedgwick 2008, 43). Jarman (1992) comments:

> AIDS showed up an inheritance for a confusion. Faced with the prospect of writing about it, I faltered; there were too many stories I wanted to record. There had been no disease since syphilis so trapped in preconception and sexual stigma; exaggerated by the (erroneous) perception that it was only transmitted between homosexual men – 'AIDS, AIDS, AIDS', shouted the kids in the playground, 'Arse Injected Death Syndrome'. (83)

In addition to the mediatic distortion of the disease, the Thatcher government actively endorsed the marginalisation of the gay community, especially through Section 28 of the Local Government Act of 1987–88, which explicitly prohibited the promotion of homosexuality while implicitly promoting homophobia (see Thorp and Allen 2000). In this way, Thatcherism championed conservative values, such as heterosexual marriage and nationalism, while depriving homosexuals of their civil rights, forcing them into behavioural constraints and considering them an abjection. British politics staged an interplay of AIDS, homosexuality and morality, constructing homosexuality as an external, and abject, other to public society.

Gay communities, while removed from the social sphere as active agents, were thrown into the public arena via the equation of homosexuality, immorality and AIDS. When Jarman decided to make a film about AIDS in the first person – as a white, gay, British man with AIDS – he could not ignore the problematics of representing AIDS and the mediatic and political twisting of the disease. In the media, the representation of the PWA is based on the absence of the first person, of the scandalous 'I/We', to maintain a reassuring distance between image and heterosoc, the illusory belief that the disease does not concern 'me/us' but 'them'. In his confronting heterosoc, even before the making of *Blue*, Jarman (1992) describes as fundamental his resolution 'to start putting in the "I" rather than the "they"; and having made the decision about the "I" to show how things related to me so that I wasn't talking of others – *they* were doing this and *they* were doing that' (27). In *Blue*, the choice of the first person configures itself as a taking on of responsibility to break the ignorant silence surrounding AIDS, as well as Jarman's way of becoming an invisible yet subjectivised witness. In this sense, *Blue* can be understood as an ethico-political form of testimony.

With *Blue* and its absence of figurative images, Jarman is therefore doing two things at once: he is subverting the negative representation of the PWA and forcing spectators into experiencing his own blindness due to the disease. Indeed, Jarman gives a personal identity back to the ill subject – himself – by leaving the AIDS body invisible through the use of a blue monochromatic screen as the only image track of the film. *Blue* is a negation of the spectacularised image of the PWA, whose identity is restored through the sound track, and obliges spectators to experience the same blindness as Jarman. Not least, it is also Jarman's way to acknowledge the inexhaustible nature of AIDS:

> No ninety minutes could deal with the eight years HIV takes to get its host. Hollywood can only sentimentalise it, it would all take place in some well-heeled west-coast beach hut, the reality would drive the audience out of the cinema and no one viewpoint could mirror the 10,000 lives lost in San Francisco to date, so we are left with documentaries and diaries like mine and even they cannot tell you of the constant, all-consuming nagging, of the aches and pains. (Jarman, quoted in Peake 2011, 514)

Thus, the blue monochromatic screen as that which annuls any figurative image constitutes an ethical rejection of a stereotypical and comprehensive representation of the PWA. What is more, the film's iconoclastic aesthetics, in its withholding of a reassuring visual or aural depiction of AIDS, unsettles spectators, encouraging them to acts of empathic, imaginative engagement.

At the Limits of the Visible and the Audible

Blue operates a subversion of stereotypical images of the PWA through an ethics of representation based on invisibility. The non-representational choice of the monochrome bears witness to figuration's failure to represent AIDS and death, thereby tracing ethical limits for artistic mimesis. Jarman explicitly endorses the second commandment, longing for an iconoclastic aesthetics which he achieves with *Blue*'s ultramarine screen: 'For accustomed to believing in image, an absolute idea of value, his world had forgotten the command of essence: "Thou Shall Not Create Unto Thyself Any Graven Image", although you know the task is to fill the empty page. From the bottom of your heart, pray to be released from image'.

The film's iconoclasm hinges on the rejection of spectacle-images of the PWA as well as on the unrepresentable and ultimately unspeakable nature of death connatural to the disease. In the face of a euphemistic over-determination of the PWA, Jarman withdraws from the realm of mimesis to open a space of imaginative potentiality, within which the medium's inadequacy to figuratively represent certain models emerges. If mediatic images of the PWA are *eidōla*, false and harmful mimetic representations which can at best elicit pity, the film's non-representational image encourages a relationship between figuratively unrepresented content and spectator in terms of openness and unsettlement. The lack of mimetic images in *Blue* visually renders an absolute rejection of the image as deceptive copy, in an overall understanding of figuration as inescapably affirmative – which is reminiscent of Gérard Wajcman's (1998) argument on artistic mimesis as 'a negation of death and loss. A negation of absence' (242). Moreover, while mimetic reproduction necessarily excludes, monochromes retain a much more inclusive potential. Rather than limiting, by figuratively delimiting, the experience of AIDS and suffering, Jarman's blue screen references its model without however reducing it to a consumable mimetic image and invites spectators to engage with the imaginative power of colour.[2]

In the seventy-six minutes of ultramarine blue screen that constitutes *Blue*'s image track, Jarman develops a stratified, partially unintelligible sound track made up of four voice-overs (Nigel Terry, Tilda Swinton, John Quentin, Derek Jarman), residual whispers, music, environmental and electronic noises, silence and the obsessive leitmotifs of a tolling bell and the injured melody of a broken music box. The visual blankness, paired with such highly layered aural dimension, complexifies the viewers' engagement with the film and elicits the experiencing of 'empathic unsettlement' (Ellis 2009, 244), whereby the sharing of someone else's suffering leaves spectators disturbed and displaced, in this way also maintaining alterity as irreducible. Additionally, the collage narrative structure further complicates the viewers' access to the film for its interweaving of Jarman's personal recount of living with AIDS with socio-political critique and reflections on the problematics of representation.

According to Andrew Moor (2000), *Blue* is an example of 'a cinema of denial' and 'achieves for queer cinema what Laura Mulvey had advocated for feminist film practice in the mid-70s, namely an ascetic denial of visual pleasure' (49). The film, in its hindering of a mimetic access to the PWA, denies the pleasure that may derive from the spectacular image of the queer body. Jarman completely subverts the negative portrayal of the PWA by refusing figuration and exploiting the aural dimension: the ill body disappears (into the monochromatic blueness), and only subjectivity remains (in the sonorous articulation). Rather than an aesthetics of displeasure, however, *Blue*'s colour and sounds allow for the pleasure of the imagination, which balances the possible displeasure of the eye.

Into the **Blue**

Blue brings the discussion on cinematic iconoclasm and colour to the extreme by employing a blue monochromatic screen as the only image track of the film. What is more, Jarman selects a deep, ultramarine blue hue patented by the French artist Yves Klein, who named it International Klein Blue (IKB) and whose work is strongly related to monochromes. In Klein's Neoplatonic view, this hue expresses the unity between what is intelligible and what is sensible (Bois 2007, 87–88) and represents the colour of harmony between every existent as opposed to division and conflict (Solnit 2005). Jarman purposely employs the IKB because of its connotations and uses it to express a tension between the negation of mimetic forms (the monochromatic image) and the access to an intellectual vision (the interrogation and understanding of AIDS and homosexuality in heterosoc, blindness, solitude and death). In this single, ultramarine blue screen, Jarman conveys his total refusal of the film image as spectacle, abolishing the image's limits imposed by mimesis and figuration.

Different from the blank screens analysed in the book so far, Jarman's blue monochromatic screen results from a 'chromatic cancellation' (Venzi 2013, 61) of images which configures itself not as a destructive void (as it occurs, for instance, in Guy Debord's black and white screens), but as a surface of pure potentiality. Vivian Sobchack's phenomenological engagement with the film in 'Fleshing Out the Image: Phenomenology, Pedagogy, and Derek Jarman's *Blue*' (2011) elaborates on the peculiarity of the image track, refusing to describe it as a blank screen or a non-visual image. *Blue*, she contends, does offer a clear image, if only *'referentially indeterminate'*; namely, it offers a 'plenitude of blueness' (197) which permits 'a sensually-enhanced mode of audiovisual experience' (193). Indeed, colour's omnipresence slowly seeps into the viewer and is even reinforced by the continual aural references to blue: we see blue, we hear blue, we can potentially feel this blue. *Blue*'s non-representational image track qualifies as iconoclastic *eikōn*, for it maintains a relationship with the unrepresentable model without providing a mimetic access to it: the individual experience of AIDS is omnipresent, articulated via an extremely evocative sound track, and yet visually irrecoverable.

The blue monochrome also reproduces Jarman's subjective point of view: rendered blind by the AIDS-related cytomegalovirus, he literally places viewers into his own visual impossibility, forcing them to share a perceptual hiatus. Peter Wollen (2004) explains:

> Blue was the colour Jarman saw when eye-drops were put in his eyes, in the hope of alleviating his blindness. Paradoxically, blindness allowed Jarman to see beyond the distraction of images, directly into the realm of colour, as Yves Klein had wished. Aids was too important to Jarman for it to be represented by images. (118)

For both director and spectators, the halting of sight opens up the possibility of vision as a way to interrogate the realm of images – something which Klein's ultramarine blue deliberately encourages. Klein abandoned the reproduction of figurative features of the sensible world to favour an iconoclastic expression of the infinite. In delineating his 'indefinable pictorial sensibility', the French artist recounted an episode from his childhood:

> Once, in 1946, while still an adolescent, I was to sign my name on the other side of the sky during a fantastic 'realistico-imaginary' journey. That day, as I lay stretched upon the beach of Nice, I began to feel hatred for birds which flew back and forth across my blue, cloudless sky, because they tried to bore holes in my greatest and most beautiful work.
>
> Birds must be eliminated. (Klein [1961] 2013)

Declaring the blue sky as his own artwork, Klein endorsed anti-mimetic art to bridge the gap between the material *here* and the infinite *there*. Klein's blue monochromes thus concretise the dichotomy between what is sensible and what is intelligible: on the one hand, the incorporeality of the monochrome is the ultimate expression of the breaking with mimesis in search for the super-sensible; on the other hand, the materiality of colour renders the visceral connection with the sensible sphere. In establishing an intimate relationship between transcendence and immanence, the IKB allowed Jarman to position his film between 'the sublime and the relentlessly physical' (Wymer 2005, 178). The blueness of the screen at once abstracts from physical reality and is vividly material – a tension which the sound track further emphasises, alternating lyrical fragments with painstaking descriptions of bodily deteriorations, in an inextricable entanglement of the spiritual and the carnal.

As a colour expressing a tension towards the heavenly infinite, the IKB also qualifies as a unifying principle able to transcends borders and divisions, epitomised by Klein's monochromatic world maps. Grenoble, Nice, as well as France and Algeria lose their political borders in the transcending blue colouring. The visually beautiful signs of colonising powers – the ships, the flags, the dragons in the rough seas – the 'known world' of the colonisers and the 'unknown' of the colonised, the Terra Incognita, are covered by colour. Rebecca Solnit (2005) comments: 'Painting the world blue made it all a terra incognita, indivisible and unconquerable, a ferocious act of mysticism' (179). Jarman builds on the powerful unifying force and anti-war value of the IKB, remarking that '[b]lue transcends the solemn geography of human limits' and, later in the film, '[f]or Blue there are no boundaries or solutions'. In its omnipresence, the IKB permits the transcending of political borders and of the limits of figurative representation, which Jarman articulates through the binary between physical sight and intelligible vision.

Polysemous colour, the IKB in *Blue* tinges everything, constantly oscillating between positive and negative connotations – blue is the colour of love and nature ('Blue of my heart', 'Blue of my dreams', 'Slow blue love', 'Blue skies'), but also of AIDS, death and Jarman's blindness ('Blue drags black with it', 'The Blue Bearded Reaper', 'Empty sky blue after-image', 'I place a delphinium, Blue, upon your grave'). Such a 'semiotic slipperiness' (Remes 2015, 116) of the colour blue, which eschews a single meaning in both Klein's and Jarman's use, progressively increases. If early in the film blue retains a more positive valence, it slowly interweaves with the names of Jarman's dear dead ones and his hospital treatments. In line with Klein's understanding of ultramarine blue, *Blue*'s monochromatic screen consists of a space of pure potentiality, within which negative and positive meanings coexist in the dissolution of mimesis. What Jarman decidedly adds to his understanding of colour is its identification with queerness (Galt 2011, 75–96; Jarman 1994; Remes 2015, 115). As opposed to the rigidity of line and form, colour is a destabilising force in its materially impregnating of surfaces with an image not ascribable to an aesthetics of transparency. In *Chroma* (1994), Jarman traces a queer history of colour, from queer artists' and intellectuals' interest in colour to the Nazi use of pink, each time emphasising the interconnectedness of colour, queerness and politics. Rosalind Galt (2011) asserts that 'colour is where Jarman's films make their stand against hetero culture, where they propose utopian spaces, and where they locate a valuable queer life' (81). Thus, colour in *Blue* is also a fundamental component of the film's queer aesthetics.

The film visually opens on a black screen which rapidly changes to the IKB, requiring spectators to look at the visual gap left by an inaccessible image – a gap which figurative representation can no longer occupy. Jarman puts to test the relationship between sight and vision throughout *Blue*, in a progressive distancing of the two faculties. While earlier in the film, he fears the loss of his capacity of creative insight as consequence of the loss of eyesight ('If I lose half my sight will my vision be halved?'), later he acknowledges the autonomy of vision from sight, to the point of wondering whether the two might be inversely proportional. Like Tiresias in the *Oedipus Rex* (Sophocles 429 BCE) who, blinded for having seen the unseeable, obtains the ability to foresee as well as to see the present with more clarity, Jarman accesses an augmented vision with the gradual worsening of his physical sight. Variously addressed as 'blind bard' (Wymer 2005, 176), 'gifted magus' (Moor 2000, 64) and a seer (Higginson 2008), Jarman, like a modern Tiresias, guides the spectator in the blue blindness of the film through sound. Joining the twentieth-century suspicion of sight, Jarman acknowledges the discrepancy between physically seeing and knowing:

One can know the whole world
Without stirring abroad
Without looking out of the window
One can see the way of heaven
The further one goes
The less one knows
[...]
If the doors of perception were cleansed then everything would be seen as it is.

Such poetic reflections on expanded vision are interwoven with painstaking descriptions of Jarman's hospital visits, medical treatments and worsening health. According to Kate Higginson (2008), the 'utilization of the logic of sacrificial blindness is circumscribed, tempered, by the film's frequent turns to the corporeal' (88). While the film negates access to any figuration of the PWA, it nonetheless conveys the body in pain with extraordinary vividness. Like Klein's Neoplatonic approach, Jarman's IKB brings together sensible matter – the body, here in its most earthly manifestation as ill body – and the intelligible realm of blind vision. Patrizia Lombardo (1994) effectively notes:

> With a violent leap, the most bodyless film ever produced projects the human body in its most cruel and unspeakable presence: pain, illness, suffering at the borderline between the physical and the mental, the conscious and the unconscious, life and death. *Blue* comes from the most extreme philosophical reflection upon the conditions themselves of twentieth-century art, and radicalises the form of cinema, renouncing it, abstracting the essence of seeing from the concrete shapes where sight can dwell. (133)

Corporeality paradoxically impregnates a monochromatic film. There are no representational depictions of the yellowish pus in the eye or the irritated skin; yet, the detailed descriptions evoke a vivid image of the wasting away of the body. These accounts not only belong to Jarman's autobiographical experience, but also are an integral part of his critique of the spectacularisation of AIDS. Instead of reassuring depictions of the PWA which spectacle-images provide by maintaining an exclusively mimetic relationship with the referent, there is a disturbingly fleshy yet unfigurable image, which intelligibly references its model. Colour echoes Jarman's blindness and renders the invisibility proper to the virus, which not only becomes visible in the utterly individual manifestations of AIDS-related complications, but also significantly alludes to the forced invisibility of the gay community within the visible socio-political context (see Ashton 2012). AIDS's and homosexuality's problematic relation to visibility (that is, the invisibility of pain and the disease and homosexuality's societal invisibility) finds a non-spectacularised mode of expression in *Blue*'s iconoclastic focus on the body: omnipresent but never exhibited. The body, always positioned at the centre of Jarman's cinematic oeuvre – from the sun-drenched bodies of *Sebastiane* (1976) to the violently entangled bodies of *Jubilee* (1978) and the abundant male nude bodies of *Edward II* (1991) – continues to exert its privileged role even in the absence of its own image. With *Blue*, 'we learn to stop looking and to start listening instead' (Smith 1993, 19). That which provides a sensuous, meaningful yet fragmented access to the visually inaccessible body is, indeed, the film's sound track, through the plurality of voices and sounds it offers.

Aural Resonances

Blue's aural dimension partially balances the film's halting of mimetic vision, giving access to the invisibility at the core of the film. However, the stratified aural pastiche of voices, noises, silence, choral singing and music is ultimately irreducible to meaning. A slow-paced, almost idyllic sonorous (of music, singing,

Nigel Terry's soothing voice) restlessly alternates with the violence of quotidian noises, the uniform beeping of hospital machines, the sound of bombs and war. The contrast is discomforting, both when the change is sudden and when it occurs progressively – for instance, in the slow, menacing shifting of the music from instrumental to electronic. In addition to the aural tension between the heavenly ethereal and the darkly material, silence and voices alternate clarity with evocative unintelligibility. As much as Jarman develops his film around the potentialities of the aural dimension, there remains nonetheless an inaudible spot which chimes with the blind spot that is the film itself. Even the most meticulous description shuns comprehensive mimesis, thereby returning aural fragments.

As the monochrome sets limits for the eyes, so does sound for the ears, negating the possibility of hearing everything in the philosophical sense that Jean-Luc Nancy develops in *Listening* (2007). According to Nancy, there is a significant difference between 'to hear' (*entendre*) and 'to listen' (*écouter*). While 'to hear' corresponds with understanding the textual or contextual meaning of something aurally conveyed, 'to listen is to be straining toward a possible meaning, and consequently one that is not immediately accessible' (6). In the latter sense, sound produces a tension towards meaning:

> To be listening is always to be on the edge of meaning, or in an edgy meaning of extremity, and as if the sound were precisely nothing else than this edge, this fringe, this margin – at least the sound that is musically listened to, that is gathered and scrutinized for itself, not, however, as an acoustic phenomenon (or not merely as one) but as a resonant meaning, a meaning whose sense is supposed to be found in resonance, and only in resonance. (7)

Nancy's resonance refers not only to the quality of sound to reverberate, but more importantly to sound's ability to evoke a response in the listening subject, and specifically a response to something irreducible to meaning. Listening promotes an ontological openness – to the world, to others – and therefore exposes to the possibility of being-with. Paul Hegarty (2008), expanding on Nancy's account, argues that 'this type of listening subject is in the process of creating a community with all that is around and whoever is around' (198). Understood as such, listening, as that which occurs before meaning, is conducive to the formation of a community of listeners who share in an openness brought about by the lack of exhaustive meaning – an openness, therefore, to the irreducible alterity of the other.

Blue encourages spectators to an 'attentive listening' (Corradi Fiumara 1990, 11; see Chapter 5), to a being open to the sounds of the other, articulating the sonorous in both Nancean hearing and listening. That is, sound is the only means for expressing what remains without images, which resonates with Nancy's *entendre*; and yet, throughout the film, sound also echoes the image's insufficiency, incapable of expressing a meaning placed beyond intelligibility, and encourages openness, which recalls Nancy's *écouter*. Thus, we hear Jarman's account of his hospital visits, the excruciating list of side effects of DHPG, the denouncing of the spectacularisation of AIDS. However, music, noises, silence, voices and the whispered names of Jarman's loved dead ones point to the impossible rendering of subjective experience and death a hearing. The repeated whispering of 'David. Howard. Graham. Terry. Paul . . .', for instance, parallels the absence inscribed in the blue screen, because the spectator is penetrated by blueness and the evocative yet un-hearable sonorous, thereby tending towards meaning but never able to intelligibly grasp it in its fullness. The irreducible nature of part of *Blue*'s sonorous opens to the possibility (and potentiality) of listening, in which sound and sense continuously miss the encounter with each other but nonetheless strive towards it. The aural dimension thus refuses access to complete intelligibility and exhaustive description because of the ultimately uncommunicable nature of suffering – especially a suffering that has been so overly spectacularised. Nancy (2007) emphasises the significance of

> an insurmountable and necessary – even desirable – distance between sound and sense, a distance without which sonority would cease to be what it is. Even by continuing to use a dated vocabulary, one would have to say that the 'ineffable' does not constitute an oversignification, but, on the contrary, a beyond-significance [*outre-signifiance*] that it is not possible to enter and analyze under any kind of code. (58–59)

The non-correspondence between sound and sense endows listening with the potential for resonance in which something is always lost to intelligibility. 'David. Howard. Graham. Terry. Paul . . .' reverberate throughout *Blue*, but only an irreducible pain resonates. The names are repeated several times with a progressive lowering of the whispering voice to the point of almost silence. In this distressing echo, Jarman, via Nigel Terry, is both the producer of the original sound and the one who repeats it, because he is the only one left alive with a voice to remember and, in so doing, witness.

Adriana Cavarero, in her philosophical account of the voice, elaborates on the resonance of the voice through the mythic figure of Echo – the nymph condemned to repeat others' sounds, who falls in love with Narcissus and who, consumed by her unrequited love, physically disappears. The myth also suggests the conflicting relationship between voice and image:

> As a pure voice that refracts another voice, Echo makes the musicality of language sing. The poet Ovid wisely places her alongside Narcissus. The eye and the voice, which so tormented Plato, thus encounter one another in the Latin fable. And as with Plato, in Ovid's text there is no shortage of mirroring effects or produced copies – Narcissus' reflected image, and Echo's reverberating voice. The story tells of their impossible reconciliation. (Cavarero 2005, 165)

The 'impossible reconciliation' of image (Narcissus) and voice (Echo) stems from the cultural self-referentiality of the former contra the relationality of the latter. Nancy, too, elaborates on such discrepancy, defining the image as mostly mimetic and sound as primarily methexic. That is, while the visual is always on the verge of yielding to the temptation of mimetic reproduction, of a visual doubling complete in itself, sound tends towards a relation, 'participation, sharing, or contagion' (Nancy 2007, 25). If sound is more often methexic – namely, it involves a relationship (although of unintelligible resonance in the liminal case of listening) – it follows that there cannot be aurality without some form of co-participation. (When Narcissus – the image – ceases to talk, Echo completely loses her voice because of the lack of the other's sounds to repeat.) It is in this sense that *Blue* allows for establishing a relationship between film and spectator: we participate in someone else's suffering, without ever being able to reduce it to a fully intelligible image or concept.

In the absence of figurative images, sound – and especially the human voice – is entrusted with evoking visuality in its attesting to a unique corporeality: there is a physical being who is emitting this vocal sound. But the sound of a voice, while referencing the body which has produced it, also appeals to other bodies (to other ears), thereby qualifying as potentially highly relational; that is, a voice is in search of a body who can listen. According to Cavarero (2005),

> destined for the ear of another, the voice implies a listener – or better, a reciprocity of pleasure. [. . .] it is no longer a question of intercepting a sound and decoding or reinterpreting it, but rather of responding to a unique voice that signifies nothing but itself. There is nothing ulterior behind this voice that would make it into a mere sonorous vehicle, an audible sign. (7)

Here Cavarero's position resonates with that of Nancy: in both philosophers, when the sonorous ceases to be a question of semantic, it becomes irreducibly relational. In *Echo and Narcissus: Women's Voices in Classical Hollywood Cinema* (1991), Amy Lawrence develops an argument relevant to my approach to *Blue*'s aurality. Like Cavarero, Lawrence employs Ovid's fable to account for the unbalanced relationship between sound and image in the cinema, interpreting Echo's loss of her own voice (that is, the possibility of articulating her own thoughts) as the prerequisite for Narcissus's unrestrained fascination with himself. Accordingly, 'sound's absence [is] established as a precondition for the image's irresistible allure' (Lawrence 1991, 2). It is no wonder, then, that in a film explicitly against the beguiling temptation of images such as *Blue*, sound is that which makes the film possible in a move to contrast the image's seductive power. Jarman removes the body from the visible realm, returning instead an imaginative, carnal aurality which attests to his individual experience with AIDS; furthermore, he renders the voice a listening which at once presupposes someone who listens and marks its own insufficiency in the face of suffering. Thus, 'David. Howard. Graham. Terry. Paul . . .' haunt the blue screen and the spectator's ears with their paradoxical a-visual corporeality. Higginson (2008) observes:

> The obsessive repetition of this nominal mantra marks it as unresolved; the names standing as an indicator of the fact that the other (the beloved one grieved for) the proper name (inadequately) denotes remains incompletely internalized. Sarah Brophy has observed that in 'attempting to embrace those he has lost, [Jarman] finds that although he may repeat their names, their persons are somehow not tractable to representation'. (91)

What we listen to are sounds of absence – not only a visual (figurative) absence, but a corporeal, phenomenal absence of the dear dead ones. Their status parallels that of sound in cinema, which 'is itself a kind of echo, re-presented and reproduced, never actually "there"' (Lawrence 1991, 3). A sense of incommensurate loss resounds throughout *Blue*: sounds of absence, sounds about the absents. Jarman's whispered invocation remains a self-referential echo, thereby marking his role as witness – the one still alive, who still has a voice.

Blue's aurality is therefore essential for the film's overcoming of the spectacularisation of the PWA. It is not only the monochromatic screen but also the irreducible nature of the sonorous which allow for transcending spectacular images of the disease, in an unfathomable echoing of the invisibility and silencing of the gay community. In *Blue*, Jarman 'creates an anonymous acoustic space that maintains its sounds and voices as irrecuperable – or rather, it bears witness to a sonic ambience that cannot be transmuted back into spectacularization and intelligibility' (Khalip 2010, 97). The spectacular representation of the PWA also involved the aural dimension, which Jarman references most emblematically when he decries: 'I shall not win the battle against the virus – in spite of slogans like "Living with AIDS". The virus was appropriated by the well, so we have to live with AIDS while they spread the quilt for the moths of Ithaca across the wine dark sea'. The condemnation of the AIDS spectacularisation inexorably intersects with the misinformation surrounding the disease and with queerness ('Three quarters of the AIDS organisations are not providing safer sex information. One district said they had no queers in their community, but you might try district X – they have a theatre'). Echoing the queer visuality of the blue monochromatic screen, *Blue*'s sound track is distinctly queer in its exploitation of noise, silence and stratified voices (see, for instance, Khalip's [2010] compelling analysis).

In its challenging of fixed, heteronormative conceptions of sexual identity and representations of the PWA, *Blue* resists the audio-visual aesthetics that has traditionally supported them. While queerness is obviously not fixedly located in either the sound track or the image track, but depends on context, interpretation and use, it is nonetheless evident that *Blue* employs sonic devices and practices which facilitate the understanding of a sound as both disruptive of (hetero)normative codes and indicative of non-normative desire, such as dissonances, noises and silences.[3] Refusing to reduce the experience of AIDS to a hearing and therefore to an exhaustive sense, *Blue* uncomfortably compels us to an opening to listen to alterity, providing us with a cinematic iconoclastic *eikōn* which encourages an empathically unsettling encounter with AIDS, suffering and death.

Concluding Remarks

Blue is an example of a radically iconoclastic approach to cinema in which both figurative images and intelligible sounds are conceived as inadequate for the representation of the model. Jarman realises an IKB monochromatic film where the necessity to show his personal experience with AIDS meets an ethical and political need to not trespass into obscenity. The non-representational image track rejects spectacular images of the PWA and any attempt at a mimetic rendering of pain and suffering via colour which, in a paradoxical move, subtracts the ill body from the visible field to preserve it as individualised subject. What is more, the aural dimension echoes the inaccessible quality enshrined in the image track in that it alternates the clarity of hearable sounds to those irreducible to meaning. *Blue*'s poetics is thus framed within a broader ontological blindness and ineffability, which evidence the limits of artistic mimesis. Composed of a single, flickering image and haunted by aural resonances, Jarman's *Blue*, however, does not show the exclusively cinematic process by which an iconoclastic *eikōn* is produced. Ingmar Bergman's *Cries and Whispers* and Krzysztof Kieślowski's *Three Colours: Blue*, instead, display via fades how a figurative shot is progressively destroyed by means of colour.

7 Crumbling Faces: Ingmar Bergman's *Cries and Whispers*

INGMAR BERGMAN'S OEUVRE, from theatre to cinema and television, is aesthetically captivating and ethically fraught. Stylistic and thematic concerns recur in his plays and films, blurring the edges between reality and illusion, and eliciting the spectator's active participation through emotion and imagination. Illusion, in particular, acquires an ever-growing significance in its close link with issues of authenticity, to the point of becoming 'necessary' (Michaels 1999, 1), or even 'inevitable' (Hubner 2007, 3); that is, illusions allow individuals to cope with a potentially meaningless life. Thus, places and faces are troubled by unresolved dilemmas and irrational desires.

The search for glimpses of sense concretises more powerfully in the faces during the extreme close-ups, enigmatically lit by Sven Nykvist and Gunnar Fischer. In *Cries and Whispers* (*Viskningar och rop*, 1972), the intense facial close-ups, which disclose something about the characters' painful interiority, are also the target of destruction by means of an equally intense colour – red. While the film is overall figurative, it nonetheless contains several images which go beyond mimesis through an iconoclastic use of the colour red. Colour therefore becomes fundamental for complicating a simple reproduction of the phenomenal world, in an attempt to produce an ethical representation of the other's pain. What is more, the film offers an exquisitely cinematic passing from the moving image as iconophilic icon – the facial close-up – to the moving image as iconoclastic *eikōn* – the monochromatic red screen.

This chapter thus proposes an interpretation of Bergman's *Cries and Whispers* as emblematic of an iconoclastic ethics. It argues that the recurrent fades to red which punctuate the film are a way of representing the others' suffering in a manner respectful of its, at least partially, invisible and ineffable character.

Through an overview of the importance of colour and an in-depth analysis of the film and its central themes of grief and lack of empathy, the chapter demonstrates that the fades and the resulting red monochromatic screens are examples of iconoclastic *eikones* in which a mimetic, potentially spectacular image is replaced by an image that hints at its model without exhibiting it in a figuratively accessible manner. The film therefore supports an iconoclastic perspective because the gap between the intelligible content and its visible form is unbridgeable.

The Figurative Image Disappears into Sheer Colour

Like Derek Jarman's *Blue* and Krzysztof Kieślowski's *Three Colours: Blue* (see Chapter 8), one of the most striking features of Bergman's *Cries and Whispers* is colour. While Jarman makes colour the constitutive image track of the film, Bergman and Kieślowski punctuate theirs with fades to colour and monochromatic screens, thereby exhibiting how a mimetic image slowly vanishes into colour. All three films are significantly built around a consistent, anti-naturalistic use of a dominant colour, which assumes connotations and meanings independent from the coloured objects. Bergman's recurrent fades to red which suspend figuration, decomposing the magnified female faces, demonstrate colour's potential for the iconoclastic rendering of a cinematic world.

While early film theorists such as Béla Balázs ([1945] 1970, 242–45) and, more emphatically, Sergei Eisenstein (1957, 117–53) stressed the importance of colour as autonomous element of film, very few narrative films have used it in this way. More often, colour in film is rendered and thus perceived matter-of-factly, as something belonging to the mimetic reproduction of the world and as a means for heightening the impression of reality.[1] In Bergman's film, however, as in Kieślowski's, colour is essentially separated from the thing represented and, therefore, is fundamentally liberated from mimesis. In saying this, I do not mean that colour exists in a fluctuating state – it is, in fact, embodied in the screen; thus, it phenomenally exists as the colour of a physical object. But in the film's economy and its overall experience, colour is abstracted from visible forms to produce a dominant-colour-feeling experience; that is, in our experience of the film, we suddenly experience red or blue (the being-red or being-blue of the screen).

The idea of a colour-feeling experience, which may or may not be dependent upon a colour-representing experience, is a key notion in the philosophical debate over colour. Such ongoing issue originates from and addresses two problematics concerning colour: colour seems to be both a property of objects – something is in a specific colour – and a property of someone's experience – I perceive something as being in a specific colour (Byrne and Hilbert 2001; Levine 1998; Maund 2012). Various philosophical approaches tackle the issue in different manners, and the overall debate is complex and goes considerably beyond the scope of the present book. It suffices to consider how the debate centres on colour-feeling experience (how one experiences a colour) and colour-representing experience (how a colour is embodied in a physical object), as well as the ways in which these two kinds of experiences (mind-dependent and mind-independent) occur (Byrne and Hilbert 2001, xii–xix). For instance, if we consider a red apple, there are a number of questions that could be raised in relation to the red-feeling experience and the red-representing experience (on which I will not dwell), such as: if one, under normal conditions, is having a red-representing experience (a red apple), does this imply that one is also having a red-feeling experience? Is this proposition reversible (red-feeling → red-representing)? Is it possible for one to have, for instance, a blue-feeling experience while having a red-representing experience? And so on.

There is no conclusive outcome to the philosophical debate on colour. In cinema, I conceive of colour as both a property of objects of the mise-en-scène and as absolute entity; namely, colour as loosened from any tie with the objectual world. In this latter usage, colour is employed as autonomous and, thus, its chromatic presence on the screen acquires meanings that go beyond those related to the mimetic reproduction of such colour in phenomenal reality. Accordingly, Bergman's red and Kieślowski's blue are not mere attributes of the coloured objects because the red of an apple is not just an apple being red, in much the same way as a blue lollipop is not just a lollipop being blue; rather, they chromatically resonate with the being red and being blue of the films. That is, red and blue objects, as well as filters and lighting, enhance and create the possible meanings that these two colours assume in the films. Bergman's red and Kieślowski's blue[2] recur not only in the totalising monochromatic screens, but also in the objects of the mise-en-scène – from the burning red of the walls to the bright red of the blood; from the slightly dark blue of the room to the clear blue of the swimming pool's water. In both films, therefore, colour is also employed with autonomous value and becomes 'an abstract, un-objectual [*inoggettuale*] entity that *flows in the film through things*' (Venzi 2006, 25). Colour thus exhibits itself in two ways: by concretising in objects of the mise-en-scène, which can already produce a first departure from mimesis to something more symbolic and at times anti-naturalistic, albeit remaining in the figurative realm; and by offering itself as colour separated from any object, in a monochromatic screen.

Consequently, the experience of a film wherein one specific colour is employed in such manner is likely to elicit a dominant-colour-feeling experience. Bergman's *Cries and Whispers* encourages red-feeling experiences, even though not every object of the mise-en-scène allows for a red-representing experience. This overall red-feeling experience of the film is evoked by the continual and insisted recurrence of the colour red, not only in physical objects, but also and especially in the fades and the monochromatic screens. On the one hand, scenes are lit in a way that tends towards a single dominant colour, and props are also chosen in red, thus producing a slightly anti-naturalistic mise-en-scène; on the other hand, there are several fades to red and red monochromatic images, in which the anti-naturalism of the mise-en-scène turns into explicit abstraction. Such autonomy of colour carries out the metaphorical destruction of the mimetic shot, thereby creating iconoclastic *eikones* in the encounter between the film and the spectator.

A Film of Red and Faces

Cries and Whispers is Bergman's only film where colour is treated as essentially autonomous. Colour is also at the basis of the film's seminal idea, as evident in Bergman's own telling about the haunting images which pushed him into making the film: 'the first image kept coming back, over and over: the room draped all in red with women clad in white' (Bergman 1994, 83). This is *Cries and Whispers* reduced to its minimal form. In its use of colour, this film is also Bergman's most cinematic work. Contra Hubert I. Cohen (1993) who claims that '*Cries and Whispers* is [. . .] novelistic and theatrical' (250), I argue that the film's force resides in the facial close-ups and extreme close-ups, which do not exist in theatre, and in the tearing apart of these faces by the fades to red, which is impossible in both literature and theatre. *Cries and Whispers* is, therefore, only apparently 'novelistic and theatrical', given that it is profoundly based on inherently cinematic techniques. While for Cohen (1993) 'the film's fabric is woven of mise-en-scène more than giant close-ups' (250), I contend that the extreme close-ups and their destruction in the fades to red construct the most powerful sense of the film; namely, the impossibility to fully express, in both visible and audible terms, a person's inner life and inner inferno.

The film follows two sisters, Maria (Liv Ullmann) and Karin (Ingrid Thulin), taking care of a third, Agnes (Harriet Anderson), who is dying of womb cancer. Anna (Kari Sylwan), a servant devoted to Agnes, is however the person physically and emotionally looking after Agnes. To accompany Agnes in her final days, the women find themselves together in the manor of their childhood: outside, there is the large park lit by a faint Nordic sun; inside, where most of the story occurs, there are the claustrophobic, intensely red rooms. While Agnes embraces her pain, maintaining compassion and gratitude, her sisters remain entrapped in their inability to empathise. Both unhappily married, Maria indulges in fleeting moments of superficial tenderness, and Karin hides her overwhelming hatred behind a stiff coldness. Agnes dies, and the sisters dismiss Anna in a heartbeat, before harshly departing from each other.

The film is structured around a continuous alternation between present and past, in which the boundaries between reality and its distortion are increasingly thin. Three flashbacks and a dream interrupt the unfolding of the events in the present, and a last flashback concludes the film. Each of these interruptions belongs to one of the female characters, conveying a sense of their personality – Agnes's capacity to love unconditionally, Maria's narcissistic egotism, Karin's inability to overcome the hatred for both herself and others, Anna's compassionate love. Maria's and Karin's flashbacks and Anna's dream are shot and edited in the same manner. A figurative shot fades to red and the screen turns into a red monochromatic image. Then, an extreme facial close-up of the character, in which only one half of the face is lit, appears. This face slowly decomposes into another fade to red, leaving the screen completely red for a second time. Then the flashback, or the dream, begins. At the end of the flashback, the same transition is repeated backwards: the figurative shot fades to red; the screen becomes a red monochromatic image; an extreme facial close-up of the character, in which this time the other half of the face is lit, appears and then plunges into a fade to red; then the screen becomes completely red for a fourth time. Accompanying these transitions from the face to the monochromatic red screen are indecipherable whispers and, from time to time, the feeble sound of a distant bell. Agnes's flashbacks, however, differ from Maria's, Karin's and Anna's because they are not introduced by a fade to red, but by a dissolve,[3] and for the fact that there are no extreme close-ups of Agnes's face in between the fades. The sisters' flashbacks and Anna's dream, in which the fades to red signal the transition to and from the past, are the most cinematic scenes in the film and those which lead to iconoclastic *eikones*, as I shall explain.

The first flashback belongs to Agnes; differently from the ones that will follow, it is dominated not only by the colour red but also white, and it partially occurs in the well-lit, open space of the manor's park. After we are introduced to the character and her pain in the present, Agnes reminiscences about her childhood and her beloved mother, played by Liv Ullmann. During a magic lantern show on the Twelfth Night, Agnes gazes at her mother's blithe enjoyment of Maria's company, remembering how the mother could be, instead, 'playfully cruel' with

Agnes. From Agnes's past emotional discomfort, we are taken back to her current physical agony. The presence of a doctor, David (Erland Josephson), called to assist Agnes, leads to Maria's flashback. While in the present David refuses Maria's advances, in the past, when he was called for Anna's dying daughter, he spent the night with Maria. In an intense monologue in front of a mirror, Maria and David acknowledge their shallowness and selfishness. The day after, Maria's husband, Joakim (Henning Moritzen), who has returned from a work trip and, having sensed the cheating, is caught stabbing himself with a paperknife by an uncaring and slightly repulsed Maria. Back in the present, Agnes dies, and the priest recites a surprisingly agnostic sermon for her, before Karin closes the chamber's doors and everything fades to red. Karin's flashback coils around the disgust for her husband, Fredrik (Georg Årlin), twenty years her senior, and her self-harm. In a loveless atmosphere of tension and uneasiness, Karin and Fredrik are dining when she accidentally breaks a glass, spilling red wine over an immaculate white sheet. After she has returned to her room, Karin uses the shard of glass broken at dinner to cut her vagina and then smears her face with the blood, defiantly smiling at a repelled Fredrik who has come to claim his matrimonial rights. Finally, there is a dreamlike sequence of Agnes's resurrection, shot as if it were a flashback of Anna. Hearing someone crying, Anna rushes into the bedroom where Agnes supposedly lies dead. Caught in a liminal state, Agnes resurrects, beseeching her sisters to assist her trespassing. First Karin enters the room but, overcome by repulsion, she runs away. Then Maria approaches Agnes with seeming tenderness. However, when the dead sister begins to touch the living sister, who is capable of only superficial displays of affection, Maria screams in disgust and hastily leaves the room. Only Anna remains beside the unrested dead, taking Agnes in her arms in the manner of a *pietà*. Additionally, there is a further flashback which concludes the film. Like the first flashback, it belongs to Agnes, is introduced by a dissolve, is white-dominated and shot in the sunny park. It is a reminiscence of Agnes's joyous day with her sisters and Anna. The sisters, dressed in white gowns, with Anna in grey, share a startling moment of grace in the warmly lit park of the manor.

While there are a variety of possible themes to explore in relation to *Cries and Whispers*, my analysis will primarily focus on the magnified female faces consumed by the fades to red and their value as iconoclastic *eikones*. Existing scholarly analyses discuss a cluster of topics: there is the idea, supported by Bergman himself (1977), of the female characters as representing different aspects of Bergman's mother (Cohen 1993, 249; Cowie 1992, 277; Gado 1986, 409–22; Sitney 1989), the possible interpretations of the dreamlike sequence of Agnes's resurrection (Hubner 2007, 108–16; Törnqvist 1996, 157–58), the analogy between Christ and Agnes (Cohen 1993, 257–60; Gado 1986, 409, 416–19; Kalin 2003, 134–41, 145; Törnqvist 1996, 153) and the significance of the extensive presence of the colour red in both mise-en-scène and editing (Cohen 1993, 250–51; Kalin 2003, 147–49; Misek 2010, 63–64; Törnqvist 1996, 149; Venzi 2013).

One of the most examined sequences is that of Agnes's resurrection, which incorporates some of Bergman's stylistic and thematic concerns. While establishing a parallel between Agnes and Christ as both *agni Dei* (Kalin 2003, 134–62; Törnqvist 1996, 146–59), the scene also provides a lyrical blurring of reality and illusion through its style. Laura Hubner (2007) considers the scene's contradictory status of a dream which is stylistically shot as if it were real – it is, in fact, shot in the same manner as the previous flashback sequences. According to Hubner, the opposition between content and style contributes to making Agnes's resurrection the most startling and horrific scene in a film where the boundaries between reality and hallucination are incredibly thin. However, while in her account 'this image of the corpse rising has to be seen as truly horrific' (Hubner 2007, 114), I find it instead tender and disarmingly lonely. Agnes's skeletal hands are not the brutal hands of a zombie, but a desperately poetic metaphor of the loneliness of death. It is instead the white-dominated flashback that concludes the film which consists of the most dreamlike sequence of *Cries and Whispers* because of its style and overall atmosphere. This scene is stylistically at odds with the rest of the claustrophobic, intensely red film, in which resentment and selfishness regulate most of the relationships among characters – except for that between Anna and Agnes. This concluding image of the four female characters dressed in white, harmoniously spending time together, seems a shared fantasy, or an impossible image, because of its light colours, outdoor spaces and unexpected peacefulness which are absent from the rest of the film. The white is so candid and the calm so sweet that it seems impossible for them to exist in the harshly red reality that dominates the film. As Frank Gado (1986) notes, 'this idyllic finale' is a 'gentle illusion' (421).

Indeed, while this final flashback is drenched in luminous white, the rest of the film visually reverberates in ominous red. Such colour becomes an objective correlative of the grief and pain which dominate the film and whose representation is however never obscene. The reality of the others' suffering is preserved and respected in the cries on the magnified faces and in the whispers on the red screens. Physical pain does take a visible form in Agnes's body writhing in agony, Joakim's suicide attempt and Karin's self-harm. However, the presence of the fades to red and the red screens, in which we sense that something deeply and painfully violent is invading the screen, functions as a means to safeguard the invisible and inexpressible quality of a person's interiority, thereby refusing to spectacularise suffering. The obsessive presence of the colour red – in the mise-en-scène, the fades and the monochromatic screens – and its autonomy from mimetic reproduction or conventional meaning constitute the most astonishing and innovative element of the film.

Bergman (1994) conceived of 'the color red as the interior of the soul. When I was a child, I saw the soul as a shadowy dragon, blue as smoke, hovering like an enormous winged creature, half bird, half fish. But inside the dragon everything was red' (90). Following Bergman's likening of red and soul, the red in *Cries and Whispers* has been variously connected to the character's troubled inner life as representing 'raw emotion' (Hubner 2007, 114), or 'some mood of rawness or passion or anger, some feeling of interiority' (Harcourt 1974, 252). It is also linked to blood, thereby becoming 'symbolic of the widespread physical and mental wounds' (Mosley 1981, 161), as well as 'of life but also of sacrifice, of death. It is the color of erotic love, passion' (Törnqvist 1996, 149). The close association of red and interiority leads Jesse Kalin (2003) to claim that, 'when we enter the manor at the film's beginning, we thus enter the human soul with all its mysteries' (149), while Peter Cowie (1992) elaborates on the unsettling red-feeling experience that the film elicits, paralleling 'Bergman's vision of the interior of the soul-monster [. . .] with the sensation of bloodletting that the film transmits' (280). Resonating with aspects of the philosophy of colour, Richard Misek (2010) also emphasises the totalising presence of red in the film, suggesting to 'watch the film in an unlit room with white walls, and these walls too become drenched in red' (63). That is, someone's experience of *Cries and Whispers* is likely to produce an overall red-feeling experience, even if the spectator is not having a red-representing experience (for instance, the white walls). Besides the absolute redness of the monochromatic screen and the progressive one of the fades, red objects infest the film's mise-en-scène, impregnating everything to the point that 'the film emerges from red, returns to red in the spaces between scenes, and concludes with red' (Misek 2010, 64).

What is however remarkable about *Cries and Whispers* are the fades to red, which are unusual in film, where such transitions are mainly by means of fades to black. There is something in the fades to red which goes beyond the conventional meaning of the fade as signalling a passage of time. Clearly, the fades to red in *Cries and Whispers* are associated with a passage of time, since they precede and conclude the flashbacks. However, because of the autonomy which the colour red acquires throughout the film, such fades also point to something else: a subtly violent force that surfaces on the screen. The redness seems to swell while the figurative image recedes, as if, in a blushing triggered by inner disquiet, blood was rising to the surface of the screen. Thus conceived, the fade to red assumes an iconoclastic value, troubling the spectator's look, as opposed to the more widespread conventional sense of the fade to black. Luca Venzi (2013) observes:

> In the first case [fade to black], spectators read the black as a purely syntactical scan and fill in, without disorientation, the absence of image confronting them: what they encounter is a discursive convention rather than a visual transformation; in the second case [fade to colour], the spectators' capacity to detect a discursive note in the film, which the film is continuously asking them, has to be replaced by the fact that a figurative image has gradually become a colour. (62–63)

Venzi goes on to briefly outline the use of the fade to red in *Cries and Whispers* as that which destroys the figurative image, concretely manifesting 'the wide, amorphous lump of a suffering not fully representable' (68). Similarly, Cohen (1993, 250) dwells on the film's fades to red and their violent character. The fade to red both tries to give visibility to a hidden, brutal impulse and challenges the spectator's look through the sudden destruction of figuration. Tied to a disquieted interiority, which arises in its unfigurability in the red screens, the colour red concretely dismantles figurative shots, producing iconoclastic *eikones*. Furthermore, the fade to red replaces the figurative facial close-up of female characters with the iconoclastic close-up of their tormented interiority. What we experience in the red's swelling is an inner life, with its demons and unilluminated corners, slowly emerging on the surface of the screen.

From Iconophilic Icon to Iconoclastic Eikōn

While there are numerous fades to red in the film, I will primarily consider those which precede and follow the flashbacks, because these transitions, where faces crumble in a red screen, concretely illustrate the passage from the iconophilic icon to the iconoclastic *eikōn*. In these fades to red, we pass from the moving image as iconophilic icon – the facial close-up – to the moving image as iconoclastic *eikōn* – the red monochromatic screen. As in Jean Epstein's ([1921] 1977) and Béla Balázs's ([1945] 1970, 52–88; [1924] 2010, 38–45, 100–11) accounts, in which the face in the close-up is that through which interiority surfaces on an exterior, visible means, the facial close-ups in *Cries and Whispers* attempt to convey something of a person's inner life. Concurrently, however, this possibility is partially negated by the fades to red which dismantle the figurative shot, giving rise to iconoclastic *eikones*: the intensely red screens. Sound similarly remarks on language's failure to express a human being's inner state. Thus, we pass from the cries on the magnified faces to the whispers on the red screens; in both cases, we are confronted with sounds which ultimately remain indecipherable.

The status of the film's disquieted interiorities, their being beyond figurative representation and intelligible expression, is directly linked to suffering, which constitutes that place of our interiority where we never go back easily. *Cries and Whispers* is a film of decomposing faces apt for a non-representational rendering of physical pain and inner suffering. From the film's inception, close-ups of Agnes's face contorted in a grimace of pain, followed by her literally writing and underlining that she is in pain, fill the screen. Physical pain recurs also through Joakim's stabbing and Karin's mutilation. However, pain in the film is not solely physical, but includes emotional pain to which none of the main characters is immune – from the most superficial of Maria's disappointment for her unfulfilled desire for David, over Karin's failed attempts to face her deepest emotions, to Anna's grief for her daughter. Being a film on pain, it is also a film on empathy and its absence. Empathy is here intended in its etymological meaning of 'to suffer with' and refers to an individual's capacity to find in themselves that place of sorrow which enables them to suffer with someone else; namely, to imaginatively share the pain of others. Robert Sinnerbrink (2016) observes that 'empathy is *feeling with*' (92) another person and consists in 'the capacity to imaginatively adopt the other's perspective [. . .] from a first-person point of view' (93). In her thorough account of film and empathy, Jane Stadler (2017) also stresses the relevance of 'moral imagination' together with 'embodied resonance' (325) in empathic processes and delineates how narrative and stylistic cues can attune us to others' emotional state. For instance, cinematic close-ups, both visual and aural, can cognitively and affectively move us, move something in us, through the powerful encounter with a magnified face or sound of the other which invests our eyes or ears. In *Cries and Whispers*, in addition to the narrative and the giant facial close-ups, also the non-representational red screen insistently urges spectators to confront the other's pain, inviting to an empathic effort. The empathy which the film encourages is uncomfortable, because it demands us to affectively imagine someone else's pain through a resonance with the pain that we ourselves may have experienced, without however reducing the other's suffering to our own. That is, the empathy we may feel for these characters is disconcerting, also because the pain which is surfacing on the screen is not our pain.

Cries and Whispers shows a wide spectrum of behaviours towards others, from Agnes's unworldly compassion to Fredrik's complete inability to feel with others. Agnes is physically in pain because of her cancer and emotionally capable of empathising with others. Anna utterly empathises with Agnes, yet she seems unable to understand or relate to Karin's suffering, refusing to forgive her after being slapped. The late mother blissfully spends time with Maria, reserving a cold and un-empathic attitude to Agnes as a child. Maria and Karin both lack empathy and recoil at Agnes's imploration of love during the resurrection scene. However, while Karin is at least practical when it comes to Agnes's illness, Maria is visibly uncomfortable in front of Agnes's physical pain. Finally, David does not hesitate to humiliate Maria both in the present and in the past, and Fredrik is selfishly indifferent to everybody. Therefore, to the exclusion of Agnes, who is a true sacrificial *agnus Dei*, a general inability to empathise affects all the characters at different levels: more clearly Fredrik, David and Maria, who is not afraid of physically touching because she remains at the epidermal surface of things, as well as Karin, who abhors being touched because she understands its profundity, and Anna, who can empathise with Agnes but 'refuses even to make a gesture or an attempt to recognise what Karin feels or see how wounded she is' (Kalin 2003, 141).

Agnes, Maria and Karin are the most fascinating characters because of their painfully conflicted interiority, the complexity of their personality and the intensity of their facial close-ups. The face in the close-up as iconophilic icon – namely, the figurative image of the face as that which can reveal something of a person's interiority – recurs throughout the film. According to Irving Singer (2009), *Cries and Whispers*, like other Bergman's films, 'rel[ies] extensively upon close-ups of faces that disclose what is happening in a character's innermost feelings' (83). The characters' tormented inner life undoubtedly surfaces in the facial close-ups through the often-subtle epidermal changes of expression; however, the film also acknowledges the limits of the figurative representation of interiority. The facial close-ups which plunge into a red screen are symptomatic of the impossibility to figuratively reveal such 'innermost feelings'. Bergman searches the magnified faces which, by means of progressive changes in the expression, convey a sense of the character's inner state. However, a person's inner suffering eventually remains beyond mimetic reproduction.

The Face as Icon

Cries and Whispers is rife with close-ups of faces, and each of these close-ups does express something about the character, thereby constituting what

Figure 7.1 Close-up of Agnes in pain

can be addressed as iconophilic icon. The facial close-up as iconophilic icon is present from the beginning of the film when we are first introduced to Agnes (Figure 7.1). Agnes's face writhing in pain, her eyes closed tight, the mouth curved into an excruciating grimace and the head slowly turning in distress, as if looking for some solace somewhere, effectively disclose the character's state. Here, an internal, invisible pain surfaces in the exteriority of the face and offers itself to viewers. In much the same manner, the moving image concluding the film before the last pouring of red is a close-up of Agnes's serene face during a moment of grace. Such peacefulness is enhanced by its being at odds with Agnes's aching face in the rest of the film; on this peaceful face, which seems more angelic than terrestrial, we read the serenity of her soul.

Maria's facial close-ups also disclose something about her character. Her uncomfortable smirks and unrested eyes give a glimpse into her nervous beguilement and overall shallowness: she shuns seriousness and seemingly cannot focus on anything but for a fleeting moment. In her flashback, there is a mirror scene which at once affirms and negates the possibility of expressing a person's interiority through the exteriority of the face. Maria and David are reminiscing about the past when David puts her in front of a mirror. With Maria's face occupying most of the frame in an extreme close-up (Figure 7.2), David starts listing the almost imperceptible changes that have occurred on her face as evidence of her inner alterations:

Figure 7.2 Extreme close-up of Maria and David in front of the mirror

>DAVID: I want you to see that you've changed. Now you cast rapid, calculating sidelong glances. You used to look directly, openly, undisguisedly. Your mouth, once soft, has an expression of discontent and hunger. Your complexion is pallid, you use make-up. Your fine, broad forehead now has four wrinkles above each eyebrow. You can't see them in this light, but you can in daylight. Do you know where they come from?
>MARIA: No.
>DAVID: Indifference, Maria.
>[David's lower face, primarily his lips, enters the frame beside Maria's face]
>DAVID: And this fine contour, from ear to chin-point, is no longer so implicit. It shows that you're easy-going and indolent. Look here, at the nostrils: why do you sneer so often? You sneer too often; do you see, Maria? Beneath your eyes the sharp, barely visible wrinkles of boredom and impatience.
>MARIA: Can you see all that?
>DAVID: No, but I feel it when you kiss me.

Throughout the scene, Maria's expression, at first curiously amused, slowly changes into an uncomfortable smile. We follow David's account while searching Maria's face for these signs. And we see them. We notice the faint wrinkles, we become aware of the make-up covering her cheeks. The micro movements of Maria's face, which allow for her inner state to become visible, recall Balázs's physiognomy and Epstein's *photogénie*. As if following Balázs's claims about the power of physiognomy to disclose a character's emotions, or Epstein's account of the close-up as that which augments our knowledge of the magnified reality, Maria's continuous and subtle changes of expression from an apparent self-confident smile to a self-conscious smirk reveals her uneasiness at David's words. However, Bergman investigates the limits of this epidermal, cognitive enhancement throughout the film. In this scene, the faith in the facial close-up as that which discloses a person's interiority is verbally dismissed. David cannot read this inner state on Maria's face, but he can feel it when they kiss. While formally Ullmann's face remains to dominate the frame, the facial close-up as iconophilic icon is partially negated by David's words; thus, interiority seems to resist mimetic rendering even in the presence of figuration.

Finally, Karin's facial close-ups are soaked in intense distress; in a way, they complement Agnes's: while the latter's close-ups are mainly expressions of a physical pain, the former's give a visible shape to an emotional suffering. From the extreme close-up of her face in doleful bewilderment introducing her flashback (Figure 7.3), over her face smeared with blood, to that following an attempt at intimacy with Maria, Karin's close-ups reveal her status as wounded beast. Shortly after Karin's flashback, there is a sequence for the most part composed of facial close-ups and extreme close-ups against a red wall, which displays a first failed attempt at a more profound bond between Karin and Maria. The two sisters look for each other, Maria tenderly caressing Karin, who at first refuses to be touched before dolefully abandoning herself to the caresses. It seems as if an emotional bond has been established. But suddenly Karin jumps away from Maria with a desperate cry, throwing herself against the wall. Her cries act as a counterpart of Agnes's: there, it is a physical pain devouring the character; here, it is an emotional suffering trying to find an outflow. On Karin's face, where everything is deformed by a profound and sharp anguish, we read her soul's disquietude. While she relentlessly repeats 'don't touch me', first in a cry, then in whispers, her face slowly disappears, swallowed by a fade to red.

The Becoming Red of the Face

Indeed, the sisters' facial close-ups as iconophilic icons are, in some instances, consumed by fades to red. In the fades to red and in the red screens which follow, interiority is denied a figurative form. Something interior can be expressed in the face, but there always remains something else which is impossible to mimetically bring to the surface. Thus, the fade to red progressively covers what is figurative, and the soul – Bergman's red – invades the screen. The subtle yet palpable violence of the monochromatic screen is also enhanced by other reds which occur throughout the film: first and foremost, the red of blood – of Joakim, who stabs himself and bleeds onto his white shirt; of Karin, who cuts her vagina and then rubs blood on her sadly satisfied face. It is also the red of the suffocating house, which itself seems to be bleeding, and the dark red of the wine that stains the candid sheet. It is, therefore, a violent, intense red, tied to destructive impulses – not a red belonging to a soul at rest, but the colour of a disquieted interiority.

Given that, in Bergman's view, red is the colour of the soul, the fade to red can be read as a fade to the soul, the soul surfacing on the red monochromatic screen. As such, the soul is at once that which can transpire from the changes of expression occurring on a face and that which remains, at least partially, unrepresentable in mimetic terms. Cinema's failure to figuratively express a person's interiority is rendered both visually and aurally: the red monochromatic screen bears witness to that which lies beyond mimetic reproduction and intelligible words. Thus, whispers accompany the red screens without articulating the clear meaning that intelligible sentences have. *À propos* of *Cries and Whispers*, Bergman (1994) states: 'Words will ultimately become meaningless, and the behavior will be out of sync; illogical forces that one cannot account for will come into play' (89). While in quotidian, social life individuals are most often expected to live according to logic, as the characters in the film strive to do, interiority follows its own, not necessarily logical laws of desire. Words, like figurative images, fail to express such inner life. Echoing Bergman's account of language, Törnqvist (1996) explains: 'Bergman distrusts language as a means of establishing contact. On the contrary, he maintains, language is normally used to build walls between people behind which they may hide' (15). The characters in *Cries and Whispers* do not establish a profound bond through words, and the most powerful scenes in which they manage to express something about their troubled interiority occur without words being spoken. Cohen (1993) remarks: 'Bergman knows that words cannot convey what humans feel or what feelings do' (258–59). Thus, we hear evocative whispers in the transitions from a face to a red screen, which hint at both something obsessively tormenting the character and the possibility of a sincere emotional bond beyond the misunderstandings brought by words.

Moreover, in the fade to red transitions, there is the passage from an image as iconophilic icon to an image as iconoclastic *eikōn*. We first see a facial close-up that augments our knowledge of the character, and then we are confronted with an image beyond mimesis; we hear whispers, at times accompanied by stifled cries and the tolling of a bell. The extreme facial close-up being decomposed by the fade to red thus exhibits the very process of destruction of the icon

(Figures 7.3–5). What is most striking in terms of iconoclasm in *Cries and Whispers* is the fact that we see the process of the un-making of the giant faces, not only the result. That is, an iconoclastic *eikōn* is concretely produced before the spectator's eyes. Most importantly, cinema can show this process because of its being movement. As Balázs ([1945] 1970) had realised,

> the filming of colours in movement [. . .] could open up a vast domain of human experience which could not find expression in any other art, least of all in painting. For a painter may paint a flushed face but never a pale face slowly being warmed to rose-red by a blush; he can paint a pale face but never the dramatic phenomenon of blanching. (242)

A monochromatic painting, for instance, can only display the result of destruction, but not how something has been progressively destroyed. Cinema, instead, can film how a face gradually vanishes into colour. In Bergman's film, we first see a figurative, magnified face, and we can almost 'taste the [character's] tears' *à la* Epstein ([1921] 1977, 13); then, progressively, tragically, we witness the decomposition of this face, its slowly dissolving into a red screen. The showing of this process also attests that, while a face can expose something of a person's interiority, inner life exceeds our capacity to give it a fully figurative and intelligible form. Interiority and intimate suffering cannot be exhausted by mimetic images or comprehensible words because they also comprise an inexpressible part, which nonetheless exists and demands to be acknowledged as such. This is what takes place in the transitions to and from the flashbacks, and more generally in the fades to red. It is here where the inherently cinematic force of *Cries and Whispers* rests: not only do we see an iconoclastic image (the red screen), but we also witness the process of destruction of iconophilic icons and of production of iconoclastic *eikones*. In front of our eyes, a figurative shot crumbles because of the unbridgeable gap that separates it from its referent.

The magnified faces decomposed by the fades to red are icons shattered into red fragments; then the fragments recompose themselves into a red screen. Introducing Maria's and Karin's flashbacks, as well as Anna's dream, we see an enigmatic, vivid close-up of one of the female characters: Maria's lips forming a self-conscious smirk, her eyes incapable of settling on anything; Karin's straight look, her eyes and mouth wide open in fear, before she shuts them in sorrow and resignation (Figures 7.3–5); and Anna's blank expression, as if incapable of having thoughts of her own. Then, each time, the red swallows the sisters' troubled faces and Anna's inscrutable face, and the screen becomes a red monochrome. Each face offers a fleeting glimpse into the character's interiority – we can

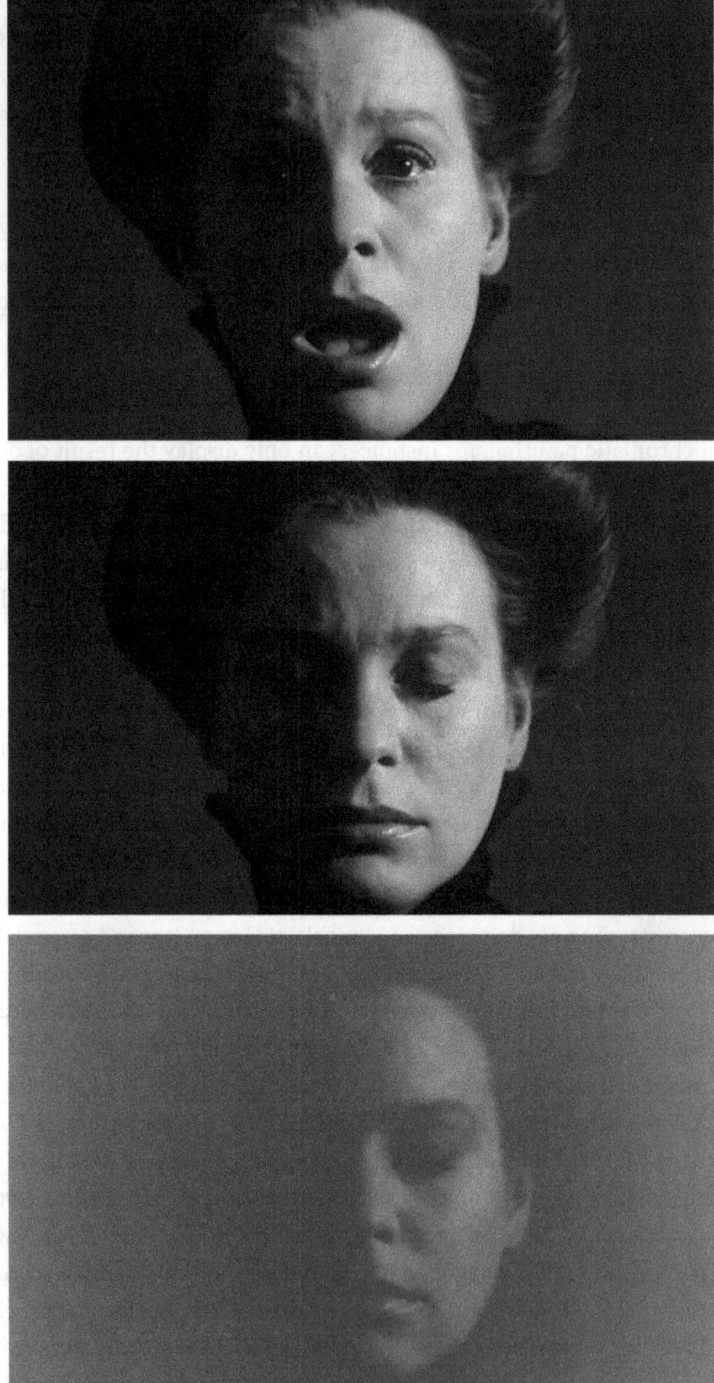

Figures 7.3 to 7.5 From Karin's facial close-up to the fade to the red screen

almost feel Maria's discomfort, Karin's emotional wounds and Anna's saintly devotion. But we can only gain access to a minuscule fragment of their doleful state, which remains beyond visual or aural representation. The fades to red and the red screens which intermittently interrupt the narrative, thereby destroying figurative shots, as well as the whispers accompanying them, express the failure to audio-visually represent a person's inner life. These monochromatic red screens qualify as iconoclastic *eikones* for they are the iconoclastic close-ups of that which is viscerally private and unrepresentable. Ultimately, interiority – with all its demons and desires – is located beyond mimesis, in a blinding vision of red surrounded by wistful whispers.

Concluding Remarks

Cries and Whispers displays the very process of destruction of the icon and production of iconoclastic *eikōn* through the female faces first consumed by the red and then hesitantly reconstructed from the red. In an exclusively cinematic manner, a movement from the iconophilic icon to the iconoclastic *eikōn* is produced via colour: from a figurative face on which something interior reveals itself to a monochromatic red screen where the unrepresentable face of the soul appears. The depiction of the others' suffering, always in danger of falling into obscenity, is respected in these movements from a restless face to a red screen; and in the unfolding of such process, we read at once the possibility to evoke something on a face and the insufficiency of mimetic images to account for a person's intimate suffering. The face, and particularly the female face, qualifies as a privileged site for both the sacralisation and destruction of the image, for the face is the most emotionally charged part of the human body. Kieślowski's film, the analysis of which concludes this book, similarly produces a dismantling of the female face via an iconoclastic usage of colour and fades, echoing Marian iconography in that it binds the feminine to the maternal and sorrow, as well as an iconoclastic tradition fearful of the Holy Mary icon.

8   Blocks of Suffering: Krzysztof Kieślowski's *Three Colours: Blue*

KRZYSZTOF KIEŚLOWSKI HAS explored in cinema the boundaries between what can be figuratively shown and what does not have a visible equivalent in phenomenal reality. Profoundly interested in intimate stories in both documentary and fiction, he concluded his film-making career with a trilogy that investigates, through the extremely physical medium of film, ideals and concepts that pertain to the domain of metaphysics. This chapter focuses on the first film of the trilogy, *Three Colours: Blue* (*Trois Couleurs: Bleu*, 1993), which is a narrative, overall figurative film four times interrupted by fades to black. My contention is that these four fade-outs constitute iconoclastic *eikones* because they are a visible negation of mimetic reproduction in the face of an unfigurable and uncognisable grief.

As in Ingmar Bergman's film, in Kieślowski's, too, the dismantling of the mimetic image occurs on the face of the female character, recalling the Christian iconoclastic tradition which targeted, among others, icons representing Holy Mary. The face of the grieving mother is also a significant motif in Marian iconography, in which womanhood is primarily understood as motherhood and inextricably tied to suffering (Mondzain 2013, 187–231). Thus, throughout *Three Colours: Blue*, there is an interplay of the face as that which allows emotions to surface and an iconoclastic refusal to render maternal sorrow an accessible, uncomplicated image. In the four fade-outs, spectators see what the protagonist's feel: a grief beyond thoughts or figurative images.

This chapter first introduces some ideas on the Western concept of the face, engaging with its representation in the cinematic close-up and in Marian iconography. It then provides an overview of Kieślowski's shift from documentary to fiction since it had to do with the ethical risk of mimetically recording another person's intimacy. The forsaking of documentary, which originated from questions regarding the possibility of filming everything, brings Kieślowski to explore in fiction the tension between cinema's ability to visually represent that which cannot be seen, and its ultimate insufficiency attested by the presence of undecipherable images in his films. The investigation of such a strain is at the centre of *Three Colours: Blue*, a film caught between the aestheticism of mimetic images and the blankness of monochromatic screens. The thread that ties this chapter together thus concerns the limits of mimetic representation and the ethical implications of showing the intimate suffering of others.

Notes on the Western Concept of Face

The Western concept of face is dense with meaning and has undergone various semantic shifts throughout history. Camille Chamois, Daphné Le Roux and Benjamin Levy (2012) identify some of the main shifts and define the face as a 'semiotic construction'; namely, as something that constitutes itself through culture and changes meaning accordingly, rather than as a natural given. An essential shift in the Western interpretation of the face occurred in the seventeenth century when 'the face is not anymore the effect of an external impression but becomes the place of revelation of a peculiar interiority' (Chamois et al. 2012). That is, the face became the place for the revelation of the soul (*âme*), although it was characterised by an essentially one-way movement from interiority to exteriority, rather than an interchange between the two dimensions. Another important change took place in the nineteenth century when the face configured itself as dual: it was at once the place for the expression of individuality and the manifestation of a type (Chamois et al. 2012). The face was that which not only allowed individuality to surface through facial expressions, but also permitted the often-harmful categorisation of human beings into different types.[1] Then, at the beginning of the twentieth century the face, albeit maintaining its duality, shifted from individuality-type to interiority-exteriority, or individuality-universality. The face, thus, becomes the locus where the universal and the particular meet, an interpretation that can be found in Jean Epstein's ([1921] 1977) and Béla Balázs's ([1924] 2010) accounts; their engagement with the facial close-up maintains an iconophilic quality given by the correspondence between an invisible inner life and its visual surfacing on the magnified face.

Both Epstein's and Balázs's work on the cinematic close-up have a mystical tone that intersects with an idealistic perspective which conceives of the face as a totality belonging to a complete being. While Balázs identifies as facial close-up primarily the human face and its micro movements, Epstein recognises any object of a close-up as belonging to the category of face, including landscapes, body parts and inanimate objects. Through the notions of *photogénie* and physiognomy, they develop a religious vocabulary of the face in film and a theory of the cinematic close-up as that which allows for an enhanced knowledge of reality. Epstein expands on Louis Delluc's concept of *photogénie*, maintaining its ambiguity. Delluc ([1920] 1985) vaguely presents '*photogénie* [. . . as] the agreement between cinema and photography' (36) and develops it as a somewhat mysterious rite between a referent and the film medium. There are things which are photogenic in themselves (such as the flesh or light-coloured eyes [53]), but an agreement between objects and the film medium is required for *photogénie* to occur (56, 59). Likewise, Epstein ([1926] 2012) defines as 'photogenic any aspect of things, beings, or souls whose moral character is enhanced by filmic reproduction' (293). Despite the vagueness of definitions, both theorists stress *photogénie*'s essential capacity of enhancing aspects of phenomenal reality. *Photogénie* thus expresses a correspondence between the qualities of an object/person and the properties of the cinematic medium; that is, it bespeaks 'an accordance between reality [. . .] and its representation' (Carluccio 1992, 59). Described as such, *photogénie* would be a property of specific objects and beings that the film medium can record and reveal but is unable to create from scratch. It remains ambiguous insofar as it is a quality belonging to certain phenomenal referents – not everything can be photogenic – that cinema can make visible (or more visible).[2]

In this scenario, the close-up is that which increases the photogenic aspect of living things and inanimate objects by virtue of its dimension, thereby producing a sensory and cognitive magnification. Enlarged on the screen, the object of the close-up intensifies the viewer's perception of that portion of reality, establishing a close link between spectator and phenomenal world. Epstein ([1921] 1977) outlines the overwhelming power of the close-up to display and amplify emotions as follows:

> The close-up modifies the drama by the impact of proximity. Pain is within reach. If I stretch out my arm I touch you, and that is intimacy. I can count the eyelashes of this suffering. I would be able to taste the tears. Never before has a face turned to mine in that way. Ever closer it presses against me, and I follow it face to face. It's not even true that there is air between us; I consume it. It is in me like a sacrament. Maximum visual acuity. The close-up limits and directs the attention. As an emotional indicator, it overwhelms me. I have neither the

right nor the ability to be distracted. (13)

The close-up has the capacity to bring onto the epidermal surface of the face an inner life which affectively addresses the viewer. As a secular sacrament, it opens a new dimension of reality, positing itself as a visible mediator between interiority and exteriority.

Similarly, Balázs discusses the revelatory power of cinema and the emotional amplification produced by the close-up, focusing on the notion of physiognomy. This concept refers to cinema's capacity to reveal the multi-faceted dimension of human beings through the continuous changes of facial expressions. The body and its movements convey inner life and, by virtue of cinema and the magnification of the close-up, 'the whole of mankind is now busy relearning the long-forgotten language of gestures and facial expressions' (Balázs [1924] 2010, 10). Like Epstein, Balázs conceives of the close-up as a mediator between the individual and the universal and emphasises its capacity to unconceal a forgotten, hidden life. At the core of this renewed visibility there is the gesture, even the almost imperceptible movement of the face's skin. Inner life, to become visible, needs to acquire a corporeal form in the facial expression which takes the form of a proper revelation in the magnification of the close-up: 'close-ups are often dramatic revelations of what is really happening under the surface of appearances' (Balázs [1945] 1970, 56). The face in the close-up visually expresses inner transformations and manifests a human essence, configuring itself as a place for the interchange between an individual inner life and a universal external dimension.

Delluc, Epstein and Balázs often employ a quasi-liturgical vocabulary in their discussions of the facial close-up (for instance, their consistent yet vague use of the terms 'soul' and 'revelation'), which is indicative of the influence of Christianity on the Western concept of face and therefore on Western accounts of the face in the cinematic close-up. The recourse to a religious, primarily Christian, lexicon is also distinctive of Gilles Deleuze and Félix Guattari's (1987, 167, 172, 176–79, 182) argument on the face and is found in scholars commenting on these primary sources (Aumont 2003, 134, 145; Dalle Vacche 2003, 15; Grespi 2013, 41–42, 46–47; Turvey 1998, 35). Barbara Grespi (2013) poignantly observes that 'the Christological icon [. . .] is fundamental for the entire path of sacralisation of the filmic image' (46), because the concept of face in Western culture is profoundly linked to Christ's face and Christ as face. Christianity represents one of the main cultural roots of Western Europe and has exercised its influence also through the sacred icon of Christ. The Christological icon is significant not only for iconophilic approaches to the cinematic close-up but also for non-iconophilic accounts, which maintain the reference to the face of

Christ and Christ as the quintessential Western face (see, for example, Deleuze and Guattari 1987, 176–84).

Indeed, an important aspect concerning the Western notion of face is its link with religion, primarily that of the Old and New Testament, found in, among others, Georg Simmel's ([1901] 1959, 276–81) and Emmanuel Levinas's (1969) analyses, which have considerably influenced film studies. Simmel ([1901] 1959, 278–79) attributes the process by which the face is associated with the expression of the soul to Christianity, since it promoted the chaste covering of the body, leaving the face as the only unveiled body part. As such, the face became that which allowed for an exchange between the individual and others; namely, it came to constitute the primary and most immediate tool for social interaction. In Simmel's perspective, as in the iconophilic interpretation of the cinematic close-up, the face is a means for reciprocating the other's gaze and for revealing the soul – a quite positive understanding which hinges on Simmel's overall conception of the face as belonging to a complete being, which is far from the fragmented subjectivity of the post-World War II period. While also in Levinas's account (1969) the face becomes the tool for the encounter with the other, the meaning of this encounter radically changes, assuming an iconoclastic quality reminiscent of the Biblical ban on any graven image (see Chapter 5).

While less often discussed, the face of Holy Mary in the icon has also influenced Western depictions and understandings of images. In binding motherhood to suffering, Marian iconography reworks the troublesome issue of maternal sorrow. Marie-José Mondzain (2013) explores the relevance of the mother for Christian and later Western conceptualisations of images, claiming that 'the mother, phantasmatic site of original fusion, was the most dreaded figure by the adversaries of the image' (190). In her fascinating study, Mondzain traces how Holy Mary's relation to the incarnation has been rendered as a relation with death. While God the father assumes a super-sensible function, that of the mother is grounded in the sensible; namely, to give God a carnal, hence perishable body. Accordingly, 'without woman God cannot make himself visible. But, if he becomes visible through her, he also becomes mortal' (Mondzain 2013, 197). Thus, the incarnation brings about the mother's and Christ's sorrow; that is, Christ suffers on the cross because of his mortal body given to him by the mother. After the resurrection, the mother and her grief no longer have a place in the Scriptures; such unbearable sorrow instead becomes the subject of plastic arts from the eleventh century: 'it is up to art alone to make her visible, problematic icon of an idolatrous moment' (Mondzain 2013, 203).

There is indeed a strand of Marian iconography which focuses on Holy Mary's maternal, incommensurable grief: the more explicit Our Lady of Sorrows and the Virgin of the Passion types, as well as the Eleousa icon, in which the mother's grief for her son's death is tragically experienced proleptically.[3] In *Three Colours: Blue*, the mimetic depiction of maternal sorrow is set in tension with its figurative cancellation. The face is an exterior surface capable of expressing something of a person's inner state; however, when grief becomes most acute, the protagonist's painful interiority is visually rendered through an anti-mimetic form. Like with Bergman, so with Kieślowski, too, the female face is the target of figurative destruction; here, however, the iconoclastic gesture is directed towards not only a female face, but a mother's face (Julie [Juliette Binoche] suffers insofar as she is a mother who no longer has a living daughter). While Christian iconophilia figuratively celebrates the *mater dolorosa*, Kieślowski's film uses monochromatic screens to render too sharp a grief. Such grief refuses mimesis because it refuses a form which could – visually and metaphorically – contain it.

From Real Tears to Glycerine

Kieślowski began his career as a documentarist filming a Polish social reality foreclosed by official media. His documentaries mainly focus on the lives of individuals 'working for, or fighting against, State institutions' (Andrew 1998, 13), such as factory workers or surgeons on exhausting shifts. Polish politics and social issues play an essential role in Kieślowski's documentary oeuvre since they shape the lives of individuals, thereby determining their choices. Such an attention to the socio-political climate continues in his early Polish fiction films, where the context influences and interferes with the lives of the characters. In his later European co-productions, however, explicit socio-political issues are placed in the background of highly intimate stories, which follow emotionally fragmented female characters.

The passing from documentary to fiction and from Polish fictional films to European co-productions has triggered various readings, which range from interpreting this shift as an abandonment of political engagement in favour of metaphysical dilemmas (Haltof 2004, 108–14; Sobolewski 1999) to understanding it as a continuation of Kieślowski's attention to individuals and their quotidian struggles (Andrew 1998, 13–14; Coates 1999, 32–53; Reyland 2012, 81–89). Slavoj Žižek (2001b, 72) proposes a compelling interpretation which identifies Kieślowski's forsaking of documentary for fiction as primarily ethical, and Kieślowski's own account of his turning to fiction lends itself to such a reading:

> *Not everything can be described.* That's the documentary's great problem. It catches itself as if in its own trap. The closer it wants to get to somebody, the

more the person shuts him or herself off from it. And that's perfectly natural. It can't be helped. If I'm making a film about love, I can't go into a bedroom if real people are making love there. If I'm making a film about death, I can't film somebody who's dying because it's such an intimate experience that the person shouldn't be disturbed. And I noticed, when making documentaries, that the closer I wanted to get to an individual, the more the subjects which interested me shut themselves off. That's probably why I changed to features. There's no problem there. I need a couple to make love in bed, that's fine. Of course, it might be difficult to find an actress who's willing to take off her bra, but then you just find one who is. Somebody's supposed to die. That's fine. In a minute, he'll get up again. And so on. I can even buy glycerine, put some drops in her eyes and the actress will cry. I managed to photograph some real tears several times. It's something completely different. But now I've got glycerine. I'm frightened of those real tears. In fact, *I don't know whether I've got the right to photograph them. At such times I feel like somebody who's found himself in a realm which is, in fact, out of bounds.* That's the main reason why I escaped from documentaries. (Kieślowski, quoted in Stok 1993, 86; my emphasis)

Kieślowski's abandonment of documentary seems to be responding more to an ethical urgency rather than a will to exclude politics and social issues from his work. The director questions the rightfulness of recording and reproducing real, highly intimate experiences such as sex, death and sorrow. He does not, however, renounce the filming of fictional experiences – we are, for instance, shown Weronika's (Irène Jacob) death on a stage, and Véronique and Julie making love and crying, in *The Double Life of Véronique* (*La Double Vie de Véronique*, Krzysztof Kieślowski, 1991) and *Three Colours: Blue*, respectively. Elaborating on the above quote, Žižek (2001b) inquires: 'How, then, is Kieślowski's ban on real tears related to the Old Testament ban on images?' (74). The philosopher concludes that Kieślowski's fictional works are characterised by an aesthetics in contrast to the dictates of Christian iconoclasm:

> Kieślowski seems to share the Old Testament injunction to withdraw the domain of what really matters from degrading reality. However, in a spirit which runs counter to Old Testament iconoclasm, he supplements the prohibition to depict intimate moments of 'real' life with, precisely, *fiction*, with 'false' images. While one should not show 'real' sex or intimate emotional moments, actors can *feign* them, even in a very 'realistic' way (as they definitely do in Kieślowski's films). (Žižek 2001b, 74)

Žižek continually opposes Kieślowski's fictional works to Christian iconoclasm for their realistic (figurative) representation of intimacy. Undoubtedly, at first glance it seems that the director has no issue in showing fictional intimacy in a decidedly mimetic manner. And yet, even in the arthouse European co-productions, where bodies are exhibited in both pleasure and pain, there is always at least one out-of-focus image, a blurred image, an undecipherable image that suspends mimesis. Above all, in *Three Colours: Blue*, via the annulling of any possible figurative image in the four black-outs, Kieślowski acknowledges that not everything can be mimetically represented, even in fiction.

One essential aspect for an understanding of Kieślowski's work as ethical is the importance given to that which cannot be seen but can only be hinted at. The director himself has stated:

> The moment something is named, the possibility of free interpretation is cut off. The moment you leave something unnamed, and leave the place of the name open, that place can be filled by anyone [. . .]. If *I* fill that space, it cannot be filled by the viewer. (Kieślowski, quoted in Coates 1999, 169)

Kieślowski neither tells nor shows it all; rather, he leaves it to the spectator to make sense of the fragmentary or missing images, encouraging through the incompleteness of form the exercise of our ethical imagination. He now has glycerine, films entwined naked bodies and shows life suddenly leaving a human being. But he never trespasses into the obscenity of the showing it all. This capacity for rendering visible – without stepping into excessive mimesis – that which pertains to the invisible sphere brings together iconoclastic reminiscences with an iconophilic approach to visibility. While issues of invisibility/unrepresentability run through Kieślowski's entire oeuvre, rendered through gaps encompassing the narrative, visual and aural levels, they are most clearly present in the *Colours* trilogy, in which 'very often everything that's most important takes place behind the scenes, you don't see it. Either it's there in the actors' play, or it isn't. Either you feel it, or you don't' (Kieślowski, quoted in Stok 1993, 216). Indeed, in the trilogy, dialogue is thinned out, at times reduced to the minimum, and images alternate mimetic clarity with out-of-focus, blurring or destruction of figuration. There are fictional tears (all three films end with one of the main characters crying), there is sex, there is death; and yet, the point remains that not everything can be filmed because 'not everything can be described'. This impasse – which concerns not only the film medium (can/should everything be filmed?), but also reality (can everything be cognised and made intelligible?) – is that which the *Colours* trilogy set to explore.

A Trilogy on Entangled Love

The *Three Colours* trilogy is a French, Polish and Swiss co-production and marks Kieślowski's last film-making efforts before his retirement. Kieślowski's long-time collaborator, Krzysztof Piesiewicz, suggested the basic idea for the trilogy; namely, exploring the ideals of the French Revolution – liberty, equality and fraternity – from an intimate, personal perspective. Accordingly, the first film, *Three Colours: Blue*, deals with personal freedom and its limits; the second, *Three Colours: White* (*Trois Couleurs: Blanc*, 1994), investigates the precarious equilibrium between individuals who are supposedly equal but practically one is more equal than the other; and the last one, *Three Colours: Red* (*Trois Couleurs: Rouge*, 1994), engages with the ways in which people can touch and positively change each other's lives through acts of kindness.

Albeit grouped in a trilogy and replete with mutual references, the three films are to be considered, in the director's words, as 'individual, [. . .] separate films' (Kieślowski, quoted in Stok 1993, 220). Each film focuses on the protagonist's personal experience of liberty (Julie in *Blue*), equality (Karol in *White*) and fraternity (Valentine in *Red*) and how these ideals intersect with the concept of love, specifically love as *agapē/ἀγάπη*. This specific type of love makes its literal appearance at the end of *Three Colours: Blue*, in the chorus sung in Ancient Greek where the word *agapē* recurs several times. In the New Testament, *agapē* primarily refers to Christ's deeds, the love of God towards humankind and God himself, therefore maintaining the meaning of a gratuitous love par excellence (see, 1 Corinthians 13:1–13; 1 John 4:8). In the *Colours* trilogy, *agapē*, free of any religious connotation, comes to signify a love which stems from 'the acceptance of others' (Žižek 2001b, 161); that is, from accepting that one cannot live far removed from the world and is inextricably entwined with the lives of others. Accordingly, Nicholas W. Reyland (2012) argues that '[t]he films propose, in their tales and their tellings, a journey one might take to live better in late-modern times: the transition from solipsistic individualism to the mutually beneficial practises of *agapē*' (3). This resonates with Žižek's (2001b) claim that 'each part of the trilogy focuses on the voyage from a certain mode of radical self-withdrawal to the acceptance of others' (161), as well as with that of Dave Kehr (1994), who observes how 'three films that seemed to have been carefully distinguished by tone, content and appearance turn out to be the same film, telling the same story of [. . .] isolation subsumed by a sense of infinite interdependence' (20). The *Colours* trilogy can, thus, be understood as an ode to love in all its subtle and peculiar manifestations. In particular, the montage coda at the end of *Three Colours: Blue* expresses the mutual entanglement which ties together the three films.

Three Colours: Blue follows Julie's life after she survives a car accident in which her husband Patrice (Hugues Quester), a famous composer, and her daughter Anna lose their lives. Consumed by grief, she sells everything and moves to a flat in Paris where nobody knows her. However, Olivier (Benôit Régent), her husband's collaborator who is desperately in love with her, finds her and tries to convince her to finish Patrice's *Concerto for a Unified Europe*. At first Julie refuses, in an attempt to shut herself from the world; but gradually she begins to establish relationships with the people around her: she befriends Lucille (Charlotte Véry), a prostitute and stripper who lives in her building, and leaves her house to Sandrine (Florence Pernel), Patrice's mistress now pregnant with his child. Slowly accepting that she cannot withdraw herself from the world, Julie finishes the *Concerto* and makes love with Olivier. The film ends with Julie finally breaking into tears, followed by an extremely evocative coda. Four shots, each showing one character who has inevitably affected Julie, are linked through fades and accompanied by a chorus sung in Ancient Greek. The lyrics are taken from Saint Paul's First Letter to the Corinthians, which proclaims the primacy of love above all things, thereby tying together the shots forming the film's coda. As Žižek (2001b, 175–78) and Tammy Clewell (2000, 204) observe, Julie's tears signal her acceptance of others. She is able to cry only after having come to terms with the fact that she cannot live without others, shutting herself from the world because of her fear of losing (and therefore suffering for) someone else again. The four consecutive shots are paired with music in B minor (a key fraught with anticipation and nostalgia), whose fragments were heard throughout the film, either played by a single or a few instruments. Now, instead, the orchestral and choral version of the *Concerto* aurally renders Julie's journey from isolation and withdrawal to entanglement and communion, conveying the lovingly painful sense that one's life is in mysterious and inextricable ways connected to the life of others.

When Blue Turns Black: A Grief Observed

A most striking feature of *Three Colours: Blue* is the presence of four fade-outs, which are visible black-outs that punctuate the otherwise figurative film, interrupting the flow of images. Anticipating and accompanying such interruptions is a funereal music which is a variation of the funeral march in G minor heard during Anna and Patrice's funeral early in the film. This ghostly music concretely overwhelms the protagonist, plummeting her into the core of her unbearable grief which takes the shape of a monochromatic black screen.

Significantly, the four black-outs occur in those moments when Julie's thought is brought to the death of her husband and daughter. However, even thought refuses to think these deaths. Thus, the four black-outs can be understood as iconoclastic *eikones* which, bearing witness to the unthinkable nature of these deaths (especially Anna's), allow for the representation of grief without making it obscene. The questions underlying the analysis concern if and how it is possible to represent in images and words such a grief: is it ethical to mimetically reproduce others' grief, and specifically a mother's grief for her child? (After all, even language lacks a term for a parent who has lost a child.) How can grief be represented without running the risk of making it obscene? To explore these issues, I will first touch on the significance of the colour blue and music as the fundamental elements for the representation of the protagonist's sorrow. I will then look at the four black-outs, spelling out their ethical value as iconoclastic representations of grief.

Although scholarly approaches and arguments may differ, existing literature nevertheless share the idea of *Three Colours: Blue* as being strongly related to the theme of mourning (Andrew 1998, 37; Clewell 2000; Haltof 2004, 129; Reyland 2012, 176; Venzi 2006, 124–29; Wilson 1998, 350; Žižek 2001b, 167). Whether the film is understood as a journey through mourning or towards mourning, it is undoubtedly centred on the protagonist's grief for the tragic loss of her husband and daughter. Throughout, Patrice is primarily embodied in music and Anna in colour, both of which are achingly melancholic; together, the musical cues and the colour blue represent the becoming audible and visible of Julie's grief.

While Ingmar Bergman's *Cries and Whispers* was bathed in red, Kieślowski's *Three Colours: Blue* is haunted by blue, from its title to its opening (blue filters, blue objects). Due also to its being a cold primary colour, blue is commonly associated with moods of melancholy and sadness (Andrew 1998, 25; Haltof 2004, 129; Reyland 2012, 111–12; Žižek 2001b, 164). In addition to this general connotation, blue in this film is profoundly linked to the past, embodied in objects that once belonged to either Patrice or Anna, thereby recurring throughout the film as a painful reminder of the past and as a visual correlative of Julie's grief. According to Luca Venzi (2006), blue is

> the most immediate and insisting symbolic-expressive manifestation of Julie's *grief* and, more generally, of the past that she obstinately tries to remove from her existence. But the past stays close to her: in *Trois couleurs: Blue* the past *preserves itself in the colour*. (128)

Through the use of blue filters and blue objects, the whole film is pervaded by this colour. Most evidently, blue is the colour of Anna's candy wrapper in the opening scene, Anna's bedroom, Anna's crystal lamp (which is the only object that Julie brings with her in the Parisian apartment), Anna's lollipop (which Julie dolefully and furiously devours), Patrice's book binders, the notes written on Patrice's musical sheets and the swimming pool where Julie takes refuge from the world. Thus, the colour blue becomes the 'indelible trace of an absence, [the] cristallisation of a lack [. . . and] of an unfillable void, [. . . as well as] the past which preserves itself and the grief which renews itself' (Venzi 2006, 128–29).

However, the four fade-outs punctuating the film are black, not blue. Venzi (2006, 125–29) proposes a convincing reading of the colour black in these four fades as an intensified blue. That is, while the fade-outs are figuratively black, they are symbolically blue and express the extreme point of grief – that in which blue turns black. Similarly, Emma Wilson (1998), quoting the abstract painter Wassily Kandinsky, argues that 'when it [blue] sinks almost to black, it echoes a grief that is hardly human' (350). In the film's economy, black can indeed be understood as an intensification of the colour blue; namely, as the point in which grief and the doleful past (blue) are so intolerably present that they become black. Defined as such, blue stands for a clotted grief located inside Julie – the four fades to black – and around her – in the omnipresent blue objects. 'Blue is the invisible becoming visible', Yves Klein (quoted in Weitemeier 2001, 19) once argued. In *Three Colours: Blue*, the painful past concretises itself in the blue objects of the mise-en-scène, and Julie's unfigurable grief becomes visible in the four blue-turned-black fade-outs.

While the blue objects mostly embody the memory of Anna, Patrice comes back through music, which is the other element haunting Julie throughout the film. Not only does music play a fundamental role in the narrative (Patrice was a composer; Olivier tries to complete the unfinished *Concerto* commissioned by the European Council; Julie completes the *Concerto*), but it is also an essential stylistic component which meta-diegetically evokes the painful past. The music, which seems to be coming from an elsewhere, de facto blurring the boundaries between diegetic and non-diegetic sound, bursts suddenly, like a fragilely dormant grief, provoking Julie's black-outs. Reyland (2012) remarks that, 'throughout *Blue*, Julie is haunted, terrified and, occasionally, beguiled by the music from the *Concert[o]* and elsewhere' (119). Whether a variation of the funeral theme or fragments from the *Concerto*, music permeates Julie's experience of reality and comes to signify the aural equivalent of the fades to black.

The four interruptions that bring back the past and its grief, plunging Julie in a state beyond words or mimetic images, are composed of fades to black, visually, and music, aurally. The music precedes, accompanies and follows the fades, thence disappearing when the scene resumes. Besides the black-outs, in which a figurative shot is destroyed, there are also two moments in which images are on the verge of disappearing. The first time occurs when Julie is at the hospital, asleep on an armchair, when suddenly the music erupts, waking her up, and the figurative shot falters under an almost-fade to blue. That is, Julie almost disappears swathed in the blue. The second time a figurative shot seems to be disappearing (now in an almost-fade to black), and yet resists such fading, occurs in the Parisian café where Julie habitually goes. Here, too, it is music which firstly threatens the image. While in the previous case the music was meta-diegetic, on this occasion it is diegetic: a mendicant outside the café plays with the flute the melody from the *Concerto* that Patrice was composing. Julie's coffee cup is traversed by black shadows that seem on the verge of swallowing it in a fade to black which, however, does not happen. Both cases display the fragility of the figurative image when confronted with the eruption of grief. In the four black-outs, however, the figurative image collapses, devoured by a blue-turned-black.

The first black-out occurs at the hospital, soon after the almost fade to blue, while Julie is watching her husband and daughter's funeral on a TV. Julie sits in an armchair, when suddenly a voice off-screen says 'Hello', and Julie turns and looks with hollow eyes at the off-screen space. The funeral music erupts with Julie's facial close-up, the scene fades to black, the screen remains black for six seconds, and then the scene resumes from the moment in which it was interrupted. Julie replies, 'Good morning', and has a quick and unpleasant exchange with a journalist who wants to exploit her tragedy. The second black-out happens when Julie meets Antoine (Yann Trégouët), the hitch-hiker who witnessed the fatal accident at the beginning of the film. He has contacted her to give her back a golden necklace which he found near the car and which belonged to Anna. Antoine asks Julie if she has any questions since he got to the car just after the accident. She replies with a blunt 'no', and the music from Patrice and Anna's funeral bursts onto screen. The scene fades to black, and the screen remains black for nine seconds, before the scene continues with Antoine asking a question to Julie regarding Patrice's last words (which, as we find out, were the conclusion of a joke he was telling Julie and Anna before the accident). The third black-out occurs in the swimming pool where Julie takes refuge from the world. Julie is swimming when she sees Lucille by the pool. Surprised to find her there, Julie swims towards her. To Lucille's question, 'Are you crying?' the music erupts, followed by a fade to black on Julie's blankly stunned face. While the screen remains black for nine seconds, 'two separate and, in both symbolic and musical sense, opposed themes are brought into conflict' (Reyland 2012, 220): the funeral march in G minor and the memento from the *Concerto* in B minor intersect. Then the scene resumes with Julie replying: 'It's the water' (Figures 8.1–4). The fourth and last black-out takes place in Olivier's apartment when Julie finds confirmation of Patrice's long-term mistress. Olivier questions Julie about her intentions now that she has found out about the adultery – and hence that Patrice was not the irreprehensible and perfect husband she had built in her head. The music from the *Concerto* erupts, and the scene blackens for eleven seconds. Then, surprisingly smiling, Julie replies: 'I'm going to meet her'.

The black-outs take place either soon after or while Julie is exposed to something regarding the past, which demands her to confront it. In the first case, it is a voice from the outside world: 'Hello' (the journalist, who knew both Julie and Patrice before the accident). In the other three cases, it is a question that anticipates the black-outs: 'If you want to ask me something . . .' (Antoine); 'Are you crying?' (Lucille); 'What are you going to do?' (Olivier). It is not solely something from the past that plunges Julie into this black stillness of time (memory only needs a sound or an image to awaken, violently), but it is also the request to confront such a past that triggers Julie's black-outs. Unable to express her grief in verbal or image form because that would be tantamount to accepting what has happened as incontrovertibly real, Julie abandons herself to thought's incapacity to deal with a reality too painful.

An Unfigurable and Ineffable Grief

Like the fades to red in Bergman's *Cries and Whispers*, the fades to black in *Three Colours: Blue* transcend the conventional function attributable to the fade – that of signalling a considerable passage of time. In Bergman, it was the fading to colour, specifically to red, which broke the traditional usage of the fade, thereby troubling the spectator's look; in Kieślowski, it is a convention – the fade to black – which is made out to be other than itself. That is, instead of signalling the passage of a substantial calculable time, the fade to black is here employed to express the stillness of experiential time of the individual in the face of grief. The fades to black in *Three Colours: Blue*, thus, represent something akin to a suspension of time: they interrupt a scene which then continues as if nothing had happened. Kieślowski himself has explained the meaning of these four fade-outs as follows:

186 | ICONOCLASM IN EUROPEAN CINEMA

Figures 8.1–8.4 The third black-out at the swimming pool

There are various fade-outs. There's the typical elliptical fade-out: time passes. A scene ends, there's a fade-out and a new scene begins. And there are four fade-outs which bring us back to exactly the same moment. The idea is to convey an extremely subjective point of view. That is, that time really does pass but for Julie, at a certain moment, it stands still. (quoted in Stock 1993, 215–16)

In the black-outs, therefore, spectators see what Julie feels. In the face of a grief which she cannot, at this point, cognise, we see Julie experiencing the shutting down of her thought. The becoming black of the image is nothing other than the intensification of the blue, with all its implications, and therefore bears witness to Julie's raw, unthinkable and unfigurable grief. The first black-out imposes itself, unfathomably, upon spectators, who experience a halt of vision and the cancellation of a figurative shot without being able to attribute a meaning to it. The repeating of the black-outs, however, allows viewers to 'comprehend that it is a colour which they see recurring in the becoming black of the image' (Venzi 2006, 127). Thus, spectators can progressively read in the destruction of the figurative shot Julie's inner state, her incommensurable grief, becoming visible.

It is no coincidence that the black-outs occur on Julie's petrified facial close-ups, something which resonates with Bergman's fades to red. Like in *Cries and Whispers*, in *Three Colours: Blue*, mimetic reproduction cannot account for the most intimate and painful states of a person. Julie never explicitly talks about her grief, only mentioning matter-of-factly her husband and daughter's death on rare occasions (with the journalist; with her mother). She might say that they are dead, but she avoids expressing how she feels or what she thinks because hers is an unspeakable and unrepresentable grief. Only in the removal of mimesis can her feeling acquire a visible form. Notwithstanding Kieślowski's claim about the lack of problems posed by fiction because actors feign, he nevertheless does not put Julie's grief into words or show her thoughts by means of figurative images. The four black-outs can thus be understood as iconoclastic *eikones* in the sense I have attributed to this term. They are, indeed, images of Julie's impossibility to cognise her grief, and they are iconoclastic because they refuse to spectacularise suffering; namely, to transform something extremely intimate into a visual spectacle. In *Three Colours: Blue*, the destruction of figurative shots by means of fade-outs is of ethical nature. The sudden fade-outs that interrupt the regular narrative flow are a way to express and respect the unrepresentability of Julie's grief, as well as a refusal to spectacularise death and grief, making them inaccessible to the world of mimetic representation. Rather than concealing the unbridgeable gap between grief and its depiction by means of figurative images and intelligible words, Kieślowski inserts four fade-outs, leaving it to the viewer to make sense of them.

According to Wilson (1998), 'this is a film caught in contradiction between representation and its refusal' (351). While making an overall figurative film, Kieślowski challenges the film medium's capacity to represent: he now has glycerine and actors who feign; yet, shots are destroyed by fades to black, and intelligible speech is replaced by a funereal, evocative music. A medium such as cinema, which is based on moving images of recorded phenomenal referents, is therefore employed to represent that which cannot be seen – a mother's grief and the memory of her dear dead ones. Kieślowski could have used figurative metaphors to illustrate Julie's mournful mind state; instead, he opts for the destruction of any figuration, turning grief/the past into one colour that covers everything. In an interview, the director commented: 'Film is very materialistic: all you can photograph, most of the time, is *things*. You can describe a soul but you can't photograph it; you have to find an equivalent. But there isn't really an equivalent' (quoted in Andrew 1998, 82). There exists a gap between certain aspects of reality and their possible representation which an iconoclastic aesthetics can make visible without rendering mimetically accessible, in this way appealing to the viewer's ethical imagination. An image of imagelessness thus replaces any figurative metaphor of grief, thereby preserving the invisible nature of that which lacks a sensible counterpart, to attest that not everything can enter the world of mimetic representation without complications.

Concluding Remarks

There is a tension, in Kieślowski's work, between cinema's capacity to mimetically reproduce reality and its ability to hint at that which does not have a phenomenal equivalent. In *Three Colours: Blue*, Julie's uncognisable grief is embodied in the blue objects of the mise-en-scène, the actress's petrified face and the funereal music; but it also finds powerful expression in the visual black-outs that allow the audience to see what she feels. The four black-outs, therefore, constitute the becoming present of a grief which cannot find a figurative form, iconoclastically displaying Julie's thought in its refusal to think about Patrice's and Anna's deaths. Accordingly, the four interruptions configure themselves as iconoclastic *eikones* insofar as they represent their unfigurable model without spectacularising it. In so doing, they also leave the spectator free to fill the gaps, imagine and attribute meaning. The negation of mimetic, self-explanatory images, thus, contributes to the creation of a 'pensive spectator' (Bellour 2012, 86) by fostering ethical imagination and providing the conditions for a communal sharing of sense.

Conclusion: A Communal Vision through Broken Images

'NO ONE EVER writes something meaningful that is not [also] a love letter' (2019, 308), Marie-José Mondzain writes. This book is my love letter to cinema, especially to its images and sounds at the edge of representability and its potential as a means for sharing complex and challenging experiences. It is also a reflection on the power of images to create or destroy a communal vision. Images can create it by hinting at that which cannot become a completely accessible image and destroy such a vision through excessive mimesis and the obscenity of the showing it all. In this scenario, iconoclasm has proven to be a particularly suitable tool for investigating the ways in which we conceive and relate to images. While historically iconoclasm carries a violently destructive drive directed against the other's point of view, in the arts it can become a stimulating, potentially ethical perspective to challenge more habitual forms of image-making and image-viewing. In positing the existence of an unbridgeable gap between an image and its model, iconoclastic stances highlight the ethical limits of artistic mimesis and the persistence of a contradictory attitude, among others, in the West: a yearning for an easily accessible representation which, however, most often ends up being interpreted as an appearance far removed from truth. Entangled in an ancient dichotomy, the contemporary image at once enjoys the status accorded to the *eikōn* and suffers the deficiencies of the *eidōlon*.

Examining a tendency which sinks its roots in ancient philosophy and medieval theology, this book has instantiated the potentialities and ethical correspondences that the cancellation of film images can have, thereby contributing to current debates on images and the technologies of vision through the fascinating prism of iconoclasm. The existence of a conflicting attitude about cinema which recalls the *eikōn-eidōlon* dichotomy constitutes the premise of this book.

Throughout, I have established an iconoclastic aesthetics of cinema that comprises various gestures and techniques, which range from the literal manipulation of the film strip to the metaphorical dismantling of film as mimetic moving images of a recorded reality. What had started as an exploration of iconoclastic acts directed towards the visual image in the cinema eventually also developed into my becoming enamoured with disruptive approaches to film sound. The films discussed, in fact, accompany a reflection on the visual image with a privileging of the aural dimension – a privileging which can develop in terms of intelligible voices to counterbalance the falsehood proper to the image, as in the works of Guy Debord, Jean-Luc Godard, Marguerite Duras and, to some extent, Isidore Isou, or it can unfold as language's failure to articulate meaning, thereby aurally paralleling the visual destruction of figuration, as in the films of Carmelo Bene, Derek Jarman, Ingmar Bergman and Krzysztof Kieślowski. Hence, the study of cinematic iconoclasm progressed as an investigation of the lacerating, intimate yet conflicted relation that the film image can establish with sound.

This iconoclastic aesthetics also carries ethical concerns, which include Isidore Isou's chiseled images against war, Guy Debord's *détourned* images of consumer society, Carmelo Bene's absurdist critique of moralist standards via a frenzy of anti-mimetic images and sounds, Jean-Luc Godard's composite images apt for the expression of the unrepresentable, Marguerite Duras's de-synchronised images of desire, and Derek Jarman's, Ingmar Bergman's and Krzysztof Kieślowski's monochromatic screens for a non-spectacular rendering of the other's suffering. In all these cases, an imaginative effort is required from spectators to overcome and make sense of the audio-visual impasse displayed in the films.

This book has also emphasised that cinema (and, in general, any visual medium) cannot account, always and in all cases, for every possible reality. While cinema should be able to consider everything, it needs, nonetheless, to match its images and sounds to its content. Accustomed to images' pervasive presence and our distracted viewing, the halting of a mimetic, accessible audio-vision that cinematic iconoclasm provokes can elicit more pensive engagements with images and can promote a taking on of responsibility in regard to the visual field – to what we allow to enter and therefore share. Issues of image-making and image-consuming go back to ancient philosophy and find one of their most forceful, literal expressions in the destruction of icons of Christ during the Byzantine controversy. Significantly, many of the iconoclastic destructions in the analysed films occur on the face – faces literally destroyed through the physical aggressions against the film strip (Isou, Debord, Bene); faces slowly plunging into blankness (Godard, Bergman, Kieślowski); visually absent faces (Duras, Jarman); faces lacerated by superimpositions (Godard).

In all these cases, iconoclasm echoes its historical roots: from Christ's icon to cinematic close-up, the face remains the privileged site for destruction.

From Christ's Icon to Film Images: A History of Destroyed Faces

This book has explored some iconoclastic approaches to cinema and cinema's ability to subvert historical iconoclasm's violently destructive force against the other into a means for reflecting on film images and their ethical potential. More specifically, the emphasis on the dichotomy between the image as *eikōn* and the image as *eidōlon* has allowed me to investigate different facets of the film image in its relationship with a model, situating the image at the centre of a web of relations: What does an image represent? Who makes film images of what? Who watches these film images?

Visual images are the object of intense debate because of their being placed within such a relational system (involving model, image, image-maker and image-consumer), which I have briefly unfolded in the Prologue. Plato's concerns about images of art as copies of a copy (Idea → sensible thing → image) and their consequent potential for deception originate from the series of relations in which the image finds itself and which involve the model, the maker of images (imitator), the image (imitation of an imitation) and the viewer. In a similar manner, the Plotinian revaluation of images, which become intermediaries between humans and the One, derives from their relational character; that is, images and the One, as well as the viewer, belong to the same realm, only at a different ontological level. However, in both Plotinus and Plato, the image is ultimately inadequate to represent intelligible models – Plato's ideas and Plotinus's the One are, in fact, beyond any possible mimetic rendering. Subsequently, the Christian theology of the image reworks Platonic and Plotinian philosophy, together with the Biblical ban on graven images and the Christian concept of the incarnation of God. As a result, a division opposes those who allow the material image to figuratively represent God to those who fully reject such a position, interpreting it as idolatrous. Therefore, the image can be an intermediary between two elements otherwise separated (*eikōn*), but it can also be inadequate, blasphemous or obscene (*eidōlon*) – a binary which persists in some contemporary Western attitudes about visual representations.

Cinema, for its being founded on moving images, is a privileged medium for the study of the image in its troublesome relationship with a referent. Cinema's original contribution to the debate on iconoclasm is its possibility of showing the very process of image destruction and not solely the result of destruction thanks to its being in motion. That is to say, cinema has always the option of temporalising the *eidōlon* and the *eikōn* and, as such, it provides a variety of devices to destroy images. Techniques such as slow-motion and freeze-frame can be used to dismantle mimetic movement; similarly, through fades, colour and monochromatic screens, cinema can display the sudden disappearance of figurative images into a monochromatic screen (an image of imagelessness). I have therefore focused my analysis on cinema's broken images – broken in their mimetic relation with a model that eschews figurative reproduction. Cinematic iconoclasm, thus, constitutes a possible answer to the modern and contemporary iconic overload so reliant on a mimetic aesthetics.

Part I centred on explicitly destructive approaches to cinema, which are reminiscent of philosophical and Christian iconoclasm in their fierce critique of the film image as deceptive copy. The cinema of Isou, Debord, Bene and Godard consists in a questioning of the film image's status, its complicity with dominant ideology and its ability to represent reality. Their iconoclastic aesthetics underlies ethico-political concerns and an overall distrust about certain self-evident, mimetic images which are understood as illusory *eidōla*. Already in the playful and anarchic spirit of Isou's *Traité de bave et d'éternité* is it possible to find defaced images expressing a condemnation of war and French foreign politics, as well as an attention to cinematic iconoclasm's potential for a refreshing relationship between film images and spectators. Political critique is the main thrust behind Debord's films, which aim at demolishing a capitalist worldview and promoting critically active forms of spectatorship via a consistent use of *détournement*. From his first to his last film, Debord subverts the images of capitalism (and consequently, also that of narrative and auteur cinema for their supposed connivance with dominant ideology), making films that are difficult to sit through because of their aesthetics of displeasure. Bene's ecstatic embracing of non-sense, which encompasses the narrative, visual and aural domains, carries out a fierce attack against society and moralism. Thus, in *Our Lady of the Turks*, aphasia and apraxia proceed to tear apart Catholic precepts, social decorum and the idea of subjectivity itself. Finally, in Godard's oeuvre, political and ethical preoccupations mingle not only to complexify those film images which reiterate a capitalist ideology, but also to interrogate cinema's ability to represent reality. In his films, a critique of the illusionism of certain film images – the *eidōla* of capitalism – is accompanied by a belief in relationships between images able to convey something about the world – the iconoclastic *eikones* of a cinema 'that can't be seen' (*Histoire(s) du cinéma*, 1988–98).

From Isou's appeal for the destruction of cinema to Godard's multi-layered images, in Part I, I have engaged with some of the most explicit stances against the film medium: 'I proclaim the destruction of cinema', Daniel/Isou argues in

Traité; 'the cinema, too, must be destroyed!' Debord insists in *Sur le passage* (1959); 'Cinema should be destroyed', Bene emphatically declares ([1970] 2011e, 60); 'let us destroy that [i.e., of the bourgeoisie] image', Godard urges in *British Sounds* (1969). What is more, through the analysis of Isou's *Traité de bave et d'éternité*, Bene's *Our Lady of the Turks* and some of Debord's and Godard's films, I have discussed the major iconoclastic devices at work in the cinema, that of the blank screen, which consists in an image of imagelessness and can qualify as a metaphor for an impossible image, altered motion, which goes against cinema's reproduction of habitual perception of movement, image-sound disjunctions, which mar the harmonious, comprehensible relation between the image track and the sound track, and the voice as *phoné*, which hinders the more traditional status of the verbal in film as that which conveys meaning.

Such disruptive aesthetic forms are also found in the films discussed in Part II, where the film image's complex relation with reality is further tested through invisible and unrepresentable referents which resist mimesis and strongly call into question the domain of ethics. Duras's *Le Navire Night* disassociates image and sound because of the threat that figuration poses to the sharing of desire; thus, the film unfolds the impossible relationship between desiring voices and desired bodies. Jarman's *Blue* articulates an utter rejection of spectacular images of persons with AIDS by means of a monochromatic ultramarine blue screen to preserve the individual experiences of the disease as irrecoverable to mimetic representation. Bergman's *Cries and Whispers* and Kieślowski's *Three Colours: Blue* insert sudden audio-visual hiatuses in their overall figurative fabric to render the otherwise unrepresentable experience of suffering. In all these cases, mimesis results insufficient to represent the others' emotional life without running the risk of producing an obscene representation.

In Part II, I have paid particular attention to the ethical value of iconoclastic *eikones*, arguing for an ethics of (in)visibility that such images encourage. It is an ethics of both image-making and image-viewing which insists on the importance of interrogating our complicity in the construction and destruction of a shared vision. On the one hand, *Le Navire Night*, *Blue*, *Cries and Whispers* and *Three Colours: Blue* refuse a mimetic, accessible representation in favour of images at the edge of invisibility that could preserve the partially unrepresentable character of the model. On the other hand, spectators of these films 'share the invisibility of a sense' (Mondzain 2019, 177) in the absence of self-explanatory images and are therefore free to imaginatively fill the visual gaps on screen. Part II complements the analyses of Isou's, Debord's, Bene's and Godard's films in Part I, making explicit the ethical charge that, in cinema, iconoclasm can present as a way to challenge uncomplicated representations of reality. That is, cinematic iconoclasm puts into crisis the value of those images which, through mimesis and distracted attention, contribute to the destruction of a communal vision. The broken images of cinematic iconoclasm, instead, have the potential to elicit more reflective, ethically imaginative responses by giving space to the invisibility required for a shared vision. At the edge of the unrepresentable and the ineffable, iconoclastic film images are powerful means at our disposal to actively engage not only with the cinema, but also with the current visual sphere in which we live and build relationships.

Notes

Introduction

1. For French scholarship not available in English, translations are mine.
2. Unless otherwise specified, all translations from Latin and Ancient Greek are mine. I have used Lewis and Short's *A Latin Dictionary: Founded on Andrews' Edition of Freund's Latin Dictionary; Revised, Enlarged and in Great Part Rewritten* (1900), and Liddell and Scott's *A Greek-English Lexicon* (1966).
3. Following house style, Ancient Greek terms have been transliterated without diacritics.
4. For Italian scholarship not available in English, translations are mine.

Prologue

1. The debate is far more complex and involves the key concepts of 'image' (the issue of Christ as *the image of* God and of man as *in the image of* God) and 'similarity' (the man-God relationship of likeness echoing that between copy and prototype). For a thorough discussion of this debate in early Christianity, see Besançon (2000, 81–148), Ladner (1953) and Mondzain (2005).
2. For the iconophiles, too, there is no consubstantiality between the icon and the divine model. However, while iconophilia does not require identity of substance between image and prototype, iconoclasm demands consubstantiality as a necessary condition for any image.

Part I

Chapter 1

1. I have maintained the original French title throughout the book because of 'the unfortunate series of (mis)translations to which the film has been subjected' (Uroskie 2011, 23). The French *bave* can translate as 'slobber' or 'saliva', the latter being more appropriate for Isou's film. Thus, a possible translation for the title could be *Treatise on Saliva and Eternity*. However, the most widespread English translation of the film is *Treatise on Venom and Eternity*.
2. Following academic tradition for the spelling of 'chiseled' with one 'l'.
3. For an analysis of Kandinsky's and Malevich's art in terms of iconoclasm, see Besançon (2000, 330–73) and Wajcman (1998).
4. Because of the lack of translations of Mauthner's work on language, I base my overview on the following scholars commenting on it: Bredeck's *Metaphors of Knowledge: Language and Thought in Mauthner's Critique* (1992), Pisano's 'Misunderstanding Metaphors: Linguistic Scepticism in Mauthner's Philosophy' (2016), Weiler's *Mauthner's Critique of Language* (1970) and Weller's 'The Language Crisis: From Mallarmé to Mauthner' (2018).
5. While there is affinity between Mauthner and one of the most eminent philosophers of language, Ludwig Wittgenstein (Pisano 2016, 98–99; Weiler 1970, 299–306), I engage exclusively with the former, for his radical critique of language is closely tied to the literature of the unword to which Lettrist poetry belongs. In the *Tractatus Logico-Philosophicus* (1968), Wittgenstein at once agrees with Mauthner's postulate and dismisses his method (4.0031). According to Wittgenstein, there exists a language capable of describing the world; that is, there is a relation between language and world (4.014) which allows for propositions to be a picture/image of reality (4.01) – something absent from Mauthner's radical language scepticism.
6. For a discussion of Mauthner's and von Hofmannsthal's perspectives as opposed to Wittgenstein's, see Nordmann's 'Thought Experiments' (2005).
7. For a thorough account of literary and philosophical approaches to language in the twentieth century, see Weller (2018).
8. For an in-depth account of the influence of Jewish mysticism on Lettrism, see also Sjöberg (2015).
9. Judaism displays some affinities with scepticism, as Mauthner himself had noticed (see Pisano 2016, 118–19), for God is ultimately unknowable, unnameable and unrepresentable.
10. For the present analysis, I have used the 1951 final version of *Traité* which contains figurative images in every chapter.

11. Although the protagonist is played by Isou and the commentary exposes his ideas on cinema, the voice-over associated with the character of Daniel is not Isou's, but that of Albert J. LeGros, which produces a further disassociation between what is seen – Isou – and what is heard – LeGros (see *Traité*'s opening credits).
12. It should be noted that the sadism of Isou's discrepant cinema differs from Aaron's (2007, 51–52) discussion of 1970s film theory's understanding of cinema as sadistic. In the latter, sadism stands for classical cinema's depriving the spectator of agency. Conversely, Isou's sadism consists of his desire to metaphorically and physically hurt spectators. More importantly, Isou's sadism implies an actively engaged spectator as opposed to the allegedly fixed, passive spectator of classical cinema.

Chapter 2

1. See Debord ([1961] 2006) and *Internationale situationniste* ([1969] 2006a; [1966] 2006c). For a detailed account of this invective, see also Dall'Asta and Grosoli (2011, 20–27).
2. For instance, the monochromatic screen can have a diegetic function (Ugenti 2013, 75–76) or a conventional punctuation function, signalling a passage of time primarily in the form of the fade to black (Burch 1981, 57; Venzi 2013, 62).
3. I use silence in the meaning of deliberately devoid of voices, noises, or music; nevertheless, there are still 'involuntary' sounds such as the projector's.
4. For an analysis of *Hurlements*' eliciting of an iconoclastic mental cancelling of images, see Cooper (2019, 135–40).
5. The term cinema, short for the French *cinématographe*, comes from the Ancient Greek words of *kinēma/κίνημα*, which means movement, and *grafō/γράφω*, which translates (among other possible meanings) as 'I write'. Additionally, the term *kinēma* derives from the stem of the verb *kineō/κινέω*, which means 'I move', and the suffix *–ma/–μα* which designates the result of the action of the verb, thus translating as that which has moved. Therefore, cinema etymologically translates as writing of that which has moved.
6. I address as mimetic the film movement which mimics our most habitual perception of movement.
7. For a discussion of the SI's critique of urbanism, see Plant (1992, 56–61).
8. 'In love the separate does still remain, but as something united and no longer as something separate; life [in the subject] senses life [in the object]' (Hegel [1798] 1971, 305).

Chapter 3

1. Unless otherwise specified, the translations from Bene are mine. I have tried to render at best his ideas, which he often expressed through invented neologisms and aural re-/dis-sonances.
2. There are inconsistencies with the numbering of the English translations of Eckhart's German sermons; see McGinn's Foreword to *The Complete Mystical Works of Meister Eckhart* (2009). I have used Walshe's numbering.
3. For a critical appraisal of Derrida's argument on Western logocentrism as phonocentric, see Cavarero (2005, 213–41), Dolar (2006, 36–43) and Kane (2014, 186–93).
4. For a further account of Bene's exoticism/eroticism, see Simsolo ([1973] 2011, 119–20).

Chapter 4

1. There are several models of faith which do not necessarily entail belief; see Bishop (2016).
2. The issue of belief and cinema has been developed by several scholars using different approaches. For a discussion of cinematic belief as a way to recover a belief in the phenomenal world, see, for instance, Bazin (1967, 9–16), Deleuze (1997a), Rushton (2011, 42–78), Cavell (1979) and Sinnerbrink (2012). For an argument on cinematic belief as emotion, see Sorfa (2017).
3. For further accounts of images as relational entities, see Mondzain (2019).
4. While Godard and most scholars identify the shots of the concentration camps in this fragment as filmed in Auschwitz and Ravensbrük, Witt (2013, 132) sustains that they were filmed in Dachau instead.
5. For a thorough discussion of *Histoire(s)* and the representation of the Shoah, see Saxton (2004; 2008).
6. The discourse on a possible redemptive power of film images resonates with Kracauer's (1960) argument on cinema's power to reveal aspects of physical reality that otherwise would go unnoticed. However, while in Kracauer's theory cinema can redeem reality by mechanically reproducing it – namely, by indexically bearing the traces of the recorded reality – in Godard's *Histoire(s)* cinema's revelatory capacity derives from the possibility of establishing new relationships between diverse images which coexist in a single frame. That is, Kracauer's trust in cinema's ability to mimetically reproduce phenomenal referents as a way to redeem the otherwise concealed reality is put to the test by Godard's multiple images.
7. Godard's images of and claims on Christianity in *Histoire(s)* are close to some arguments of mysticism (especially that of Meister Eckhart) and apophatic theology.

For instance, while Godard in *Histoire(s)* is claiming for an audio-visual representation of the Shoah, he nonetheless preserves its void through incomplete, stratified film images.

Part II

Chapter 5

1. Levinas delineates the difference between 'like' and 'same'. While to be like implies an identification coming from outside, because 'like' needs a second term of comparison, to be the same is instead an identification coming from within. Levinas (1969) affirms that 'the identity of the individual does not consist in being like to itself, and in letting itself be identified *from the outside* by a finger that points to it; it consists in being the *same* – in being oneself, in identifying oneself from within' (289).
2. In Aaron's discussion there is a distinction between ethics and morality, wherein the former involves issues of responsibility and requires a reflective response, while the latter refers to a socially coded emotional response aimed at reassuring the spectator rather than unsettling their moral beliefs.
3. Mondzain (2013; 2017; 2019) elaborates on the constitutive relational character of the image as *eikōn*, building on its etymological meaning and ancient and medieval philosophy's interpretations. While my understanding of iconoclasm in an artistic context diverges from Mondzain's, I nevertheless share her definition of the *eikōn* as relational.
4. For further accounts of noise as interruption, disturbance and transgression, see Attali (1985) and Hegarty (2008; 2020).

Chapter 6

1. Jarman's term for moralistic heteronormative society.
2. For a further account of *Blue*'s imaginative potential, see Cooper (2019, 76–87).
3. For an account of the queer potential of film sound-track, see Buhler (2013); for a discussion of sonic practices for a queering of the sound-track, see Davis (2008) and Suárez (2017).

Chapter 7

1. The more frequent use of colour in cinema is that of which Arnheim (1958, 154–60) and Münsterberg (1916, 146–48) were critical, for a mimetic use of colour

threatens cinema's art status by reducing the distance between the film image and its phenomenal referent.
2. While the monochromatic images in *Three Colours: Blue* are black, I sustain Venzi's (2006, 129) claim that, in this film, black acquires the symbolic value of an intensified blue. Pastoureau (2009), too, points out the closeness between black and blue, arguing that 'for a long time, blue, an unobtrusive and unpopular color, remained a sort of "sub-black" in the West or a black of a particular kind. Thus, the histories of these two colors can hardly be separated' (12).
3. While a fade signals the passage from an image to a blank screen, thereby implying a stark interruption of figuration, a dissolve indicates the gradual transition from one shot to another. As Bordwell (1985) explains, 'visually, the dissolve is simply a variant of the fade – a fade-out overlapped with a fade-in – but it is a fade during which the screen is never blank' (46). In this film, dissolves are used only for Agnes's flashbacks to partially deprive her character of the violence proper to the fades to red.

Chapter 8

1. For example, Cesare Lombroso's ([1876] 2006) study on the correlation between physiognomy and criminology, where he identifies criminal types based on their bodily, especially facial, appearance.
2. While the relationship involving the referent, its cinematic image and the photogenic aspect remains ambiguous in Delluc and Epstein, in the Russian formalists' appropriation of the term, *photogénie* is developed in a more defined manner. *Photogénie* becomes a quality entirely given by the film medium through the stylistic manipulations of the phenomenal referent, which is not photogenic in itself (Eikhenbaum [1927] 1982, 5–31; Tynyanov [1927] 1982, 32–54). Conversely, in Delluc and Epstein, cinematic devices can only accentuate the photogenic aspect, which remains distinctive of certain objects and subjects.
3. Interestingly, there is a historical association with Holy Mary and the colour blue in religious painting, which has been variably interpreted; see for instance, Gage (2009, 129–30) and Murray, Murray and Devonshire Jones (2014, 65).

Glossary

Circumscribability: literally 'draw a line around'. In the Christian theological debate over sacred images, it refers to the inscription of God's divinity into a material frame and expresses the act of defining, enclosing or limiting the divine nature of God by means of his figurative representation in the icon. During the Byzantine iconoclastic controversy, circumscribability constituted one of the major conflicting points between iconophiles and iconoclasts: while the former denied that the icon circumscribes the divinity, the latter contended that depicting Christ in figurative terms corresponds to enclosing the nature of the divine, which is unlimited by definition, inside a material medium.

Consubstantiality: the identity of substance between copy and prototype. In the case of sacred images, the relationship of identity involves the divine nature of the model (God) and the artificial nature of the copy (icon). Accordingly, there is the natural image, which is generated and is by nature (for instance, Christ the son is the natural image of God the father), and the artificial image, which is created by imitation (for example, the icon). During the Byzantine iconoclastic controversy, both iconoclasts and iconophiles agreed on the impossibility of identity of substance between the icon and Christ. However, while the iconophiles excluded any relationship of consubstantiality between the artificial image and the natural image, the iconoclasts conceived consubstantiality as being essential for any image, whether natural or artificial.

Copy-Prototype Relationship: the ambiguous relationship between the image as copy and its prototype which is at the basis of the iconoclastic and the iconophilic positions. The diverging interpretations of this specific relationship leads to the two opposing stances – in iconophilia, the relationship is of likeness, whereas in iconoclasm, it is of alterity (the copy being inadequate for the representation of the prototype).

***Eidōlon (Εἴδωλον)*:** from *eidos*/εἶδος, 'that which is seen'. An image exclusively grounded in the visible sphere with no truthful connection with its prototype. Particularly in Plato, it translates as 'phantom' and 'image reflected in a mirror or water', therefore carrying connotations of illusion and deception. The *eidōlon* consists in an excessive similarity with its referent, thereby assuming a highly deceptive quality given by its resembling too much of the appearance of the prototype.

***Eikōn (Εἰκών)*:** from *eoika*/ἔοικα, 'to be like', and *eikos*/εἰκός, 'like truth'. An image in a relationship of likeness with its prototype. It functions as an intermediary between the sensible (visible) world and the intelligible realm.

Icon: Latinisation of the Greek *eikōn*. Used in Christian theology to define a sacred representation of God. It retains the same quality of the *eikōn*, of being an intermediary between the terrestrial world (humans) and the celestial sphere (God). Not to be confused with Charles S. Peirce's semiotic use of this term to mean a sign which mimetically resembles in its features the physical appearance of the referent. While in Peirce's use the relationship between icon and referent is imitational, in Christian theology (from an iconophilic perspective) it is relational.

Iconoclasm: from *eikōn* and *klaō*/κλάω, 'I break'; etymologically 'the breaking of icons'. From an iconophilic perspective, attitude against sacred representations of God (icons). From an iconoclastic perspective, attitude against a certain type of images understood as false copies of the referent (idols). Had the iconoclasts won the controversy over sacred images in the eighth and ninth centuries, it would have been addressed as 'idoloclasm'.

Iconoclastic *eikōn*: an image retaining the quality of the *eikōn* as that which mediates between a visual form and its model, but which does so by breaking with mimesis on the ground of an iconoclastic interpretation of the copy-prototype relationship.

Iconophilia: from *eikōn* and *phileō*/φιλέω, 'I regard with affection', 'I love'; etymologically 'love for icons'. Historically, the Christian attitude in favour of visual representations of God. In some texts on the Byzantine controversy, the term iconoduly is used in place of iconophilia (from *eikōn* and *douleia*/δουλεία, 'slavery' or 'servitude').

Idol: Latinisation of the Greek *eidōlon*. Used in Christian theology to address a false and deceptive representation of God; also, an image presenting itself as if it were a god.

Image: in this book, a referential representation perceivable through the senses; namely, a copy of something else (image *of* something). Within the Western Platonic tradition, the image as a secondary mode of being presupposes, as a direct consequence, a prototype that pre-exists it. On the one hand, the copy has to resemble its prototype to be recognisable as the image *of* such a prototype; on the other hand, the image has to be sufficiently different from the prototype in order to be its representation instead of positing itself as presence. The uniqueness of the prototype ceases once it is possible to transpose it into an image, hence a copy, at least at the level of the visible form. Contra the prototype, which by definition is one of a kind, a copy is always potentially plural. As consequence, whatever is conceived as unique – Platonic ideas; God in the monotheist religions of Judaism, Islam and Christianity – cannot be shaped into a sensible form, otherwise the uniqueness of the being would be lost. This is at the core of the Jewish and Muslim prohibition of sacred images, while also constituting the basis for the distinction between iconophiles and iconoclasts in Christianity.

Figurative: used in the sense employed in figurative arts as opposed to abstract and non-figurative art. That which reproduces recognisable aspects of phenomenal reality.

Mimesis: from *mimēsis*/μίμησις, 'imitation'. In art, it implies a relationship of likeness with a world, be it phenomenal or fictitious. In this book, I follow a 'world-reflecting' model of artistic mimesis according to which 'mimesis incorporates a response to a reality [...] that is believed to exist outside and independently of art' (Halliwell 2002, 23).

Model: the original used for subsequent copies; namely, 'an object of imitation' (*Oxford English Dictionary* 2022, II). Here interchangeable with prototype, original and referent since they all stand for the original type used for possible copies.

Prototype: from *prōtos*/πρῶτος, 'first', and *typos*/τύπος, 'mould', 'form', 'model', therefore 'original model' for subsequent copies.

Spectacularise: to produce something which exclusively addresses the eyes of the viewer. More generally in this book, to reduce something invisible/intelligible/unrepresentable to an object grounded in the visible sphere only. Drawn from the Latin *spectaculum*, which comes from the stem of the verb *spectāre*, intensive form of *specere*, which translates as 'to look at something'.

Bibliography

Aaron, Michele. 2007. *Spectatorship: The Power of Looking On*. London: Wallflower.

Adorno, Theodor W. 1967. 'Cultural Criticism and Society'. In *Prism*, translated by Samuel and Shierry Weber, 17–34. London: Spearman.

Alazet, Bernard. 1992. *Le Navire Night de Marguerite Duras: Écrire l'effacement*. Lille: Presses Universitaires de Lille.

Allen, Richard. 1993. 'Representation, Illusion, and the Cinema'. *Cinema Journal*, 32(2): 21–48.

Agamben, Giorgio. 2002. 'Difference and Repetition: On Guy Debord's Films'. In *Guy Debord and the Situationist International: Texts and Documents*, edited by Tom McDonough, 313–19. Cambridge: MIT Press.

Amerini, Fabrizio. 2009. 'Tommaso d'Aquino, la verità e il Medioevo'. *Annali del Dipartimento di Filosofia*, 15: 35–63.

Andrew, Dudley. 1976. *The Major Film Theories: An Introduction*. New York: Oxford University Press.

Andrew, Dudley. 1984. 'Representation'. In *Concepts in Film Theory*, 37–56. New York: Oxford University Press.

Andrew, Geoff. 1998. *The 'Three Colours' Trilogy*. London: British Film Institute.

Aquinas, Thomas. 1923. 'Chapter LIX. That God Is Not Ignorant of the Truth of Enunciations'. In *The Summa Contra Gentiles*, translated by the English Dominican Fathers from the latest Leonine edition, 126–28. London: Burns Oates & Washbourne.

Armengaud, Françoise. 2004. 'Faire ou ne pas faire d'images. Emmanuel Levinas et l'art d'oblitération'. *Noesis*, 3. doi.org/10.4000/noesis.11.

Arnheim, Rudolf. 1958. *Film as Art*. Berkeley: University of California Press.
Ashton, Jenna C. 2012. 'Derek Jarman's *Blue*: Negating the Visual'. *Journal of Applied Arts & Health*, 3(3): 295–307.
Attali, Jacques. 1985. *Noise: An Essay on the Political Economy of Music*, translated by Brian Massumi. Minneapolis: University of Minnesota Press.
Aumont, Jacques. 2003. 'The Face in Close-Up'. In *The Visual Turn: Classical Film Theory and Art History*, edited by Angela Dalle Vacche, translated by Ellen Sowchek, 127–48. New Brunswick: Rutgers University Press.
Bachmann, Gideon. 1972–73. '*Salomé* by Carmelo Bene' [Review]. *Film Quarterly*, 26(2): 20–23.
Balázs, Béla. [1945] 1970. *Theory of the Film: Character and Growth of a New Art*, translated by Edith Bone. New York: Dover Publications.
Balázs, Béla. [1924] 2010. *Béla Balázs: Early Film Theory*, edited by Erica Carter, translated by Rodney Livingstone. New York; Oxford: Berghahn Books.
Bazin, André. 1967. *What is Cinema?* Vol. 1, translated by Hugh Gray. Berkeley: University of California Press.
Bazin, André. 1972. *What is Cinema?* Vol. 2, translated by Hugh Gray. Berkeley: University of California Press.
Bellour, Raymond. 2012. *Between-the-Images*, translated by Allyn Hardyck. Zurich: JRP Ringier.
Belting, Hans. 2002. 'Beyond Iconoclasm: Nam June Paik, the Zen Gaze and the Escape from Representation'. In *Iconoclash: Beyond the Image Wars in Science, Religion and Art*, edited by Bruno Latour and Peter Weibel, 390–411. Karlsruhe: ZKM Center for Art and Media; Cambridge: MIT Press.
Bene, Carmelo. 1970. *L'orecchio mancante*. Milan: Feltrinelli.
Bene, Carmelo. 2000. *'L mal de' fiori*. Milan: Bompiani.
Bene, Carmelo. [1976] 2002a. 'A boccaperta'. In *Opere: Con l'Autografia d'un ritratto*, 423–533. Milan: Bompiani.
Bene, Carmelo. [1995] 2002b. 'Autografia d'un ritratto'. In *Opere: Con l'Autografia d'un ritratto*, v–xxxvii. Milan: Bompiani.
Bene, Carmelo. [1969] 2011a. 'Capricci'. Interview by Noël Simsolo. In *Carmelo Bene: Contro il cinema*, edited by Emiliano Morreale, 29–35. Rome: Minimum Fax.
Bene, Carmelo. [1998] 2011b. 'Che i vivi mi perdonino . . .' Interview by Thierry Lounas. In *Carmelo Bene: Contro il cinema*, edited by Emiliano Morreale, 172–86. Rome: Minimum Fax.
Bene, Carmelo. [1995] 2011c. Interview. By Goffredo Fofi. In *Carmelo Bene: Contro il cinema*, edited by Emiliano Morreale, 166–71. Rome: Minimum Fax.

Bene, Carmelo. [1968] 2011d. Interview. By Jean Narboni. In *Carmelo Bene: Contro il cinema*, edited by Emiliano Morreale, 21–28. Rome: Minimum Fax.
Bene, Carmelo. [1970] 2011e. Interview. By Noël Simsolo. In *Carmelo Bene: Contro il cinema*, edited by Emiliano Morreale, 56–63. Rome: Minimum Fax.
Bene, Carmelo. [1978] 2011f. 'L'estetica del dispiacere'. Interview by Maurizio Grande. In *Carmelo Bene: Contro il cinema*, edited by Emiliano Morreale, 136–60. Rome: Minimum Fax.
Bene, Carmelo, and Umberto Artioli. 2006. *Un dio assente: Monologo a due voci sul teatro*, edited by Antonio Attisani. Naples: Medusa.
Bergala, Alain. 1986. 'La Beauté du geste'. *Cahiers du Cinéma*, 385: 57–58.
Bergman, Ingmar. 1977. 'Cries and Whispers'. In *Four Stories*, translated by Alan Blair, 57–94. London: Boyars.
Bergman, Ingmar. 1994. 'Cries and Whispers'. In *Images: My Life in Films*, translated by Marianne Ruuth, 83–103. London: Bloomsbury.
Besançon, Alain. 2000. *The Forbidden Image: An Intellectual History of Iconoclasm*, translated by Jane M. Todd. Chicago: University of Chicago Press.
Bettetini, Maria T. 2006. *Le radici dell'iconoclastia*. Bari: Laterza.
Bishop, John. 2016. 'Faith'. In *The Stanford Encyclopedia of Philosophy*. https://plato.stanford.edu/entries/faith/#FaiBel.
Blau, Herbert. 2011. 'Performing in the Chaosmos'. In *Reality Principles: From the Absurd to the Virtual*, 89–102. Ann Arbor: University of Michigan Press.
Bois, Yve-Alain. 2007. 'Klein's Relevance for Today'. *October*, 119: 75–93.
Boldrick, Stacy. 2020. *Iconoclasm and the Museum*. London: Routledge.
Boltanski, Luc. 1999. *Distant Suffering: Morality, Media and Politics*, translated by Graham D. Burchell. Cambridge: Cambridge University Press.
Bordwell, David. 1985. 'Time in the Classical Film'. In *The Classical Hollywood Cinema: Film Style and Mode of Production to 1960*, co-edited with Janet Staiger and Kristin Thompson, 42–49. London: Routledge.
Bredeck, Elizabeth. 1992. *Metaphors of Knowledge: Language and Thought in Mauthner's Critique*. Detroit: Wayne State University Press.
Brenez, Nicole. 1998. 'Le Film abymé'. In *De la figure en général et du corps en particulier: L'invention figurative au cinéma*, 339–60. Paris: De Boeck Supérieur.
Brenez, Nicole. 2004. 'The Forms of the Questions'. In *Forever Godard*, edited by James S. Williams, Michael Temple and Michael Witt, 160–77. London: Black Dog Publishing.
Brown, William. 2018. *Non-Cinema: Global Digital Film-Making and the Multitude*. New York: Bloomsbury Academic.

Buchloh, Benjamin H. D. 2016. 'Roundtable: Art at Mid-Century'. In *Art since 1900: Modernism, Antimodernism, Postmodernism*, edited by Hal Foster, Rosalind E. Krauss, Yve-Alain Bois, Benjamin H.D. Buchloh and David Joselit, 375–84. London: Thames & Hudson.

Buhler, James. 2013. 'Gender, Sexuality, and the Soundtrack'. In *The Oxford Handbook of Film Music Studies*, edited by David Neumeyer, 367–82. New York: Oxford University Press.

Burch, Noël. 1981. 'The Repertory of Simple Structures'. In *Theory of Film Practice*, translated by Helen R. Lane, 51–69. Princeton: Princeton University Press.

Byrne, Alex, and David R. Hilbert. 2001. *Readings on Color: The Philosophy of Color*. Cambridge: MIT Press.

Cabañas, Kaira M. 2014. *Off-Screen Cinema: Isidore Isou and the Lettrist Avant-garde*. Chicago: The University of Chicago Press.

Cappabianca, Alessandro. 2012. *Carmelo Bene: Il cinema oltre se stesso*. Cosenza: Pellegrini Editore. Kindle edition.

Carluccio, Giulia. 1992. 'La naissance du Cinéma ou la naissance de l'amour du Cinéma: Forfaiture'. *Cinema & Cinema*, 64: 53–72.

Carroll, Noël. 1996. 'Defining the Moving Image'. In *Theorizing the Moving Image*, 49–74. Cambridge: Cambridge University Press.

Cavarero, Adriana. 2005. *For More than One Voice: Toward a Philosophy of Vocal Expression*, translated by Paul Kottman. Palo Alto: Stanford University Press.

Cavell, Stanley. 1979. *The World Viewed: Reflections on the Ontology of Film*. Cambridge: Harvard University Press.

Chamois, Camille, Daphné Le Roux and Benjamin Levy. 8 September 2012. 'Visage et Subjectivité'. Seminar at Collège International de Philosophie, Paris. https://visageetsubjectivite.wordpress.com.

Chiesa, Lorenzo. 2012. 'A Theatre of Subtractive Extinction: Bene without Deleuze'. *Mimesis*, 1(2). doi.org/10.4000/mimesis.248.

Chillemi, Francesco. 2011. 'Carmelo Bene and the Overcoming of Logocentrism: Epiphany of the Primordial Voice in the Eclipse of Meaning'. *Annali d'Italianistica*, 29: 253–67.

Chillemi, Francesco. 2015. 'Filming Nothingness: Invisibility, Ineffability, and the Inviolable Absence of God in Carmelo Bene's *Hamlet*'. *Mimesis*, 4(2). doi.org/10.4000/mimesis.1085.

Chion, Michel. 1999. *The Voice in Cinema*, translated by Claudia Gorbman. New York: Columbia University Press.

Choi, Jinhee, and Mattias Frey (eds). 2014. *Cine-Ethics: Ethical Dimensions of Film Theory, Practice, and Spectatorship*. London; New York: Routledge.

Chouliaraki, Lilie. 2006. *The Spectatorship of Suffering*. London; Thousand Oaks; New Delhi: SAGE Publications.
Cléder, Jean. 2014. Introduction to *Marguerite Duras: Le cinéma*, 3–12. Paris: Lettres modernes Minard.
Clewell, Tammy. 2000. 'The Shades of Modern Mourning in "Three Colours" Trilogy'. *Literature/Film Quarterly*, 28(3): 203–9.
Coates, Paul (ed.). 1999. *Lucid Dreams: The Films of Krzysztof Kieślowski*. Wiltshire: Flicks Books.
Cohen, Hubert I. 1993. *Ingmar Bergman: The Art of Confession*. New York; Oxford: Twayne Maxwell Macmillan International.
Comolli, Jean-Luc, and Paul Narboni. 1971. 'Cinema/Ideology/Criticism', translated by Susan Bennett. *Screen*, 12(1): 27–38.
Connor, Steven. 2013. 'Sounding Out Film'. In *The Oxford Handbook of New Audiovisual Aesthetics*, edited by John Richardson, Claudia Gorbman and Carol Vernallis, 108–20. Oxford: Oxford University Press.
Cooper, Sarah. 2006. *Selfless Cinema? Ethics and French Documentary*. London: Legenda.
Cooper, Sarah (ed.). 2007. 'The Occluded Relation: Levinas and Cinema'. [Special Issue] *Film-Philosophy*, 11(2).
Cooper, Sarah. 2019. *Film and the Imagined Image*. Edinburgh: Edinburgh University Press.
Corradi Fiumara, Gemma. 1990. *The Other Side of Language: A Philosophy of Listening*, translated by Charles Lambert. London; New York: Routledge.
Coureau, Didier. 2014. '*Les Mains négatives, Césarée, Aurélia Steiner*: La voix sans visage'. In *Marguerite Duras: Le cinéma*, edited by Jean Cléder, 117–35. Paris: Lettres modernes Minard.
Cowie, Peter. 1992. *Ingmar Bergman: A Critical Biography*. New York: Limelight.
Crimp, Douglas. 2002. *Melancholia and Moralism: Essays on AIDS and Queer Politics*. Cambridge: MIT Press.
Curtay, Jean-Paul. 1974. *La Poésie lettriste*. Paris: Éditions Seghers.
Dall'Asta, Monica, and Marco Grosoli. 2011. *Consumato dal fuoco: Il cinema di Guy Debord*. Pisa: Edizioni ETS.
Dalle Vacche, Angela (ed.). 2003. 'Introduction'. In *The Visual Turn: Classical Film Theory and Art History*, 1–29. New Brunswick: Rutgers University Press.
Dalton, Mary M., and Kirsten James Fatzinger. 2003. 'Choosing Silence: Defiance and Resistance without Voice in Jane Campion's *The Piano*'. *Women and Language*, 26(2): 34–39.

Daney, Serge. 2004a. 'The Godard Paradox'. In *Forever Godard*, edited by James S. Williams, Michael Temple and Michael Witt, 68–71. London: Black Dog Publishing.

Daney, Serge. [1992] 2004b. 'The Tracking Shot in *Kapò*', translated by Laurent Kretzschmar. *Senses of Cinema*. https://www.sensesofcinema.com/2004/feature-articles/kapo_daney/.

David, Marian. 2016. 'The Correspondence Theory of Truth'. In *The Stanford Encyclopedia of Philosophy*. https://plato.stanford.edu/entries/truth-correspondence/.

Davis, Glyn. 2009. 'Hearing Queerly: Television's Dissident Sonics'. In *Queer TV: Theories, Histories, Politics*, edited by Glyn Davis and Gary Needham, 172–88. London: Routledge.

Debord, Guy. [1988] 1990. *Comments on the Society of the Spectacle*, translated by Malcolm Imrie. London; New York: Verso.

Debord, Guy. [1967] 1994. *The Society of the Spectacle*, translated by Donald Nicholson-Smith. New York: Zone Books.

Debord, Guy. [1989] 2003. 'The Use of Stolen Films'. In *Guy Debord: Complete Cinematic Works*, translated and edited by Ken Knabb, 222–23. Oakland: AK Press.

Debord, Guy. [1961] 2006. 'For a Revolutionary Judgement of Art'. In *Situationist International Anthology*, edited and translated by Ken Knabb, 393–97. Berkeley: Bureau of Public Services.

Debord, Guy, and Gil J. Wolman. [1956] 2006. 'A User's Guide to *Détournement*'. In *Situationist International Anthology*, edited and translated by Ken Knabb, 14–21. Berkeley: Bureau of Public Services.

Debray, Régis. 1992. *Vie et mort de l'image: Une histoire du regard en Occident*. Paris: Gallimard.

Deleuze, Gilles. 1983. 'Plato and the Simulacrum', translated by Rosalind Krauss. *October*, 27: 45–56.

Deleuze, Gilles. 1997a. *Cinema 2: The Time-Image*, translated by Hugh Tomlinson and Robert Galeta. Minneapolis: University of Minnesota Press.

Deleuze, Gilles. 1997b. 'One Less Manifesto'. In *Mimesis, Masochism, and Mime*, edited by Timothy Murray, translated by Eliane dal Molin and Timothy Murray, 239–58. Ann Arbor: University of Michigan Press.

Deleuze, Gilles, and Félix Guattari. 1987. 'Year Zero: Faciality'. In *A Thousand Plateaus: Capitalism and Schizophrenia*, translated by Brian Massumi, 167–91. Minneapolis: University of Minnesota Press.

Delluc, Louis. [1920] 1985. 'Photogénie'. In *Écrits cinématographiques I*, 31–77. Paris: Cinémathèque Française.

Derrida, Jacques. 1973. *Speech and Phenomena*, translated by David B. Allison. Evanston: Northwestern University Press.

Devereux, Andrew W. 2016. '"The Ruin and Slaughter of . . . Fellow Christians": The French as Threat to Christendom in Spanish Assertions of Sovereignty in Italy, 1479–1516'. In *Representing Imperial Rivalry in the Early Modern Mediterranean*, edited by Barbara Fuchs and Emily Weissbourd, 101–25. Toronto: University of Toronto Press.

Doane, Mary Ann. 2003. 'The Close-Up: Scale and Detail in the Cinema'. *Differences*, 14(3): 89–111.

Dolar, Mladen. 2006. *A Voice and Nothing More*. Cambridge: MIT Press.

Dottorini, Daniele. 2013. 'Punto cieco: Isou, Debord, Monteiro e la negazione dell'immagine'. *Ágalma, rivista culturale e di estetica*, 26: 50–58.

Downing, Lisa, and Libby Saxton. 2010. *Film and Ethics: Foreclosed Encounters*. London: Routledge.

Eikhenbaum, Boris M. [1927] 1982. 'Problems of Cine-Stylistics'. In *Russian Poetics in Translation, Volume 9: The Poetics of Cinema*, edited by Richard Taylor, translated by Richard Sherwood, 5–31. Oxford: RPT Publications in Association with Department of Literature, University of Essex.

Eisenstein, Sergei. 1949. *Film Form: Essays in Film Theory*, edited and translated by Jay Leyda. New York: Harcourt, Brace.

Eisenstein, Sergei. 1957. *The Film Sense*, edited and translated by Jay Leyda. New York: Meridian Books.

Ellis, Jim. 2009. *Derek Jarman's Angelic Conversations*. Minneapolis: University of Minnesota Press.

Epstein, Jean. [1921] 1977. 'Magnification and Other Writings', translated by Stuart Liebman. *October*, 3: 9–25.

Epstein, Jean. [1926] 2012. 'On Certain Characteristics of *Photogénie*'. In *Jean Epstein: Critical Essays and New Translations*, edited by Sarah Keller and Jason N. Paul, 292–96. Amsterdam: Amsterdam University Press.

Fargier, Jean-Paul. 1971. 'Parenthesis or Indirect Route'. *Screen*, 12(2): 131–44.

Feldman, Hannah. 2014. 'Sonic Youth, Sonic Space: Isidore Isou and the Lettrist Acoustics of Deterritorialization'. In *From a Nation Torn: Decolonizing Art and Representation in France, 1945–1962*, 77–108. Durham: Duke University Press.

Field, Allyson. 1999. '*Hurlements en faveur de Sade*: The Negation and Surpassing of "Discrepant Cinema"'. *SubStance*, 28(3): 55–70.

Fleming, David H. 2017. *Unbecoming Cinema: Unsettling Encounters with Ethical Event Films*. Bristol; Chicago: Intellect.

Foster, Hal, Rosalind E. Krauss, Yve-Alain Bois, Benjamin H. D. Buchloh and David Joselit. 2016. *Art since 1900: Modernism, Antimodernism, Postmodernism*. London: Thames & Hudson.

Furno, Raffaele. 2013. 'Carmelo Bene's *Phonè*: Radical Renovation or Reinvented Tradition'. In *The Italian Method of la drammatica: Its Legacy and Receptions*, edited by Anna Sica, 205–19. Milan: Mimesis.

Gado, Frank. 1986. *The Passion of Ingmar Bergman*. Durham: Duke University Press.

Gage, John. 2009. *Colour and Culture: Practice and Meaning from Antiquity to Abstraction*. London: Thames & Hudson.

Galt, Rosalind. 2011. *Pretty: Film and the Decorative Image*. New York: Columbia University Press.

Gamboni, Dario. 1997. *The Destruction of Art: Iconoclasm and Vandalism since the French Revolution*. London: Reaktion Books Ltd.

Girgus, Sam B. 2010. *Levinas and the Cinema of Redemption: Time, Ethics, and the Feminine*. New York: Columbia University Press.

Godard, Jean-Luc. (March-April) 1996. Interview. By Gavin Smith. *Film Comment*. https://www.filmcomment.com/article/jean-luc-godard-interview-nouvelle-vague-histoires-du-cinema-helas-pour-moi/.

Grespi, Barbara. 2013. 'L'immagine sfregiata: Il cinema e i volti del sacro'. *Ágalma, rivista di studi culturali e di estetica*, 26: 40–49.

Grønstad, Asbjørn. 2016. *Film and the Ethical Imagination*. London: Palgrave Macmillan.

Groys, Boris. 2002. 'Iconoclasm as an Artistic Device: Iconoclastic Strategies in Film'. In *Iconoclash: Beyond the Image Wars in Science, Religion and Art*, edited by Bruno Latour and Peter Weibel, 282–95. Karlsruhe: ZKM Center for Art and Media; Cambridge: MIT Press.

Günther, Renate. 2002. *Marguerite Duras*. Manchester: Manchester University Press.

Halliwell, Stephen. 2002. *The Aesthetics of Mimesis: Ancient Texts and Modern Problems*. Princeton: Princeton University Press.

Haltof, Marek. 2004. *The Cinema of Krzysztof Kieślowski: Variations on Destiny and Chance*. London: Wallflower.

Hand, Seán. 1989. 'Introduction'. In *The Levinas Reader*, 1–8. Oxford: Blackwell

Hanson, Ellis. 1991. 'Undead'. In *Inside/Out: Lesbian Theories, Gay Theories*, edited by Diana Fuss, 324–40. London; New York: Routledge.

Harcourt, Peter. 1974. 'Ingmar Bergman's *Cries and Whispers*: A Discussion'. *Queen's Quarterly*, 81(2): 247–57.

Heath, Stephen. 1974. 'Lessons from Brecht'. *Screen*, 15(2): 103–28.

Heath, Stephen. 1976. 'Narrative Space'. *Screen*, 17(3): 68–112.
Heathcote, Owen. 2000. 'Excitable Silence: The Violence of Non-violence in *Nathalie Granger*'. In *Revisioning Duras: Film, Race, Sex*, edited by James S. Williams, 75–91. Liverpool: Liverpool University Press.
Hegarty, Paul. 2008. *Noise/Music: A History*. New York: Continuum.
Hegarty, Paul. 2020. *Annihilating Noise*. New York; London: Bloomsbury.
Hegel, G. W. F. [1798] 1971. 'Love'. In *Early Theological Writings*, edited by T. M. Knox and Richard Kroner, 302–8. Philadelphia: University of Pennsylvania Press.
Higginson, Kate. 2008. 'Derek Jarman's "Ghostly Eye": Prophetic Bliss and Sacrificial Blindness in *Blue*'. *Mosaic*, 41(1): 77–94.
Hill, Leslie. 1993. *Marguerite Duras: Apocalyptic Desires*. London: Routlege.
Hirsch, Joshua. 2004. *Afterimage: Film, Trauma, and the Holocaust*. Philadelphia: Temple University Press.
Hori, Junji. 2004. 'Godard's Two Historiographies'. In *Forever Godard*, edited by James S. Williams, Michael Temple and Michael Witt, 334–49. London: Black Dog Publishing.
Hubner, Laura. 2007. *The Films of Ingmar Bergman: Illusions of Light and Darkness*. Basingstoke: Palgrave Macmillan.
Internationale situationniste. [1969] 2006a. 'Cinema and Revolution'. In *Situationist International Anthology*, edited and translated by Ken Knabb, 378–79. Berkeley: Bureau of Public Services.
Internationale situationniste. [1959] 2006b. '*Détournement* as Negation and Prelude'. In *Situationist International Anthology*, edited and translated by Ken Knabb, 67–68. Berkeley: Bureau of Public Services.
Internationale situationniste. [1966] 2006c. 'The Role of Godard'. In *Situationist International Anthology*, edited and translated by Ken Knabb, 228–30. Berkeley: Bureau of Public Services.
Isou, Isidore. 1947. *Introduction à une nouvelle poésie et à une nouvelle musique*. Paris: Gallimard.
Isou, Isidore. [1952] 1953. *Esthétique du cinéma*. Paris: Ur.
Jarman, Derek. 1992. *At Your Own Risk: A Saint's Testament*. London: Hutchinson.
Jarman, Derek. 1994. *Chroma: A Book of Colour – June '93*. London: Century.
Jay, Martin. 1993. *Downcast Eyes: The Denigration of Vision in Twentieth-Century French Thought*. Berkeley: University of California Press.
Jones, Ward E., and Samantha Vice (eds). 2011. *Ethics at the Cinema*. Oxford: Oxford University Press.
Kalin, Jesse. 2003. *The Films of Ingmar Bergman*. Cambridge: Cambridge University Press.

Kane, Brian. 2014. *Sound Unseen: Acousmatic Sound in Theory and Practice*. Oxford: Oxford University Press.

Kant, Immanuel. [1790] 1987. 'On Beauty as the Symbol of Morality'. In *Critique of Judgement*, translated by Werner S. Pluhar, 225–30. Indianapolis: Hackett Publishing.

Kaplan, Ann. 2009. 'Women, Trauma, and Late Modernity: Sontag, Duras, and Silence in Cinema, 1960–1980'. *Framework: The Journal of Cinema and Media*, 50(1/2): 158–75.

Karpf, Anne. 2017. 'Speaking Sex to Power? The Female Voice as a Dangerous Instrument'. *Imago: Studi di cinema e media*, 14: 27–36.

Kehr, Dave. 1994. 'To Save the World: Kieślowski's THREE COLORS Trilogy'. *Film Comment*, 30(6): 10–13, 15–18, 20.

Kenaan, Hagi. 2013. *The Ethics of Visuality: Levinas and the Contemporary Gaze*, translated by Batya Stein. London; New York: I. B. Tauris.

Khalip, Jacques. 2010. 'The Archeology of Sound: Derek Jarman's *Blue* and Queer Audiovisuality in the Time of AIDS'. *Differences: A Journal of Feminist Cultural Studies*, 1(2): 73–108.

Kibbey, Ann. 2005. *Theory of the Image: Capitalism, Contemporary Film, and Women*. Bloomington: Indiana University Press.

Klein, Yves. [1961] 2013. 'Manifeste de l'Hôtel Chelsea'. *Yves Klein Archives*. https://www.yvesklein.com/fr/ressources?sh=chelsea#/fr/ressources/view/document/19721/yves-klein-manifeste-de-l-hotel-chelsea?sh=chelsea&sb=_created&sd=desc.

Kobrynskyy, Oleksandr, and Gerd Bayer (eds). 2015. *Holocaust Cinema in the Twenty-First Century: Memory, Images, and the Ethics of Representation*. New York: Wallflower Press.

Kowsar, Mohammad. 1986. 'Deleuze on Theatre: A Case Study of Carmelo Bene's "Richard III"'. *Theatre Journal*, 38(1): 19–33.

Kracauer, Siegfried. 1960. *Theory of Film: The Redemption of Physical Reality*. New York: Oxford University Press.

Kupfer, Joseph. (2012). *Feminist Ethics in Film: Reconfiguring Care through Cinema*. Bristol: Intellect.

Ladner, Gerhart B. 1953. 'The Concept of the Image in the Greek Fathers and the Byzantine Iconoclastic Controversy'. *Dumbarton Oaks Papers*, 7: 1–34.

Lamberti, Edward. 2020. *Performing Ethics Through Film Style*. Edinburgh: Edinburgh University Press.

Latour, Bruno, and Peter Weibel (eds). 2002. *Iconoclash: Beyond the Image Wars in Science, Religion and Art*. Karlsruhe: ZKM Center for Art and Media; Cambridge: MIT Press.

Lawrence, Amy. 1991. *Echo and Narcissus: Women's Voices in Classical Hollywood Cinema*. Berkeley: University of California Press.

Lawrence, Tim. 1997. 'AIDS, the Problem of Representation, and Plurality in Derek Jarman's *Blue*'. *Social Text*, 52/53: 241–64.

Lengbeyer, Lawrence A. 2009. 'Belief (Philosophical Perspectives)'. In *The Oxford Companion to Emotion and the Affective Sciences*. Oxford: Oxford University Press.

Levin, Thomas Y. 2002. 'Dismantling the Spectacle: The Cinema of Guy Debord'. In *Guy Debord and the Situationist International: Texts and Documents*, edited by Tom McDonough, 321–453. Cambridge: MIT Press.

Levinas, Emmanuel. 1969. *Totality and Infinity: An Essay on Exteriority*, translated by Alphonso Lingis. Pittsburgh: Duquesne University Press.

Levinas, Emmanuel. 1989. 'Reality and Its Shadow', translated by Alphonso Lingis. In *The Levinas Reader*, edited by Seán Hand, 129–43. Oxford: Blackwell.

Levinas, Emmanuel. [1974] 2001. *Existence and Existents*, translated by Alphonso Lingis. Pittsburgh: Duquesne University Press.

Levine, Joseph. 1998. 'Colour and Qualia'. *Routledge Encyclopedia of Philosophy*. https://www.rep.routledge.com/articles/thematic/colour-and-qualia/v-1.

Lewis, Charlton T., and Charles Short (eds). 1900. *A Latin Dictionary: Founded on Andrews' Edition of Freund's Latin Dictionary; Revised, Enlarged and in Great Part Rewritten*. Oxford: Clarendon Press.

Liddell, Henry G., and Robert Scott. 1966. *A Greek-English Lexicon*, revised and augmented by Henry S. Jones and Roderick McKenzie. Oxford: Clarendon Press.

Lombardo, Patrizia. 1994. 'Cruellement bleu'. *Critical Quarterly*, 36(1): 131–33.

Lombroso, Cesare. [1876] 2006. *Criminal Man*, edited by Mary Gibson and Nicole H. Rafter. Durham: Duke University Press.

Lowe, Adam. 2002. 'To See the World in a Square of Black'. In *Iconoclash: Beyond the Image Wars in Science, Religion and Art*, edited by Bruno Latour and Peter Weibel, 544–67. Karlsruhe: ZKM Center for Art and Media; Cambridge: MIT Press.

Lukács, György. 1971. *History and Class Consciousness: Studies in Marxist Dialectics*, translated by Rodney Livingstone. London: Merlin.

MacCabe, Colin. 1974. 'Realism and the Cinema: Notes on Some Brechtian Theses'. *Screen*, 15(2): 7–27.

MacCabe, Colin. 2003. *Godard: A Portrait of the Artist at 70*. London: Bloomsbury.

Martin, Adrian. 2010. 'Surgically Imprecise Notes on the Great Carmelo Bene'. *Film Critic*. http://www.filmcritic.com.au/essays/bene.html.

Martin-Jones, David. 2018. *Cinema Against Doublethink: Ethical Encounters with the Lost Pasts of World History*. London: Routledge.

Marx, Karl, and Friedrich Engels. [1846] 1970. *The German Ideology: Part One, with Selections from Parts Two and Three, Together with Marx's 'Introduction to a Critique of Political Economy'*, edited by C. J. Arthur. London: Lawrence & Wishart.

Maund, Barry. 2012. 'Color'. *The Stanford Encyclopedia of Philosophy*. https://plato.stanford.edu/entries/color/#PrimSimpObjeViewColo.

McMahon, Laura. 2012. *Cinema and Contact: The Withdrawal of Touch in Nancy, Bresson, Duras and Denis*. London: Legenda.

Meister Eckhart. [fourteenth century] 2009. *The Complete Mystical Works of Meister Eckhart*, translated and edited by Maurice O'C. Walshe; revised with a Foreword by Bernard McGinn. New York: The Crossroad Publishing Company.

Michaels, Lloyd. 1999. 'Bergman and the Necessary Illusion: An Introduction to *Persona*'. In *Ingmar Bergman's Persona*, 1–23. Cambridge: Cambridge University Press.

Misek, Richard. 2010. *Chromatic Cinema: A History of Screen Color*. Malden: Wiley-Blackwell.

Mitchell, William J. T. 1986. *Iconology: Image, Text, Ideology*. Chicago: The University of Chicago Press.

Mitchell, William J. T. 1994. *Picture Theory: Essays on Verbal and Visual Representation*. Chicago: University of Chicago Press.

Mondzain, Marie-José. 2005. *Image, Icon, Economy: The Byzantine Origins of the Contemporary Imaginary*, translated by Rico Franses. Palo Alto: Stanford University Press.

Mondzain, Marie-José. 2013. *Homo spectator*. Paris: Bayard.

Mondzain, Marie-José. 2017. 'Spettacolo: La fine dello spettatore'. Paper presented at the Festival of Philosophy [*festivalfilosofia*], Carpi, Italy, 15 September. https://www.youtube.com/watch?v=lFAydo-3aZE.

Mondzain, Marie-José. 2019. *Le Commerce des regards: Postface inédite*. Paris: SEUIL.

Moor, Andrew. 2000. 'Spirit and Matter: Romantic Mythologies in the Films of Derek Jarman'. In *Territories of Desire in Queer Culture: Refiguring Contemporary Boundaries*, edited by David Alderson and Linda Anderson, 49–67. Manchester: Manchester University Press.

Morreale, Emiliano (ed.). 2011. *Carmelo Bene: Contro il cinema*. Rome: Minimum Fax.

Mosley, Philip. 1981. *Ingmar Bergman: The Cinema as Mistress*. London: Boyars.

Münsterberg, Hugo. 1916. *The Photoplay: A Psychological Study*. New York; London: D. Appleton and Company.

Murray, Peter, Linda Murray and Tom Devonshire Jones. 2014. 'Blue'. *Dictionary of Christian Art and Architecture*, 65. Oxford: Oxford University Press.

Nagib, Lúcia. 2011. *World Cinema and the Ethics of Realism*. New York: Continuum.

Nancy, Jean-Luc. 2005. *The Ground of the Image*, translated by Jeff Fort. New York: Fordham University Press.

Nancy, Jean-Luc. 2007. *Listening*, translated by Charlotte Mandell. New York: Fordham University Press.

Nordmann, Alfred. 2005. 'Thought Experiments'. In *Wittgenstein's Tractatus: An Introduction*, 92–125. Cambridge: Cambridge University Press.

Noys, Benjamin. 2007. 'Destroy Cinema!/Destroy Capital!: Guy Debord's *The Society of the Spectacle* (1973)'. *Quarterly Review of Film and Video*, 24(5): 395–402.

Oxford English Dictionary. 2022. 'Model'. Oxford: Oxford University Press. https://www-oed-com.ezproxy.is.ed.ac.uk/view/Entry/120577?rskey=INvQBH&result=1&isAdvanced=false#eid.

Paiano, Alessio. 2020. 'Carmelo Bene poeta del vuoto: Tracce di letteratura mistica'. *L'Ulisse*, 23: 450–70.

Pastoureau, Michel. 2009. *Black: The History of a Color*. Princeton: Princeton University Press.

Peake, Tony. 2011. *Derek Jarman: A Biography*. Minneapolis: University of Minnesota Press.

Perniola, Ivelise. 2007. *L'immagine spezzata: Il cinema di Claude Lanzmann*. Torino: Kaplan.

Perniola, Mario (ed.). 2013. 'Cinema e Iconoclastia'. [Special Issue]. *Ágalma, rivista di studi culturali e di estetica*, 26.

Pethő, Ágnes. 2011. 'From the "Blank Page" to the "White Beach": Word and Image Plays in Jean-Luc Godard's Cinema'. In *Cinema and Intermediality: The Passion for the In-Between*, 265–83. Newcastle upon Tyne: Cambridge Scholars Publishing.

Pezzella, Mario. 2011. 'Fatti dal nulla: Considerazioni sul digitale e il reale'. *Rivista di Estetica*, 46: 137–49.

Pisano, Libera. 2016. 'Misunderstanding Metaphors: Linguistic Scepticism in Mauthner's Philosophy'. In *Yearbook of the Maimonides Centre for Advanced Studies: 2016*, edited by Giuseppe Veltri, 95–122. Berlin; Boston: De Gruyter.

Plant, Sadie. 1992. *The Most Radical Gesture: The Situationist International in a Postmodern Age*. London: Routledge.

Plato. 2008. *Republic*, translated by Tom Griffith. Cambridge: Cambridge University Press.

Plotinus. 1984. *Ennead V*, translated by A. H. Armstrong, edited by Jeffrey Henderson. Cambridge: Harvard University Press.

Pohle, Joseph. 1912. 'The Dogma in Its Relation to Reason'. In *The Divine Trinity: A Dogmatic Treatise*, edited by Arthur Preuss, 194–201. Freiburg; London: B. Herder.

Poirson-Dechonne, Marion. 2016. *Entre spiritualité et laïcité, la tentation iconoclaste du cinéma*. Paris: L'Harmattan.

Rodowick, David N. 1994. *The Crisis of Political Modernism: Criticism and Ideology in Contemporary Film Theory*. Berkeley: University of California Press.

Rancière, Jacques. 2002. 'The Saint and the Heiress: Apropos of Godard's *Histoire(s) du cinéma*'. *Discourse*, 24(1): 113–19.

Rancière, Jacques. 2004. 'Godard, Hitchcock, and the Cinematographic Image'. In *Forever Godard*, edited by James S. Williams, Michael Temple and Michael Witt, 214–31. London: Black Dog Publishing.

Rancière, Jacques. 2007. *The Future of the Image*, translated by Gregory Elliott. London; New York: Verso.

Remes, Justin. 2015. 'Colored Blindness: Derek Jarman's *Blue* and the Monochrome Film'. In *Motion(less) Pictures: The Cinema of Stasis*, 111–36. Irvington: Columbia University Press.

Reyland, Nicholas W. 2012. *Zbigniew Preisner's Three Colors Trilogy: Blue, White, Red: A Film Score Guide*. Lanham; Plymouth: Scarecrow Press.

Rivette, Jacques. 1961. 'De l'abjection'. *Cahiers du cinéma*, 120: 54–55.

Royer, Michelle. 2019. *The Cinema of Marguerite Duras: Multisensoriality and Female Subjectivity*. Edinburgh: Edinburgh University Press.

Rushton, Richard. 2011. *The Reality of Film: Theories of Filmic Reality*. Manchester: Manchester University Press.

Saïd, Suzanne. 1987. 'Deux noms de l'image en grec ancient: idole et icône'. *Comptes rendus des séances de l'académie des Inscriptions et Belles-Lettres*, 2: 309–30.

Saxton, Libby. 2004. 'Anamnesis and Bearing Witness: Godard/Lanzmann'. In *Forever Godard*, edited by James S. Williams, Michael Temple and Michael Witt, 364–79. London: Black Dog Publishing.

Saxton, Libby. 2007. 'Fragile Faces: Levinas and Lanzmann'. *Film-Philosophy*, 11(2): 1–14.

Saxton, Libby. 2008. *Haunted Images: Film, Ethics, Testimony, and the Holocaust*. New York: Wallflower Press.
Saxton, Libby. 2010a. 'Blinding Visions: Levinas, Ethics, Faciality'. In *Film and Ethics: Foreclosed Encounters*, by Lisa Downing and Libby Saxton, 95–106. London: Routledge.
Saxton, Libby. 2010b. 'Ethics, Spectatorship and the Spectacle of Suffering'. In *Film and Ethics: Foreclosed Encounters*, by Lisa Downing and Libby Saxton, 62–75. London: Routledge.
Saxton, Libby. 2010c. '"Tracking Shots Are a Question of Morality": Ethics, Aesthetics, Documentary'. In *Film and Ethics: Foreclosed Encounters*, by Lisa Downing and Libby Saxton, 22–35. London: Routledge.
Scruton, Roger. 1981. 'Photography and Representation'. *Critical Inquiry*, 7(3): 577–603.
Sedgwick, Eve Kosofsky. 2008. *Epistemology of the Closet*. Berkeley: University of California Press.
Sesonske, Alexander. 1974. 'Aesthetics of Film, or a Funny Thing Happened on the Way to the Movies'. *The Journal of Aesthetics and Art Criticism*, 33(1): 51–57.
Simmel, Georg. [1901] 1959. 'The Aesthetic Significance of the Face'. In *Georg Simmel, Essays on Sociology, Philosophy and Aesthetics*, edited by Kurt H. Wolff, translated by Lore Ferguson, 276–81. Columbus: Ohio State University Press.
Simsolo, Noël. [1973] 2011. 'Carmelo Bene o della responsabilità di un'arte critica'. In *Carmelo Bene: Contro il cinema*, edited by Emiliano Morreale, 107–26. Rome: Minimum Fax.
Singer, Irving. 2009. *Ingmar Bergman, Cinematic Philosopher: Reflections on His Creativity*. Cambridge: MIT Press.
Sinnerbrink, Robert. 2012. 'Cinematic Belief'. *Angelaki*, 17(4): 95–117.
Sinnerbrink, Robert. 2016. *Cinematic Ethics: Exploring Ethical Experience through Film*. London: Routledge.
Sitney, P. Adams. 1989. 'Color and Myth in *Cries and Whispers*'. *Film Criticism*, 13(3): 37–41.
Sjöberg, Sami. 2013a. 'From Material Meaningless to Poetics of Potentiality: The Religious Dimension of Lettrist Visual Poetry'. In *Aesthetics of Matter: Modernism, the Avant-Garde and Material Exchange*, edited by Sarah Posman, Anne Reverseau, David Ayers, Sascha Bru and Benedikt Hjartarson, 370–79. Berlin: De Gruyter.
Sjöberg, Sami. 2013b. 'Mysticism of Immanence: Lettrism, Sprachkritik, and the Immediate Message'. *Partial Answers: Journal of Literature and the History of Ideas*, 11(1): 53–69.

Sjöberg, Sami. 2014. 'Fragments of Multilingualism and Anti-Realism: Paul Celan and Isidore Isou as Proponents of Romanian Jewish Experimental Literature'. *Philologica Jassyensia*, 10(1): 215–28.

Sjöberg, Sami. 2015. *The Vanguard Messiah: Lettrism between Jewish Mysticism and the Avant-Garde*. Berlin: De Gruyter.

Smith, Paul Julian. 1993. '*Blue* and the Other Limits'. *Sight and Sound*, 3(10):18–19.

Sobchack, Vivian. 2011. 'Fleshing Out the Image: Phenomenology, Pedagogy, and Derek Jarman's *Blue*'. In *New Takes in Film-Philosophy*, edited by Havi Carel and Greg Tuck, 191–206. London: Palgrave Macmillan.

Sobolewski, Tadeusz. 1999. 'Ultimate Concerns'. In *Lucid Dreams: The Films of Krzysztof Kieślowski*, edited and translated by Paul Coates, 19–31. Wiltshire: Flicks Books.

Solnit, Rebecca. 2005. 'Yves Klein and the Blue of Distance'. *New England Review*, 26(2): 176–82.

Sontag, Susan. 2002. *Illness as Metaphor & AIDS and Its Metaphors*. London: Penguin.

Sontag, Susan. 2003. *Regarding the Pain of Others*. London: Penguin.

Sorfa, David. 2017. 'Belief in Film: A Defence of False Emotion and *Brother Sun, Sister Moon*'. *Film and Philosophy*, 22: 36–57.

Stadler, Jane. 2017. 'Empathy and Film'. In *The Routledge Handbook of Philosophy of Empathy*, edited by Heidi L. Maibom, 317–26. New York: Routledge.

Stam, Robert. 1981–82. 'Jean-Luc Godard's *Sauve Qui Peut (la Vie)*'. *Millennium Film Journal*, 10–11: 194–99.

Stok, Danusia (ed.). 1995. *Kieślowski on Kieślowski*. London: Faber.

Suárez, Juan A. 2017. 'The Sound of Queer Experimental Film'. In *The Music and Sound of Experimental Film*, edited by Holly Rogers and Jeremy Barham, 234–56. New York: Oxford University Press.

Thomson-Jones, Katherine. 2008. *Aesthetics and Film*. London: Bloomsbury Publishing.

Thorp, Arabella, and Gillian Allen. 2000. 'The Local Government Bill [HL]: The "Section 28" Debate'. *Library House of Commons Research Paper 00/47*.

Törnqvist, Egil. 1996. *Between Stage and Screen: Ingmar Bergman Directs*. Amsterdam: Amsterdam University Press.

Turvey, Malcolm. 1998. 'Jean Epstein's Cinema of Immanence: The Rehabilitation of the Corporeal Eye'. *October*, 83: 25–50.

Tyagi, Ritu. 2014. 'Understanding Postcolonial Feminism in Relation with Postcolonial and Feminist Theories'. *International Journal of Language and Linguistics*, 1(2): 45–50.

Tynyanov, Yury. [1927] 1982. 'The Fundamentals of Cinema'. In *Russian Poetics in Translation, Volume 9: The Poetics of Cinema*, edited by Richard Taylor, translated by Lawrence M. O'Toole, 32–54. Oxford: RPT Publications in Association with Department of Literature, University of Essex.

Ugenti, Elio. 2013. 'I limiti del visibile nel cinema di Abbas Kiarostami'. *Ágalma, rivista culturale e di estetica*, 26: 70–78.

Uroskie, Andrew V. 2011. 'Beyond the Black Box: The Lettrist Cinema of Disjunction'. *October*, 135: 21–48.

Vatican Council I. 1868. Sess. III, *De fide et ratione*. Vatican.va. https://w2.vatican.va/content/pius-ix/it/documents/constitutio-dogmatica-dei-filius-24-aprilis-1870.html.

Venzi, Luca. 2006. *Il colore e la composizione filmica*. Pisa: Edizioni ETS.

Venzi, Luca. 2013. 'Tinte brucianti: Colore e cancellazione dell'immagine'. *Ágalma, rivista culturale e di estetica*, 26: 59–69.

Wajcman, Gérard. 1998. *L'Objet du siècle*. Paris: Éditions Verdier.

Watney, Simon. 1987. 'The Spectacle of AIDS'. *October*, 43: 71–86.

Weibel, Peter. 2002. 'An End to the "End of Art"? On the Iconoclasm of Modern Art'. In *Iconoclash: Beyond the Image Wars in Science, Religion and Art*, edited by Bruno Latour and Peter Weibel, 570–670. Karlsruhe: ZKM Center for Art and Media – Cambridge: MIT Press.

Weiler, Gershon. 1970. *Mauthner's Critique of Language*. Cambridge: Cambridge University Press.

Weitemeier, Hannah. 2001. *Yves Klein 1928–1962: International Klein Blue*. Cologne: Taschen.

Weller, Shane. 2018. *Language and Negativity in European Modernism: Toward a Literature of the Unword*. Cambridge: Cambridge University Press.

Williams, James S. 2004. 'Music, Love, and the Cinematic Event'. In *Forever Godard*, edited by James S. Williams, Michael Temple and Michael Witt, 288–311. London: Black Dog Publishing.

Williams, James S. 2016. 'Introduction'. In *Encounters with Godard: Ethics, Aesthetics, Politics*, 1–18. Albany: State University of New York Press.

Wilson, Emma. 1998. '*Three Colours: Blue*: Kieślowski, Colour and the Postmodern Subject'. *Screen*, 39(4): 349–62.

Witt, Michael. 2013. *Jean-Luc Godard, Cinema Historian*. Bloomington: Indiana University Press.

Wittgenstein, Ludwig. 1968. *Tractatus Logico-Philosophicus e Quaderni 1914–1916*, translated by Amedeo G. Conte. Turin: Einaudi.

Wollen, Peter. 1976. '"Ontology" and "Materialism" in Film'. *Screen*, 17(1): 7–25.

Wollen, Peter. 2004. 'Blue'. In *Paris Manhattan: Writings on Art*, 113–27. London; New York: Verso.

Wunenburger, Jean-Jacques. 1995. *La Vie des images*. Strasbourg: Presses Universitaires de Strasbourg.

Wunenburger, Jean-Jacques. 1999. *Filosofia delle immagini*, translated by Sergio Arecco. Turin: Einaudi.

Wymer, Rowland. 2005. *Derek Jarman*. Manchester: Manchester University Press.

Žižek, Slavoj. 2001a. *On Belief*. London; New York: Routledge.

Žižek, Slavoj. 2001b. *The Fright of Real Tears: Krzysztof Kieślowski between Theory and Post-Theory*. London: BFI Publishing.

Žižek, Slavoj. 2006. 'The Eclipse of Meaning: On Lacan and Deconstruction'. In *Interrogating the Real*, edited and translated by Rex Butler and Scott Stephens, 190–212. London; New York: Continuum.

Filmography

A Place in the Sun, George Stevens, 1951.
A Trip to the Moon / Le Voyage dans la Lune, Georges Méliès, 1902.
Alphaville: A Strange Adventure of Lemmy Caution / Alphaville, une étrange aventure de Lemmy Caution, Jean-Luc Godard, 1965.
Battleship Potemkin / Bronenosets Potëmkin, Sergei Eisenstein, 1925.
British Sounds, Dziga Vertov Group, 1969.
Blue, Derek Jarman, 1993.
Capricci, Carmelo Bene, 1969.
City Lights, Charlie Chaplin, 1931.
Cries and Whispers / Viskningar och rop, Ingmar Bergman, 1972.
Don Giovanni, Carmelo Bene, 1970.
Edward II, Derek Jarman, 1991.
Entr'acte, René Clair, 1924.
Guy Debord, son art et son temps, Guy Debord and Brigitte Cornand, 1994.
Histoire(s) du cinéma, Jean-Luc Godard, 1988–98.
Hurlements en faveur de Sade / Howls for Sade, Guy Debord, 1952.
In girum imus nocte et consumimur igni / We Wander in the Night and Are Consumed by Fire, Guy Debord, 1978.
India Song, Marguerite Duras, 1975.
Joan of Arc at the Stake / Giovanna d'Arco al rogo, Roberto Rossellini, 1954.
Johnny Guitar, Nicholas Ray, 1954.
Jubilee, Derek Jarman, 1978.
Kapò, Gillo Pontecorvo, 1960.
L'Anticoncept / The Anti-Concept, Gil J. Wolman, 1951.

L'Homme atlantique, Marguerite Duras, 1981.
Le Camion, Marguerite Duras, 1977.
Le Film est déjà commencé? / Has the Film Already Started? Maurice Lemaître, 1951.
Le Navire Night, Marguerite Duras, 1979.
Le Vent d'est, Dziga Vertov Group, 1970.
Les Mains négatives, Marguerite Duras, 1978.
Lotte in Italia, Dziga Vertov Group, 1970.
Miracle in Milan / Miracolo a Milano, Vittorio De Sica, 1951.
Nathalie Granger, Marguerite Duras, 1972.
October: Ten Days That Shook the World / Oktiabr' ili Desiat' dneĭ, kotorye potriasli mir, Sergei Eisenstein, 1928.
Our Lady of the Turks / Nostra signora dei turchi, Carmelo Bene, 1968.
Prison / Fängelse, Ingmar Bergman, 1949.
Rio Grande, John Ford, 1950.
Salomè, Carmelo Bene, 1972.
Scénario du film 'Passion', Jean-Luc Godard, 1982.
Sebastiane, Derek Jarman, 1976.
Shoah, Claude Lanzmann, 1985.
Slow Motion / Sauve qui peut (la Vie), Jean-Luc Godard, 1980.
Son nom de Venise dans Calcutta désert, Marguerite Duras, 1976.
Sur le passage de quelques personnes à travers une assez courte unité de temps / On the Passage of a Few Persons Through a Rather Brief Unity of Time, Guy Debord, 1959.
Tambours du jugement premier / Drums of the First Judgement, François Dufrêne, 1952.
The Angelic Conversation, Derek Jarman, 1985.
The Cabinet of Dr. Caligari / Das Cabinet des Dr. Caligari, Robert Wiene, 1920.
The Double Life of Véronique / La Double Vie de Véronique, Krzysztof Kieślowski, 1991.
The Last of England, Derek Jarman, 1987.
The Shanghai Gesture, Josef von Sternberg, 1941.
The Society of the Spectacle / La Société du spectacle, Guy Debord, 1973.
The Tempest, Derek Jarman, 1979.
Three Colours: Blue / Trois Couleurs: Bleu, Krzysztof Kieślowski, 1993.
Three Colours: Red / Trois Couleurs: Rouge, Krzysztof Kieślowski, 1994.
Three Colours: White / Trois Couleurs: Blanc, Krzysztof Kieślowski, 1994.
Traité de bave et d'éternité / Treatise on Venom and Eternity, Isidore Isou, 1951.

Un Chien Andalou, Luis Buñuel and Salvador Dalí, 1929.
Une Femme mariée / A Married Woman, Jean-Luc Godard, 1964.
Un Film comme les Autres, Dziga Vertov Group, 1968.
Vladimir et Rosa, Dziga Vertov Group, 1971.

Index

Note: Films are indexed under directors, who can be identified from the Filmography. 'n' indicates note.

Aaron, Michele, 122, 124, 197n, 199n
Adorno, Theodor W., 9
Agamben, Giorgio, 59–60
altered motion, 66–70, 100–1
Amerini, Fabrizio, 96
anti-mimesis, 8, 11, 18–20, 39, 87, 116, 123, 136, 144; *see also* mimesis
Aquinas, Thomas, 95–6
Armengaud, Françoise, 119
Attali, Jacques, 127–8
Aumont, Jacques, 14–15

Bachmann, Gideon, 76, 83–4
Balázs, Béla, 14–15, 155, 162, 166–7, 169, 173, 175
Bazin, André, 30, 122
belief, 54, 65, 71, 94–6, 101, 105, 109–12, 192, 198n
Bellour, Raymond, 66–7, 97, 100–1
Bene, Carmelo, 3, 5, 10, 13, 17, 21, 37, 72–80, 82–6, 89–94, 96–7, 190, 192–3
 Capricci, 83
 Don Giovanni, 79
 Othello, or the Deficiency of Women, 78
 Our Lady of the Turks / Nostra signora dei turchi, 3, 10, 21, 74, 76, 78, 83–4, 86, 89, 192–3
 Richard III, 77
 Romeo and Juliet, 77
 Salomè, 79, 83
Bergman, Ingmar, 3, 5, 10–11, 17, 22, 115, 153–7, 159–61, 164, 167–9, 172, 177, 182, 185, 187, 190, 193
 Cries and Whispers / Viskningar och rop, 3, 10, 17, 22, 153–5, 157, 159–64, 168–9, 171, 185, 193
 Prison / Fängelse, 109
Besançon, Alain, 8, 24, 26–7, 32–3, 43, 195n

Bettetini, Maria T., 2, 8, 24, 27, 29, 43
black-out, 179, 181–5, 187–8; *see also* fade
blank screen
   general, 18, 61, 193, 200n; and Bene, 79; and Debord, 56, 66, 71; and Duras, 125; and Godard, 97, 99, 110; and Isou, 43–4, 47
   all black, 6, 19–20, 61; and Debord, 61–2, 64–5; and Duras, 125–6, 130, 132; and Godard, 97–9, 105–6, 109–10; and Isou, 47, 52–3; and Jarman, 136, 146; and Kieślowski, 22, 181
   all blue *see* Jarman, *Blue*
   all red *see* Bergman, *Cries and Whispers*
   all white, and Debord, 61–2, 65
   see also monochromatic screen
Boldrick, Stacy, 7
Brenez, Nicole, 95, 98, 104
Brown, William, 120
Bruegel the Elder, 69
Buchloh, Benjamin H. D., 39
Buñuel, Luis and Dalí, Salvador
   Un Chien Andalou, 61–2

Cabañas, Kaira M., 44–6, 48, 61, 65, 71
Cage, John, 4
Cappabianca, Alessandro, 89
Carroll, Noël, 67
Cavarero, Adriana, 81–2, 128, 149–51
Chamois, Camille, Le Roux, Daphné and Levy, Benjamin, 173
Chaplin, Charlie, 50
   City Lights, 62
Chillemi, Francesco, 80, 89

Chion, Michel, 81–2
chiseled image, 38, 44–50, 52, 190
Clair, René, 50
   Entr'acte, 61
Cléder, Jean, 126
Clewell, Tammy, 181
close-up, 11, 13, 14–17, 79, 87, 90, 104, 106, 154, 157–8, 162–5, 167–9, 171–6, 184, 191
Cohen, Hubert I., 157, 162, 168
colour, 19, 115, 155–7, 192, 199n–200n; and Bene, 78–9, 86–7; and Bergman, 154, 157–8, 160–2, 168–9, 171; and Jarman, 137, 142–7, 152; and Kieślowski, 182–3, 185, 187–8
   blue *see* Jarman, *Blue* and Kieślowski, *Three Colours: Blue*
   red *see* Bergman, *Cries and Whispers*
Connor, Steven, 132
Cooper, Sarah, 119, 125–6, 197n, 199n
copy, 2–3, 5, 10–11, 13, 17–18, 24, 30, 34, 37, 45, 54, 96, 112, 117, 123, 142, 191, 195n
copy-prototype relationship, 4–6, 17–18, 27–8, 30–3, 95–6, 123, 195n
Corradi Fiumara, Gemma, 133, 148
Coureau, Didier, 131
Cowie, Peter, 161
Crimp, Douglas, 137, 139

Dall'Asta, Monica and Grosoli, Marco, 71
Dalle Vacche, Angela, 13–14
Daney, Serge, 121–2
David, Marian, 96

De Sica, Vittorio
   Miracle in Milan / Miracolo a Milano, 107
Debord, Guy, 5, 10, 12–13, 21, 32, 37, 44, 54–73, 79–80, 94, 96–7, 130, 143, 190, 192–3
   Hurlements en faveur de Sade / Howls for Sade, 3, 21, 44, 61–3, 72
   In girum imus nocte et consumimur igni / We Wander in the Night and Are Consumed by Fire, 3, 21, 63, 72
   Sur le passage de quelques personnes à travers une assez courte unité de temps / On the Passage of a Few Persons Through a Rather Brief Unity of Time, 59, 193
   The Society of the Spectacle / La Société du spectacle, 3, 21, 67–9
   and Cornand, Brigitte, *Guy Debord, son art et son temps*, 66
Debray, Régis, 13
Deleuze, Gilles, 17, 61, 73, 77–8, 80, 97, 99, 101
   and Guattari, Félix, 14–16, 175
Delluc, Louis, 14, 29, 174–5, 200n
Derrida, Jacques, 80–2
destruction, 1, 3–4, 7–8, 10–11, 17–18, 21, 27, 34, 41–2, 46, 48, 50, 52, 54–5, 72–3, 79, 94, 112, 125, 154, 157, 162, 168–9, 171, 177, 179, 187–8, 190–2
de-synchronisation *see* sound-image disjunction
détournement, 56, 62–3, 66–5, 68–9, 71–2, 192

discrepant cinema, 38, 46, 51–3, 197n
discrepant editing, 44–6, 49–51
Doane, Mary Ann, 14
Dolar, Mladen, 81–2
Dottorini, Daniele, 19, 47
Dufrêne, François
   Tambours du jugement premier / Drums of the First Judgement, 44
Duras, Marguerite, 11, 22, 115–16, 125–31, 133–5, 190, 193
   India Song, 125–8
   L'Homme atlantique, 125–6
   Le Camion, 125
   Le Navire Night, 3, 10, 22, 116, 125–6, 129–33, 193
   Les Mains négatives, 125
   Nathalie Granger, 128
   Son nom de Venise dans Calcutta désert, 126
Dziga Vertov Group
   British Sounds, 193
   Le Vent d'est, 99
   Lotte in Italia, 99
   Un Film comme les Autres, 99
   Vladimir et Rosa, 99

Eckhart, Meister, 75
eidōlon, 4–6, 10–13, 17–19, 23–6, 28–34, 37, 54–6, 68, 70–2, 75, 85, 88, 93, 96–7, 103, 117, 119, 127, 133, 142, 189, 191–2
eikōn, 4–5, 8, 14, 17, 23–9, 33–4, 96, 103–5, 123–4, 189, 191, 199n
eikōn-eidōlon dichotomy, 4, 7, 11, 17, 23–9, 33–4, 189, 191
Eisenstein, Sergei, 50, 84, 155
   Battleship Potemkin / Bronenosets Potëmkin, 61, 68

October: Ten Days That Shook the World / Oktiabr' ili Desiat' dneĭ, kotorye potriasli mir, 68
Ellis, Jim, 142
Epstein, Jean, 14–16, 166, 173–5, 200n
ethics, 10, 18–20, 22, 115–21, 125, 137, 139, 141, 154, 193, 199n

face, 11, 14–18, 48–9, 79, 106–8, 117–19, 134, 154–5, 157–9, 162–9, 171–7, 185, 188, 190–1
fade, 98, 162, 172, 181, 183–4, 187, 192, 200n
  to red, 154–5, 157–62, 167–9, 171, 185
Feldman, Hannah, 38, 45, 47, 49
Field, Allyson, 51–2, 62–3
Fleming, David H., 120
Fontana, Lucio, 18
Ford, John
  Rio Grande, 68–9
freeze-frame, 66, 69, 100–1, 192; *see also* altered motion

Gado, Frank, 160
Galt, Rosalind, 12–13, 145
Gamboni, Dario, 7
Godard, Jean-Luc, 10, 13, 37, 54, 93–112, 190, 192–3, 198n
  Alphaville: A Strange Adventure of Lemmy Caution / Alphaville, une étrange aventure de Lemmy Caution, 21, 98–9
  Histoire(s) du cinéma, 3, 10, 21, 94, 101–10, 112, 192, 198n
  Slow Motion / Sauve qui peut (la Vie), 21, 100–1
  Scénario du film 'Passion', 97

Une Femme mariée / A Married Woman, 21, 98–9
Grespi, Barbara, 14–16, 175
Grøndstad, Asbjørn, 18, 120–1
Günther, Renate, 125

Halliwell, Stephen, 24–6
Hand, Seán, 118
Hanson, Ellis, 138
Harcourt, Peter, 161
Heath, Stephen, 65
Hegarty, Paul, 128, 148
Hegel, G. W. F., 71
Higginson, Kate, 137, 146, 151
Hill, Leslie, 128
Hofmannsthal, Hugo von, 41
Hori, Junji, 111
Hubner, Laura, 154, 160–1

icon, 4, 17, 25–8, 33, 175–6, 195n
  in cinema, 154, 162, 164–5, 167–9, 171
iconoclasm, 1–2, 6–8, 18–19, 24, 27, 32, 39, 96, 117, 119, 178, 189, 191, 195n
  cinematic, 3–5, 9–14, 20–2, 29–31, 33–4, 47, 54–5, 65, 73, 77, 79, 88, 95, 115, 122–3, 142–3, 169, 190, 192–4
iconoclastic controversy, 2, 4, 17, 27–9, 32, 34
iconoclastic *eikōn*, 5, 18, 20, 32, 34, 94, 115, 121, 123–5, 127, 133–4, 152, 155, 157–9, 162–3, 168–9, 171, 173, 182, 187–8
iconophilia, 2, 13, 27, 30, 95–6
idol, 4, 25, 28, 31, 33, 57, 68
imagination, 20, 53–4, 98, 125–6, 129, 132–4, 154, 163, 179, 188

Isou, Isidore, 10, 13, 32, 37–8, 42–54, 61, 96, 130, 190, 192–3, 197n
   Traité de bave et d'éternité / Treatise on Venom and Eternity, 3, 10, 21, 44, 46–8, 51–2, 54, 61–2, 103, 192–3, 197n

Jarman, Derek, 11, 115, 135–7, 139–49, 151–2, 155, 190
   Blue, 3, 10, 22, 135–7, 141–3, 145–53, 155, 193
   Edward II, 136, 147
   Jubilee, 147
   Sebastiane, 147
   The Angelic Conversation, 136
   The Last of England, 136
   The Tempest, 136
Jay, Martin, 2, 55, 63

Kalin, Jesse, 160–1, 164
Kandinsky, Wassily, 39, 183
Kane, Brian, 81–2
Kehr, Dave, 180
Kenaan, Hagi, 116
Khalip, Jacques, 152
Kibbey, Ann, 11–13
Kieślowski, Krzysztof, 5, 11, 17, 115, 155–6, 171–3, 177–80, 182, 185, 187–8, 190
   The Double Life of Véronique / La Double Vie de Véronique, 178
   Three Colours: Blue / Trois Couleurs: Bleu, 3, 10, 18, 22, 155, 172–3, 176–83, 185, 187–8, 193, 200n
   Three Colours: Red / Trois Couleurs: Rouge, 180
   Three Colours: White / Trois Couleurs: Blanc, 180

Klein, Yves, 143–6, 183
   IKB, 143–6
Kracauer, Siegfried, 29–30, 198n

Ladner, Gerhart B., 7, 26
Lamberti, Edward, 120
Lanzmann, Claude, 19, 31
   Shoah, 31
Latour, Bruno and Weibel, Peter, 7
Lawrence, Amy, 151
Lemaître, Maurice
   Le Film est déjà commencé? / Has the Film Already Started?, 44
Lengbeyer, Lawrence, 95
Lettrism, 37–9, 42–4, 46, 53, 56, 61
Levin, Thomas Y., 60–3, 65, 67
Levinas, Emmanuel, 116–20, 176, 199n
listening, 82, 127–8, 130, 132–4, 147–51
Lombardo, Patrizia, 146
Lukács, György, 58

Malevich, Kazimir, 4, 39
Mallarmé, Stéphane, 42
Martin, Adrian, 84
Martin-Jones, David, 120
Marx, Karl and Engels, Friedrich, 56–7
Mauthner, Fritz, 41, 196n
McMahon, Laura, 127, 129, 130
Méliès, Georges
   A Trip to the Moon / Le Voyage dans la Lune, 61
Michaels, Lloyd, 154
mimesis, 2, 4–5, 10, 18–19, 21–5, 32–4, 37–40, 43, 45, 56, 60, 73–7, 85, 94, 101, 112, 115, 123, 125–6,

130, 134, 141–5, 148, 154–6, 168, 171, 177, 179, 187, 189, 193; *see also* anti-mimesis
Misek, Richard, 161
Mitchell, William J. T., 2, 57
Mondzain, Marie-José, 1–2, 8, 28, 176, 189, 193
monochromatic screen, 22, 52–3, 60–1, 63–4, 66, 98–9, 141, 143, 145, 151, 154–8, 161, 167–8, 171, 173, 177, 181, 190–1, 193, 197n; *see also* blank screen
Moor, Andrew, 142–3
Morreale, Emiliano, 83, 86
Mosley, Philip, 161
Münsterberg, Hugo, 30, 199n
mysticism, 25, 41, 89, 145
   atheistic mysticism, 108
   Christian mysticism, 74–5
   Jewish mysticism, 42–3

Nagib, Lúcia, 120
Nancy, Jean-Luc, 2, 91, 118–19, 132, 148–50
negative theology, 25, 41, 75
Noys, Benjamin, 59–60, 68

Perniola, Ivelise, 19
person with AIDS (PWA), 136–43, 146–7, 151–2
Pethő, Ágnes, 97
phoné, 73–4, 76, 80–4, 93, 193; *see also* voice
photogénie, 14–15, 166, 174, 200n; *see also* Delluc, Louis and Epstein, Jean
physiognomy, 14–15, 166–7, 174–5; *see also* Balázs, Béla
Pisano, Libera, 41

Plato, 2, 12–13, 17, 22, 24–5, 28, 34, 40, 121, 191
Plotinus, 22, 25–6, 28, 34, 191
Poirson-Dechonne, Marion, 6, 19, 45, 131
political modernism, 11–12, 29–30
Pontecorvo, Gillo
   Kapò, 121–2

Rancière, Jacques, 104
Rauschenberg, Robert, 4
Ray, Nicholas
   Johnny Guitar, 68
Remes, Justin, 137, 145
Reyland, Nicholas W., 180, 183, 185
Rivette, Jacques, 121–2
Rodowick, David N., 5, 11
Rossellini, Roberto
   Joan of Arc at the Stake / Giovanna d'Arco al rogo, 109
Royer, Michelle, 129
Rushton, Richard, 12–13

Saïd, Suzanne, 7, 24
Saxton, Libby, 9, 18, 103–4, 119–21, 124
Schaeffer, Pierre, 4
Scruton, Roger, 30
Sedgwick, Eve Kosofsky, 140
silence, 4, 41–3, 61–3, 79, 84, 86, 88, 91, 104, 128–9, 142, 147–9, 152
Simmel, Georg, 176
Singer, Irving, 164
Sinnerbrink, Robert, 120–1, 163
Sjöberg, Sami, 39–40, 42
Smith, Paul Julian, 147
Sobchack, Vivian, 143
Solnit, Rebecca, 145

Sontag, Susan, 124, 137
sound-image disjunction, 45, 47,
   51–2, 56, 71, 84, 97, 125–6,
   129–30, 132
spectacle, 2, 19, 34, 38, 122, 127, 138,
   143, 187
   and Debord, 10, 55–60, 62–71
Stadler, Jane, 163
Stam, Robert, 100
stasis, 66, 68–9, 100
Sternberg, Josef von
   The Shanghai Gesture, 68–9
Stevens, George
   A Place in the Sun, 102
stillness, 66–9; *see also* stasis

Törnqvist, Egil, 161, 168
Tyagi, Ritu, 128

Venzi, Luca, 19, 143, 156, 162, 182–3,
   187, 200n
Verlaine, Paul, 42
voice, 21, 47, 62, 68, 72–4, 76–86,
   88–9, 91, 93, 115, 126–32,
   134–5, 147–52, 190, 193; *see also*
   phoné

Wajcman, Gérard, 9, 19–20, 32–3, 39,
   122, 142
Watney, Simon, 138
Weiler, Gershon, 41, 196n
Weller, Shane, 40–1
Wiene, Robert
   The Cabinet of Dr. Caligari / Das
   Cabinet des Dr. Caligari, 61
Wilson, Emma, 183, 188
Witt, Michael, 102, 105, 110
Wollen, Peter, 144
Wolman, Gil J., 61–2
   L'Anticoncept / The Anti-Concept,
   44, 62
Wunenburger, Jean-Jacques, 2, 32
Wymer, Rowland, 144, 146

Žižek, Slavoj, 81–2, 122, 177–8,
   180–1

EU representative:
Easy Access System Europe
Mustamäe tee 50, 10621 Tallinn, Estonia
Gpsr.requests@easproject.com

www.ingramcontent.com/pod-product-compliance
Lightning Source LLC
Chambersburg PA
CBHW071710160426
43195CB00012B/1635